高等学校试用教材

建筑类专业英语

建筑工程

第二册

乔梦铎　王久愉　　　主编
王凤友　李英贤　李　斐
周桂兰　祝恩淳　高　伟　编
计学闰　　　　　　　主审

中国建筑工业出版社

《建筑类专业英语》编审委员会

前　言

经过几十年的探索，外语教学界许多人认为，工科院校外语教学的主要目的，应该是："使学生能够利用外语这个工具，通过阅读去获取国外的与本专业有关的科技信息。"这既是我们建设有中国特色的社会主义的客观需要，也是在当前条件下工科院校外语教学可能完成的最高目标。事实上，教学大纲规定要使学生具有"较强"的阅读能力，而对其他方面的能力只有"一般"要求，就是这个意思。

大学本科的一、二年级，为外语教学的基础阶段。就英语来说，这个阶段要求掌握的词汇量为2400个(去掉遗忘，平均每个课时10个单词)。加上中学阶段已经学会的1600个单词，基础阶段结束时应掌握的词汇量为4000个。仅仅掌握4000个单词，能否看懂专业英文书刊呢？还不能。据统计，掌握4000个单词，阅读一般的英文科技文献，生词量仍将有6%左右，即平均每百词有六个生词，还不能自由阅读。国外的外语教学专家认为，生词量在3%以下，才能不借助词典，自由阅读。此时可以通过上下文的联系，把不认识的生词猜出来。那么，怎么样才能把6%的生词量降低到3%以下呢？自然，需要让学生增加一部分词汇积累。问题是，要增加多少单词？要增加哪一些单词？统计资料表明，在每一个专业的科技文献中，本专业最常用的科技术语大约只有几百个，而且它们在文献中重复出现的频率很高。因此，在已经掌握4000单词的基础上，在专业阅读阶段中，有针对性地通过大量阅读，扩充大约1000个与本专业密切有关的科技词汇，便可以逐步达到自由阅读本专业科技文献的目的。

早在八十年代中期，建设部系统院校外语教学研究会就组织编写了一套《土木建筑系列英语》，分八个专业，共12册。每个专业可选读其中的三、四册。那套教材在有关院校相应的专业使用多年，学生和任课教师反映良好。但是，根据当时的情况，那套教材定的起点较低(1000词起点)，已不适合今天学生的情况。为此，在得到建设部人事教育劳动司的大力支持，并征得五个相关专业指导委员会同意之后，由建设部系统十几所院校一百余名外语教师和专业课教师按照统一的编写规划和要求，编写了这一套《建筑类专业英语》教材。

《建筑类专业英语》是根据国家教委颁发的《大学英语专业阅读阶段教学基本要求》编写的专业阅读教材，按照建筑类院校共同设置的五个较大的专业类别对口编写。五个专业类别为：建筑学与城市规划；建筑工程(即工业与民用建筑)；给水排水与环境保护；暖通、空调与燃气；建筑管理与财务会计。每个专业类别分别编写三册专业英语阅读教材，供该专业类别的学生在修完基础阶段英语后，在第五至第七学期专业阅读阶段使用，每学期一册。

上述五种专业英语教材语言规范，题材广泛，覆盖相关专业各自的主要内容：包括专业基础课，专业主干课及主要专业选修课，语言材料的难易度切合学生的实际水平；词汇以大学英语“通用词汇表”的4000个单词为起点，每个专业类别的三册书将增加1000～1200个阅读本专业必需掌握的词汇。本教材重视语言技能训练，突出对阅读、翻译和写作能力的培养，以求达到《大学英语专业阅读阶段教学基本要求》所提出的教学目标：“通过指导学生阅读有关专业的英语书刊和文献，使他们进一步提高阅读和翻译科技资料的能力，并能以英语为工具获取专业所需的信息。”

《建筑类专业英语》每册16个单元，每个单元一篇正课文（TEXT），两篇副课文（Reading Material A&B），每个单元平均2000个词，三册48个单元，总共约有十万个词，相当于原版书三百多页。要培养较强的阅读能力，读十万词的文献，是起码的要求。如果专业课教师在第六和第七学期，在学生通过学习本教材已经掌握了数百个专业科技词汇的基础上，配合专业课程的学习，再指定学生看一部分相应的专业英语科技文献，那将会既促进专业课的学习，又提高英语阅读能力，实为两得之举。

本教材不仅适用于在校学生，对于有志提高专业英语阅读能力的建筑行业广大在职工程技术人员，也是一套适用的自学教材。

建设部人事教育劳动司高教处和中国建设教育协会对这套教材的编写自始至终给予关注和支持；中国建筑工业出版社第五编辑室密切配合，参与从制定编写方案到审稿各个阶段的重要会议，给了我们很多帮助；在编写过程中，各参编学校相关专业的许多专家、教授对材料的选取、译文的审定都提出了许多宝贵意见，谨此致谢。

《建筑类专业英语》　是我们编写对口专业阅读教材的又一次尝试，由于编写者水平及经验有限，教材中不妥之处在所难免，敬请广大读者批评指正。

《建筑类专业英语》
编审委员会

Contents

UNIT ONE

Text The Preface of 《Desdign of Concrete Structure》

[1] This edition represents a major revision and expansion, as well as an update, of the previous work. However, it maintains the same basic approach: first to establish a firm understanding of the behavior of reinforced concrete structures, then to develop the methods used in current design practice and to achieve familiarity with the codes and specifications governing practical design.

[2] It is generally recognized that mere training in special design skills and codified procedures is inadequate for successful professional practice. These skills and procedures are subject to frequent and sweeping changes. To understand and keep abreast of these rapid developments, the engineer needs a thorough grounding in the basic performance of concrete and steel as structural materials, and in the behavior of reinforced concrete members and structures. ① On the other hand, the main business of the structural engineer is to design structures safely, economically, and efficiently. Hence, with this basic understanding as a firm foundation, familiarity with current design procedures, and skill in using them, is of the essence. ② This edition, like the preceding ones, serves both these purposes.

[3] Changes in format have been made, based on the author's experience in the classroom, and in response to constructive suggestions by users. Material on mechanics and behavior of reinforced concrete, formerly treated separately in an early chapter, has been integrated into the later chapters treating specific design topics such as flexure and shear, thus providing better continuity and more convenient reference to the fundamental basis of each development, and avoiding some duplication. The twelve chapters of the earlier work, some excessively long, have been subdivided into shorter chapters for easier study and reference.

[4] Enhancement of both breadth and depth of coverage has been achieved in many areas, and entirely new chapters have been added treating slabs on grade, composite construction, retaining walls, and building systems. The chapter on columns has been largely rewritten to improve its clarity and generality. For each chapter of the text, a greatly expanded reference list provides an entry into the literature for those in need of more background in detail. The number of problems for homework assignment has been greatly increased, and problems are placed at the end of each chapter for convenience of the teacher and student.

[5] All design procedures, examples, and problems are consistent with the 1983 Building Code of the American Concrete Institute (ACI) or, in the case of bridges, with the 1983 Specification of the American Association of State Highway and Transportation Officials (AASHTO). Many new design aids have been included. Thus the book should continue to be a valuable desk aid for the practicing engineer, providing him with a source of up-to-

date design information.

[6] The teacher will find the text suitable for either a one- or two-semester course in the design of concrete structures. If the curriculum permits only a single course (probably taught in the fourth undergraduate year), the introduction and treatment of materials found in Chapters 1 and 2 respectively, the material on flexure, shear, and anchorage of Chapters 3, 4, and 5, Chapter 6 on serviceability, and the introduction to one- and two-way slabs of Chapter 8, plus Chapter 12 on columns will provide a good basis. Time will probably not permit classroom coverage of frame analysis and building systems, Chapters 16 and 17, but these could well be assigned as independent reading, concurrent with the earlier work of the course. ③ In the writer's experience, such complementary outside reading tends to enhance student motivation.

[7] A second course (most likely taught in the first year of graduate study) should include an introduction to the increasingly important topic of torsion, Chapter 7, an in-depth study of slab systems using Chapters 9 through 11, and foundations and retaining walls according to Chapters 14 and 15, as well as composite construction from Chapter 13 and bridge design using Chapter 19. Prestressed concrete is sufficiently important to justify a separate course with its own text. If the curriculum does not permit this, the treatment of Chapter 18 provides an introduction to the most important concepts.

[8] The present volume is the 10th edition of a textbook originated in 1923 by Leonard C. urquhart and Charles E. O'Rourke, both professors of structural engineering at Cornell university at that time. The second, third, and fourth editions firmly established the work as a leading text for both elementary and advanced courses in the subject area. Professor George Winter, also of Cornell, collaborated with Urquhart in preparing the fifth and sixth editions, and Winter and the writer were responsible for the seventh, eighth, and ninth editions. The present volume was prepared subsequent to Professor Winter's passing in 1982.

[9] The wirter gladly acknowledges his indebtedness to the original authors. While it is safe to say that neither Urquhart nor O'Rourke would recognize very much of the detail, the approach to the subject and the educational philosophy that did so much to account for the success of this unique book would be familiar. ④ I acknowledge with particular gratitude the influence of Professor Winter. A long professional and personal relationship with him had a profound effect in developing a point of view that has shaped all work in the chapters that follow.

New Words and Expressions

revision * [ri'viʒən] *n.* 校订，修改
update * [ʌp'deit] *n.* 最新知识
codify ['kɔdifai] *v.* 编撰，整理
inadequate * [in'ædikwit] *a.* 不充足的，不适当的

sweeping [ˈswiːpiŋ]	*a.*	范围广大的
keep abreast of		保持与…并列
familiarity * [fəˌmiliˈæriti]	*n.*	精通
format * [ˈfɔːmæt]	*n.*	格式，形式
constructive [kənˈstrʌktiv]	*a.*	建设性的，结构上的
flexure [ˈflekʃə]	*n.*	弯曲，挠曲
duplication [djuːpliˈkeiʃən]	*n.*	复制，复制品
subdivide [ˈsʌbdiˈvaid]	*v.*	把……再分，把……细分
be integrated into		被并入……
enhancement * [inˈhɑːnsmənt]	*n.*	提高，增强
coverage * [ˈkʌvəridʒ]	*n.*	有效范围
retaining walls		挡土墙
clarity * [ˈklæriti]	*n.*	清晰（度），明确（性）
generality [ˌdʒenəˈræliti]	*n.*	一般（性），普遍（性）
anchorage [ˈæŋkəridʒ]	*n.*	锚固
complementary * [kɔmpliˈmentəri]	*a.*	补充的，互补的
motivation [ˌməutiˈveiʃən]	*n.*	动机
concurrent [kənˈkʌrənt]	*a.*	同时发生的，并存的
originate * [əˈridʒineit]	*v.*	开始，创造
collaborate [kəˈlæbəreit]	*v.*	合作，共同研究
acknowledge * [əkˈnɔlidʒ]	*v.*	承认，对……表示感谢
indebtedness [inˈdetidnis]	*n.*	负债，感激
profound [prəˈfaund]	*a.*	深远的，深切的

Notes

①...in the basic performance…and in the behavior…作grounding的定语。

②with this basic understanding…是独立结构，familiarity是句子的主语，...is（of essence）是谓语。

③句中well意为恰当地。

④while it is safe to say... 作状语，approach…would be…是句子的主要结构，that did so much…是定语修饰philosophy。

Exercises

Reading Comprehension

Ⅰ. Choose the best answer.

1. What's mainly talked about in the first paragraph?

A. The difference between this edition and the earlier ones.

B. The behavior of reinforced concrete structures.

C. The same basic approach maintained in all these editions.

D. The method used in current design practice.

2. Why do the engineers need a thorough grounding in the basic performance of concrete and steel?

A. In order to keep up with the rapid development of skills and procedures.

B. In order to keep abreast of the frequent and sweeping changes of the structural materials.

C. In order to keep pace with the frequent and sweeping changes of the up-to-date design.

D. In order to keep step with the frequent and sweeping changes of the codes and specifications.

3. Which of the following statements is not true?

A. Material on mechanics and behavior of reinforced concrete, formerly treated separately in the later chapters, has been integrated into an early chapter.

B. All design procedures, examples, and problems are consistent with the 1983 Building Code of the American Concrete Institute.

C. Winter and the writer were responsible for the seventh, eighth and ninth editions.

D. The number of problems for homework assignment has been greatly increased, and problems are placed at the end of each chapter.

4. The reason for rewriting the chapter on columns is ______.

A. the enhancement of both breadth and depth

B. the development of continuity

C. the attachment of advanced skills

D. the improvement of both clarity and generality

5. This edition, like the preceding ones, aims at ______.

A. mastering current procedures and skill in using them

B. designing structures economically and efficiently

C. keeping abreast of the changes and development

D. None of above.

Ⅱ. Fill in the blanks with the information given in the text.

1. What does this edition represent?

It represents ____

____

______________.

2. What are the changes in format?

Material on ____________________, formerly ____________________, has

____________________ such ____________________,

thus ____________________________.

3. The writer gladly acknowledges ________________. While it is safe to say that neither Urquhart nor U'Rourke would recognize ____________________.

Vocabulary

Ⅰ. Choose one word or phrase which is the most similar in meaning to the one underlined in the given sentences.

1. So much is happening in the world of science that it's difficult to <u>keep abreast of</u> all the latest developments.

   A. keep after　　B. keep a close watch on
   C. keep in with　　D. keep pace with

2. The company's new president made <u>sweeping</u> changes in the office.

   A. wide　　B. various
   C. rapid　　D. thorough

3. <u>Subsequent to</u> his phone call, I received a confirmation in the mail.

   A. Following　　B. Prevailing
   C. During　　D. Preceding

4. The new government promised to <u>codify</u> the laws.

   A. change　　B. arrange
   C. revise　　D. digest

5. All <u>acknowledged</u> him to have been very good-humoured and of a kind disposition.

   A. recognize　　B. accept
   C. admit　　D. confess

Ⅱ. Match the words in Column A with their corresponding definitions or explanations in Column B.

A	B
1. anchorage	a. a thick flat usu. 4-sided piece of metal, stone, wood, food, ect.
2. code	b. a course of study offered in a school, college, etc.
3. slab	c. something to which something else is fixed in order to make it firm
4. torsion	d. the size, shape, etc., in which something, esp. a book is produced
5. format	e. a system of secret words, letters, numbers, etc. used instead of ordinary writing to keep messages secret
	f. the force that moves a rod, wire, etc. back into the correct shape after it has been twisted out of shape
	g. the amount of protection given by insurance

h. any of the parts of a detailed plan or set of descriptions or directions

Translation

词 义 选 择

英汉两种语言都有一词多类（一个词有几个词性），一词多义（一个词有几个不同的意义）的现象，因而翻译时必须在理解原文的基础上，选择和确定句中关键词的词义。如"last"。

例一

He is the last person for such a job.

他最不配干这个工作。

例二

He should be the last （man） to blame.

怎么也不该怪他。

例三

He is the last man to do it.

他决不会干那件事。

Translate the following sentences into Chinese, and pay attention to the words underlined.

1. If the stove isn't made up, it will go out.
2. In this battle he accounted for five of the enemy.
3. Half the roads in the region are still to be made up.
4. She tried her best to right her husband from the charge of robbery.
5. It took Laurence Olivier more than an hour to make up for the part of "Othello".

Reading Material A

Concrete, Reinforced Concrete, and Prestressed Concrete (1)

Concrete is a stonelike material obtained by permitting a carefully proportioned mixture of cement, sand and gravel or other aggregate, and water to harden in forms of the shape and dimensions of the desired structure. The bulk of the material consists of fine and course aggregate. Cement and water interact chemically to bind the aggregate particles into a solid mass. Additional water, over and above that needed for this chemical reaction, is necessary to give the mixture the workability that enables it to fill the forms and surround the embedded reinforcing steel prior to hardening. Concretes in a wide range of strength properties can be obtained by appropriate adjustment of the proportions of the constituent materials. Special cements (such as high early strength cements), special aggregates (such as various lightweight or heavyweight aggregates), admixtures (such as plasticizers and air-entraining agents), and special curing methods (such as steam-curing) permit an even wider variety of properties to be obtained. ①

These properties depend to a very substantial degree on the proportions of the mix, on the thoroughness with which the various constituents are intermixed, and on the conditions of humidity and temperature in which the mix is maintained from the moment it is placed in the forms until it is fully hardened. The process of controlling these conditions is known as curing. To protect against the unintentional production of substandard concrete, a high degree of skillful control and supervision is necessary throughout the process, from the proportioning by weight of the individual components, through mixing and placing, until the completion of curing.

The factors that make concrete a universal building material are so pronounced that it has been used, in more primitive kinds and ways than at present, for thousands of years, probably beginning in Egyptian antiquity. The facility with which, while plastic, it can be deposited and made to fill forms or molds of almost any practical shape is one of these factors. ② Its high fire and weather resistance are evident advantages. Most of the constituent materials, with the possible exception of cement, are usually availableat low cost locally or at small distances from the construction site. Its compressive strength, like that of natural stones, is high, which makes it suitable for members primarily subject to compression, such as columns and arches. ③ On the other hand, again as in natural stones, it is a relatively brittle material whose tensile strengh is small compared with its compressive strength. This prevents its economical use in structural members that are subject to tension either entirely (such as in tie rods) or over part of their cross sections (such as in beams or other flexural members).

Notes

①特殊水泥（如高标号早强水泥），特殊骨料（如各种轻骨料，重骨料），外加剂（如塑化剂）和加气剂和特殊的养护方法（如蒸汽养护）（使混凝土）具有更多的性能。

②由于混凝土是可塑的，它具有可被浇注和填入各种实用形状的模具中的便利性，这是使它成为被普遍使用的材料的因素之一。

③就像天然石头一样，它抗压力高，这使它适用于主要受压的构件，如柱和拱。

Reading Material B

Concrete, Reinforced Concrete, and Prestressed Concrete (2)

To offset this limitation, it was found possible, in the second half of the nineteenth century, to use steel with its high tensile strength to reinforce concrete,[①] chiefly in those places where its small tensile strength would limit the carrying capacity of the member. The reinforcement, usually round steel rods with appropriate surface deformations to provide interlocking, is placed in the forms in advance of the concrete. When completely surrounded by the hardened concrete mass, it forms an integral part of the member. The resulting combination of two materials, known as reinforced concrete, combines many of the advantages of each: the relatively low cost, good weather and fire resistance, good compressive strength, and excellent formability of concrete and the high tensile strength and much greater ductility and toughness of steel. It is this combination that allows the almost unlimited range of uses and possibilities of reinforced concrete in the construction of buildings, bridges, dams, tanks, reservoirs, and a host of other structures.

In more recent times, it has been found possible to produce steels, at relatively low cost, whose yield strength is of the order of 4 times and more that of ordinary reinforcing steels.[②] Likewise, it is possible to produce concrete 3 to 4 times as strong in compression as the more ordinary concretes. These high strength materials offer many advantages, including smaller member cross sections, reduced dead load, and longer spans. However, there are limits to the strengths of the constituent materials beyond which certain problems arise. To be sure, the strength of such a member would increase roughly in proportion to those of the materials.[③] However, the high strains that result from the high stresses that would otherwise be permissible would lead to large deformations and deflections of such members under ordinary loading conditions. Equally important, the large strains is such high strength reinforcing steel would induce large cracks in the surrounding low tensile strength concrete, cracks that would not only be unsightly but which would expose the steel reinforcement to corrosion by moisture and other chemical action. This limits the useful yield strength of reinforcing steel to about 80 ksit (552 MPa) compared with 40 to 60 ksi (276 to 414 MPa) for conventional reinforcing steel.

A special way has been found, however, to use steels and concretes of very high strength in combination. This type of construction is known as prestressed concrete. The steel, usually in the form of wires or strands but sometimes as bars, is embedded in the concrete under high tension that is held in equilibrium by compressive stresses in the concrete after hardening. Because of this precompression, the concrete in a flexural member will crack on the tension side at a much larger load than when not so precompressed. Prestressing greatly reduces both the deflections and the tensile cracks at ordinary loads in such structures, and thereby enables these high strength materials to be used effectively. Prestressed concrete has extended, to a very significant extent, the range of spans of structural concrete and the types of structures for which it is suited.

Notes

①为弥补这一局限性，在19世纪后期人们发现可以使用抗拉的钢筋来强化混凝土。
②近年来人们发现可以以相对较低的造价生产屈服强度为普通增强钢材四倍的钢材。
③诚然这种构件的强度大致与那些材料成比例。

UNIT TWO

Text Design Codes and Specifications and Safety Provisions of the ACI Code

[1] The design of concrete structures is generally done within the framework of codes giving specific requirements for materials, structural analysis, member proportioning, etc. In contrast with many other highly developed countries, the United States does not have an official, national code governing structural concrete. The responsibility for producing and maintaining design specifications rests with various professional groups, trade associations, and technical institutes that have produced the needed documents.

[2] The American Concrete Institute (ACI) has long been a leader in such efforts. As one part of its activity the American Concrete Institute has published the widely recognized "Building Code Requirements for Reinforced Concrete" which serves as a guide in the design and construction of reinforced concrete buildings. The ACI Code has no official status in itself. However, it is generally regarded as an authoritative statement of current good practice in the field of reinforced concrete. As a result, it has been incorporated by law into countless municipal and regional building codes that do have legal status. Its provisions thereby attain, in effect, legal standing. Most reinforced concrete buildings and related construction in the United States are designed in accordance with the current ACI Code. It has also served as a model document for many other countries. A second ACI publication, "Commentary of Building Code Requirements for Reinforced Concrete", provides background material and rationale for the Code provisions. The American Concrete Institute also publishes important journals and standards, as well as recommendations for the analysis and design of special types of concrete structures.

[3] Most highway bridges in the United States are designed according to the requirements of the AASHTO① bridge specifications, which contain not only the provisions relating to loads and load distributions, mentioned earlier, but also include detailed provisions for the design and construction of concrete bridges. Many of the provisions follow ACI Code provisions closely, although differences will be found.

[4] The design of railway bridges is done according to the specifications of the AREA② Manual of Railway Engineering. It, too, is patterned after the ACI Code in most respects, but it contains much additional material pertaining to railway structures of all types.

[5] No code or design specification can be construed as a substitute for sound engineering judgment in the design of concrete structures. In structural practice, special circumstances are frequently encountered where code provisions can serve only as a guide, and the engineer must rely upon a firm understanding of the basic principles of structural mechanics applied to reinforced or prestressed concrete, and an intimate knowledge of the nature

of the materials. [3]

[6] The safety provisions of the ACI Code are given in the form of equations utilizing strength reduction factors and load factors. These factors are based to some extent on statistical information but to a larger degree on experience, engineering judgment, and compromise. In words, the design strength ϕS_n of a structure or member must be at least equal to the required strength U calculated from the factored loads, i. e.,

Design strength≥required strength

or

$$\phi S_n \geqslant U$$

The nominal strength S_n is computed (usually somewhat conservatively) by accepted methods. The required strength U is calculated by applying appropriate load factors to the respective service loads: dead load D, live load L, wind load W, earthquake load E, earth pressure H, fluid pressure F, impact allowance I, and environmental effects T that may include settlement, creep, shrinkage, and temperature change. Loads are defined in a general sense, to include either loads or the related internal effects such as moments, shears, and thrusts. Thus, in specific terms for a member subjected, say, to moment, shear, and thrust:

$$\phi M_n \geqslant M_u$$

$$\phi V_n \geqslant V_u$$

$$\phi P_n \geqslant P_u$$

where the subscripts n denote the nominal strengths in flexure, shear, and thrust respectively and the subscripts u denote the factored load moment, shear, and thrust. In computing the factored load effects on the right, load factors may be applied either to the service loads themselves or to the internal load effects calculated from the service loads.

New Words and Expressions

allowance * [ə'lauəns] n. 允许，考虑
rest with 由……负责
authoritative [ɔː'θɔritətiv] a. 有权威的，可相信的
countless * ['kauntlis] a. 无数的，不可胜数的
municipal [mjuː'nisipəl] a. 市的，市政的
commentary ['kɔməntəri] n. 评论，评注
rationale ['ræʃiə'nɑːli] n. 基本原理，原理的阐述
pertain * [pə'tein] vi. (to) 关于，属于
construe [kən'struː] vt. 解释，把……认作
regional ['riːdʒənəl] a. 区域的，地区的
nominal * ['nɔminl] a. 标称的，名义上的，标志的
shrinkage ['ʃriŋkidʒ] n. 收缩，减缩
subscript ['sʌbskript] n. 记号，标记

Notes

①AASHTO＝American Association of State Highway and Transportation Officials
美国各州公路与运输工作者协会

②AREA＝American Railway Engineering Association
美国铁路工程协会

③句中 where code provisions can serve only as a guide 为分割定语从句，修饰 circumstances；rely upon 后面有两个宾语，分别是：a firm understanding…，and an intimate knowledge…。

Exercises

Reading Comprehension

Ⅰ. Choose the best answer.

1. In the United States, design specifications are produced and maintained by ______.
   A. professional groups
   B. certain government departments
   C. trade associations
   D. both A and C
2. Most reinforced concrete buildings in the U. S. are designed according to the current ACI Code mainly because ________.
   A. it has an official status
   B. it is generally regarded as an authoritative statement of current good practice
   C. it has attained legal standing
   D. it serves as a model document throughout the world
3. Which statement is Not True according to the passage?
   A. AREA Manual of Railway Engineering is patterned after the ACI Code in most respects.
   B. Many provisions in AASHTO bridge specifications follow ACI Code closely.
   C. AREA is a branch of AASHTO.
   D. Neither AREA nor AASHTO belongs to ACI.
4. Which of the following is not contained in the AASHTO bridge specifications?
   A. Substitudes for sound engineering judgement.
   B. The provisions relating to loads and load distributions.
   C. Detailed provisions for the construction of concrete bridges.
   D. Provisons for designing concrete bridges.
5. Which statement is True according to the last paragraph?

A. No code or design specification can be a guide in structural practice.

B. Code provisions can be used as a sound judgement in any circumstances.

C. A firm understanding of the basic principles of structural mechanics is very essential to an engineer.

D. It is always safe for an engineer to rely on ACI Code.

Ⅱ. Fill in the blanks with the information given in Para. 2.

1. What is the ACI Code?

   It is "________________________________"

   published by ________________________________.

2. What is true about the ACI Code?

   a. It has no __________ in itself.

   b. However, it is generally regarded __________.

   c. It has been incorporated __________.

   d. It serves as a guide __________.

   e. It has also served as a __________.

3. What are strength reduction factors and load factors based on?

   To some extent, they are based on __________, but to a larger extent they are based on ________________, __________, __________.

4. In computing the factored load effects on the right, __________ either to __________ or to __________.

Vocabulary

Ⅰ. Choose one word or phrase that is the most similar in meaning to the one underlined in the given sentences.

1. His remarks have been wrongly construed.

   A. commented　　B. understood

   C. analysed　　D. reported

2. We will incorporate your suggestion in the new plan.

   A. eliminate　　B. contain

   C. include　　D. compose

3. The president and his advisors discussed matters that pertained to the war.

   A. related to　　B. happened to

   C. resulted from　　D. referred to

4. He gave an authoritative account of the recent events.

   A. detailed　　B. brief

   C. informal　　D. official

5. The specifications for the new garage are now ready.

   A. preparations　　B. locations

C. directions　　　　　　　　　　D. introductions

Ⅱ. Match the words in Column A with their corresponding definitions or expressions in Column B.

A	B
1. rationale	a. be the sign of, indicate
2. prestress	b. including many different parts
3. denote	c. be left in the charge of
4. municipal	d. that is not damaged by heat
5. rest with	e. join with one another
	f. of a town or city under its own government
	g. reason on which a system or practice is based
	h. strengthen by having stretched wires set inside

Translation

词义引伸

英汉翻译时，常常会遇到某个词在词典里找不到适当的词义，这时就应根据上下文和逻辑关系，以该词的根本词义为基础，引伸该词的意义，选择适当的译文。

例一

There is mixture of the tiger and the ape in the character of the imperialists.

帝国主义者的性格既残暴，又狡猾。

例二

The major contributors in component technology have been in the semi-conductor components.

元件技术中起主要作用的是半导体元件。

Translate the following sentences into Chinese, and pay attention to the words underlined.

1. There was no provocation for such an angry letter.
2. Fatty's Restaurant had become an institution in his life in the last seven years.
3. The trunk was big and awkward and loaded with books. But his case was a different proposition.
4. The foresight and coverage shown by the inventor of the process are most commandable.
5. The invention of machinery had brought into the world a new era-the Industrial Age. Money had become King.

Reading Material A

Safety Provisions of the ACI Code

The load factors specified in the ACI Code, to be applied to calculated dead loads and those live and environmental loads specified in the appropriate codes or standards, are summarized in Table 1. For individual loads, lower factors are used for loads known with greater certainty, e.g., dead load, compared with loads of greater variability, e.g., live loads. Further, for load combinations such as dead plus live load plus wind forces, a reduction coefficient is applied that reflects the improbability that an excessively large live load coincides with an unusually high windstorm. ① The factors also reflect, in a general way, uncertainties with which internal load effects are calculated from external loads in systems as complex as highly indeterminate, inelastic reinforced concrete structures which, in addition, consist of variable-section members (because of tension cracking, discontinuous reinforcement, etc.). ② Finally, the load factors also distinguish between two situations, particularly when horizontal forces are present in addition to gravity, i.e., the situation where the effects of all simultaneous loads are additive, as distinct from that in which various load effects counteract each other. ③ For example, in a retaining wall the soil pressure produces an overturning moment, and the gravity forces produce a counteracting stabilizing moment.

Table 1 Factored load combinations for determining required strength *U* in the ACI Code

Condition	Factored load or load effect U
Basic	$U=1.4D+1.7L$
Winds	$U=0.75\ (1.4D+1.7L+1.7W)$
	and include consideration of $L=0$
	$U=0.9D+1.3W$
	$U=1.4D+1.7L$
Earthquake	$U=0.75\ (1.4D+1.7L+1.87E)$
	and include consideration of $L=0$
	$U=0.9D+1.43L$
	$U=1.4D+1.7L$
Earth pressure	$U=1.4D+1.7L+1.7H$
	$U=0.9D+1.7H$
	$U=1.4D+1.7L$
Fluids	Add 1.4F to all loads that include L
Impact	Substitute $(L+I)$ for L
Settlement, creep, shrinkage, or temperature change effects	$U=0.75\ (1.4D+1.4T+1.7L)$
	$U=1.4\ (D+T)$

In all cases in Table 1 the controlling equation is the one that gives the largest factored load effect U.

The strength reduction factors ϕ in the ACI Code are given different values depending on the state of knowledge, i. e. , the accuracy with which various strengths can be calculated. Thus the value for bending is higher than that for shear or bearing. Also, ϕ values reflect the probable importance, for the survival of the structure, of the particular member and of the probable quality control achievable. For both these reasons, a lower value is used for columns than for beams. Table 2 gives the ϕ values specified in the ACI Code.

The joint application of strength reduction factors (Table 2) and load factors (Table 1) is aimed at producing approximate probabilities of understrength of the order of 1/00 and of overloads of 1/1000. This results in a probability of structural failure of the order of 1/100, 000.

Table 2 Strength reduction factors in the ACI Code

Kind of strength	Strength reduction factor ϕ
Flexure, without axial load	0. 90
Axial load, and axial load with flexure	
Axial tension, and axial tension with flexure	0. 90
Axial compression, and axial compression with flexure	
Members with spiral reinforcement	0. 75
Other members	0. 70
Except that for low values of axial load, ϕ may be increased in accordance with the following:	
For members in which f_y does not exceed 60, 000 psi, with symmetrical reinforcement, and with $(h-d'-d_s)$ /h not less than 0. 70, ϕ may be increased linearly to 0. 90 as ϕP_n decreases from 0. 10 $f_c' A_g$ to zero	
For other reinforced members, ϕ may be increased linearly to 0. 90 as ϕP_n decreases from 0. 10$f_c' A_g$ or ϕP_{nb}, whichever is smaller, to zero	
Shear and torsion	0. 85
Bearing on concrete	0. 70
Flexure in plan concrete	0. 65

The main body of the ACI Code is formulated in terms of strength design, with the specific load and strength reduction factors just presented. A special Code Appendix B, "Alternate Design Method", permits the use of service load design for those who prefer this older method. This appendix specifies allowable stresses for flexure, shear, bearing, etc. , that are to be used in connection with the internal effects (M, V, P, etc.) of the unfactored dead and specified service loads. For many situations, particularly with today's higher strength steels and concretes, this alternative design method is less economical than strength design.

Notes

①此外，对如恒载加活载加风力联合作用下，用一个降低系数来体现过大的活荷载不可能与大风暴同时出现。

②这些系数通常也体现了根据多次超静定的、非弹性的钢筋混凝土结构这样复杂体系的外部荷载计算内部荷载的不可靠性，况且该结构的构件由于开裂、不连续配筋等原因成为变截面构件。

③最后，荷载系数要区别两种情况，尤其是在除竖向力外，还有水平力出现时，即：在所有同时作用的荷载效应相加的情况与相互抵消的情况是不同的。

Reading Material B

Dimensions and Tolerances

Although the designer may tend to think of dimensions, clearances, and bar locations as exact, practical considerations require that there be accepted tolerances. These tolerances are the permissible variations from dimensions given on drawings.

Overall dimensions of reinforced concrete members are usually specified by the engineer in whole inches for beams, columns, and walls; sometimes half inches for thin slabs; and often 3-in. increments for more massive elements such as plan dimensions for footings. Formwork for the placing of these members must be built carefully so that it does not deform excessively under the action of workmen, construction machinery loads, and wet concrete. Accepted tolerances for variation in cross-sectional dimensions of columns and beams and in the thickness of slabs and walls are $+\frac{1}{2}$in. and $-\frac{1}{4}$ in. [15]. For concrete footings accepted variations in plan dimensions are $+2$in. and $-\frac{1}{2}$in. [15], whereas the thickness has an accepted tolerance of -5% of specified thickness [15]. The capacity reduction factor ϕ is intended to account for the situation in which several acceptable tolerances may combine to measurably reduce the strength.[①]

Reinforcing bars are normally specified in 3-in. length increments and the placement tolerances are given in the ACI Code. For minimum clear concrete protection and for the effective depth d (distance from compression of face of concrete to center of tension steel) in flexural members, walls, and compression members, the specified tolerances are as follows:

Effective Depth, d		Tolerances			
		On Effective Depth		On Minimum Clear Cover	
(in.)	(mm)	(in.)	(mm)	(in.)	(mm)
$d \leqslant 8$	200*	$\pm\frac{3}{8}$	±10	$-\frac{3}{8}$	−10
$d > 8$	200	$\pm\frac{1}{2}$	±12	$-\frac{1}{2}$	−12

* 1977 ACI Code does not include metric values; conversions are approximate.

Notwithstanding the stated tolerances on cover, the resulting cover shall not be less than two-thirds of the minimum cover specified on structural drawings or on specifications. Since the effective depth and the clear concrete cover are both components of total depth, the tolerances on those dimensions are directly related. When the tolerances on bar placement and cover accumulate, the overall dimension tolerance may be exceeded; thus field adjustment may have to be made. This may be particularly important on very thin sections such as in precast and shell structures.

For location of bars along the longitudinal dimension, and of bar bends, the tolerance is ± 2 in. except at discontinuous ends where tolerance shall be $\pm\frac{1}{2}$ in.

Accuracy of Computations

When one understands that variations exist in material strength for both steel and concrete and that variations in dimensions are inevitable (and acceptable), it becomes clear that design of reinforced concrete structures does not require a high degree of precision.

The designer should place highest priority on determining proper location and length of steel reinforcement to carry the tension forces, thus making up for that capacity which is deficient in the concrete.② Failures, when they occur, generally result from gross underestimating of tensile forces or lack of identification of how the structure or element will behave under loads. They are rarely the result of carrying too few significant figures in the design computations. However, significant figures may be lost in arithmetic operations, and gross errors may sometimes result from sloppiness. It is recommended, therefore, more for systematic control of calculations and for ease in checking than for any improved effect on the final structure, that computations in all steps be carried to three significant figures.③

Notes

①承载力折减系数ϕ用于说明几种容许误差可能累积起来明显降低强度的情况。

②设计者应该把确定受拉钢筋适当定位与长度放在首位，以弥补混凝土抗拉承载力的不足。

③因此，建议要更加重视对计算进行系统控制，要便于校核，而不是对最终结构进行改进。而且，所有的计算步骤要用三位有效数字进行。

UNIT THREE

Text Serviceability

[1] Methods have been developed to insure that beams will have a proper safety margin against failure in flexure or shear, or due to inadequate bond and anchorage of the reinforcement. The member has been assumed to be at a hypothetical overload state for this purpose.

[2] It is also important that member performance in normal service be satisfactory, when loads are those actually expected to act, i.e. when load factors are 1.0. This is not guaranteed simply by providing adequate strength. Service load deflections under full load may be excessively large, or long-term deflections due to sustained loads may cause damage. Tension cracks in beams may be wide enough to be visually disturbing, or may even permit serious corrosion of reinforcing bars. These and other questions, such as vibration or fatigue, require consideration.

[3] Serviceability studies are carried out based on elastic theory, with stresses in both concrete and steel assumed to be proportional to strain. ① The concrete on the tension side of the neutral axis may be assumed uncracked, partially cracked, or fully cracked, depending on the loads and material strengths.

[4] Until recently questions of serviceability were dealt with indirectly, by limiting the stresses in concrete and steel at service loads to the rather conservative values that had resulted in satisfactory performance in the past. Now, with strength design methods in general use that permit more slender members, through more accurate assessment of capacity, and with higher strength materials further contributing to the trend toward smaller member sizes, such indirect methods will no longer do. ② The more current approach is to investigate service load cracking and deflections specifically, after proportioning members based on strength requirements. ACI Code provisions reflect this change in thinking.

[5] In this chapter, methods will be developed to assure that the cracks associated with flexure of reinforced concrete beams are narrow and well distributed, and that short-and long-term deflections at loads up to the full service load are not objectionably large.

Cracking in Flexural Members

[6] All reinforced concrete beams crack, generally starting at loads well below service level, and possibly even prior to loading due to restrained shrinkage. ③ Flexural cracking due to loads is not only inevitable, but is actually necessary for the reinforcement to be used effectively. Prior to the formation of flexural cracks, the steel stress is no more than n times the stress in the adjacent concrete, where n is the modular ratio, E_s/E_c. For materi-

als common in current practice, n is approximately 8. Thus, when the concrete is close to its modulus of rupture of about 500 psi, the steel stress will be only $8\times500=4000$ psi, far too low to be very effective as reinforcement. ④ At normal service loads, steel stresses eight or nine times that value can be expected.

[7] In a well-designed beam, flexural cracks are fine, so-called "hairline" cracks, almost invisible to the casual observer, and they permit little if any corrosion of the reinforcement. As loads are gradually increased above the cracking load, both the number and width of cracks increases, and at service load level a maximum width of crack of about 0.01 in (0.25mm) is typical. If loads are further increased, crack widths increase further, although the number of cracks is more or less stable.

[8] Cracking of concrete is a random process, highly variable and influenced by many factors. Because of the complexity of the problem, present methods for predicti ng crack widths are based primarily on test observations. Most equations that have been developed predict the probable maximum crack width, which usually means that about 90 percent of the crack widths in the member are below the calculated value. However, isolated cracks exceeding twice the computed width can sometimes occur.

Variables Affecting Width of Cracks

[9] If proper end anchorage is provided a beam will not fail prematurely, even though the bond is destroyed along the entire span. However, crack widths will be greater than an otherwise identical beam in which good resistance to slip is provided along the length of the span. In general, beams with smooth round bars will display a relatively small number of rather wide cracks in service, while beams with good slip resistance insured by proper surface deformations on the bars will show a larger number of very fine, almost invisible cracks. Because of this improvement, reinforcing bars in current practice are always provided with surface deformations, the maximum spacing and minimum height of which are established by ASTM Specifications A615, A616, and A617. ⑤

[10] A second variable of importance is the stress in the reinforcement. Studies by Gergely and Lutz and others have confirmed that crack width is proportional to f_s^n, where f_s is the steel stress and n is an exponent that varies in the range from about 1.0 to 1.4. For steel stresses in the range of practical interest, say from 20 to 36 ksi, n may be taken equal to 1.0. The steel stress is easily computed based on elastic cracked-section analysis. Alternatively, f_s may be taken equal to $0.60 f_y$ according to the ACI Code.

[11] Experiments by Broms and others have showed that both crack spacing and crack width are related to the concrete cover distance d_c, measured from the center of the bar to the face of the concrete. In general, increasing the cover increases the spacing of cracks, and also increases crack width. Furthermore, the distribution of the reinforcement in the tension zone of the beam is important. Generally, to control cracking, it is better to use a larg-

er number of smaller-diameter bars to provide the required A_s than to use the minimum number of larger bars, and the bars should be well distributed over the tensile zone of the concrete.

New Words and Expressions

margin [ˈmɑːdʒin]	*n.*	储备量，安全系数
hypothetical [ˌhaipəuˈθetikəl]	*a.*	假说的，假设的
proportional to		与……成比例的
uncracked [ʌnˈkrækt]	*a.*	未开裂的，无裂缝的
assessment [əˈsesmənt]	*a.*	估计，评价
provisions [prəˈviʒənz]	*n.*	规定，条款
objectionably [əbˈdʒekʃnəbli]	*adv.*	该反对地，有异议地
flexural * [ˈfleksjurəl]	*a.*	弯曲的，挠曲的
prior to		在…之前
modular [ˈmɔdjulə]	*a.*	模数的
modulus [ˈmɔdjuləs]	*n.*	模数，模量
hairline [ˈhεəlain]	*n.*	细缝，毛筋
corrosion * [kəˈrəuʒən]	*n.*	腐蚀，侵蚀
complexity * [kəmˈpleksiti]	*n.*	复杂（性）
prematurely [ˈpremətjuəli]	*ad.*	不成熟地，过早地
end anchorage		端部锚固
exponent [iksˈpəunənt]	*n.*	指数，幂
alternatively [ɔːlˈtəːnətivli]	*ad.*	换句话说，另一方面

Nostes

①… with stresses… assumed …为 with＋n. ＋past participle 结构，在句中作状语，表示行为方式。

本文中还有两处类似结构：

with＋n. ＋prep. phrase

with＋n. ＋present participle

②句中 do 意为适用，行得通。

③句中 well 副词，意为相当，十分。

due to restrained shrinkage 作状语，表示原因。

④句中 psi＝pounds per square inch 磅/英寸^2。

far 用来强调程度，意为大大……，……得多。

⑤句中…height of which…，which 指代 reinforcing bars.

ASTM Specifications 美国材料试验学会标准。

Exercises

Reading Comprehension

Ⅰ. Choose the best answer.

1. What does 'for this purpose' in Para. 1 refer to?

   A. Methods have been developed.

   B. To insure that beams will have a proper safety margin against failure.

   C. The member has been sssumed to be at a a hypothetical overload state.

   D. Due to inadequate bond and anchorage of reinforcement.

2. What does Para. 4 implies?

   A. The difference in dealing with the questions of serviceability in the past and now.

   B. How to deal with the questions of serviceability.

   C. What ACI Code is.

   D. The advantage of the new method to deal with the questions of serviceability.

3. Cracking of concrete ________.

   A. can be precisely calculated

   B. is hardly predicted

   C. is irregular and changeable

   D. is a common process

4. Reinfocing bars with surface deformation ________.

   A. have good slip resistance

   B. show many cracks

   C. will not fail

   D. are provided by ASTM

5. The better way to control cracking is to use ________.

   A. a large number of bars

   B. more smaller bars and less larger ones

   C. a large number of smaller bars

   D. as many as smaller-diameter bars

Ⅱ. Fill in the blanks with the information given in the text.

1. In the past the method to deal with the question of serviceability is ____ at service load ________________________________.

2. The relations between cover and spacing of crack and crack width are that ________________________ increases ________________________ and

________________.

Vocabulary

Ⅰ. Choose one word or phrase that is the most similar in meaning to the one underlined in the given sentences.

1. As a result of <u>shrinkage</u>, the shirt is now too small to wear.
   A. loss in shape B. loss in size
   C. moving back D. moving away
2. By his <u>premature</u> action he lost the battle.
   A. ripening quickly B. developins fast
   C. done too early D. born too soon
3. Please <u>confirm</u> your telephone message by letter.
   A. make stronger B. give approval
   C. show confidence D. give advice
4. The <u>tensile</u> strength of a rope tells you how much weight it can hold without breaking.
   A. connected with force B. related to tense
   C. related to tension D. assoaciated with strength
5. The friendship between the two countries has ended in a <u>rupture</u>.
   A. damage B. ruin
   C. cutting D. break

Ⅱ. Match the words in Column A with their corresponding definitions or explanations in Column B.

A	B
1. random	a. arrangement apart
2. exponent	b. opposed to great or sudden change
3. hypothetical	c. the act of coming out
4. spacing	d. having different-sized parts
5. conservative	e. made or done without any plan
	f. a symbol which shows how many times to multiply a number by itself
	g. the tendency to go back to the natural size
	h. not based on certain knowledge

Translation

增词和减词

英汉两种语言由于表达方式不同，因此在表达同一个思想时要在译文中增加原文中没有或减掉原文中的词语。

例一　增词

The arrows in the leads identify the materials. 引线的箭头标记着材料的类型。（对“材料”增补“类型”）

例二　减词

The force required to turn a shaft depends on the length of the lever used. 使轴转动（所需）的力取决于（所用杆）臂（的）长（度）。(required 和 used 可予省略)

Translate the following sentences into Chinese, and note what should be added and what left out.

1. Being large or small, all magnets behave the same.
2. It has been thought that radium radiations might be useful in curing various diseases.
3. The first electronic computers went into operation in 1946.
4. When the pressure gets low, the boiling point becomes low.
5. Weight is down force, and therefore any object will move downward.

Reading Material A

The Gergely-Lutz Equation for Crack Width

Based on their research at Cornell University, which involved the statistical analysis of a large amount of experimental data, Gergely and Lutz proposed the following equation for predicting the maximum width of crack at the tension face of a beam:

$$W = 0.076\beta^{f}_{js}\sqrt[3]{d_c A} \qquad (1)$$

in which w is the maximum width of crack, in thousandth inches, and f_s is the steel stress at the load for which the crack width is to be determined, measured in ksi. The geometric parameters are shown as follows:

d_c——thickness of concrete cover measured from tension face to center of bar closest to that face, in

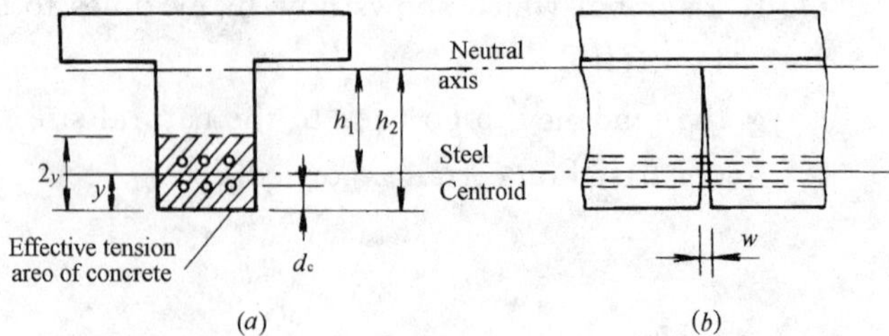

Fig. 3-1　Geometric basis of crack width calculations

β——ratio of distances from tension face and from steel centroid to neutral axis, equal to h_2/h_1

A——concrete area surrounding one bar, equal to total effective tension area of concrete surrounding reinforcement and having same centroid, divided by number of bars, in^2

Equation (1), which applies only to beams in which deformed bars are used, includes all the factors just named as having an important influence on the width of cracks: steel stress, concrete cover, and the distribution of the reinforcement in the concrete tensile zone. In addition, the factor β is added, to account for the increase in crack width with distance from the neutral axis (see Fig. 3-1*b*). ①

Permissible Crack Widths

The acceptable width of flexural cracks in service depends mostly on the conditions of exposure and should be established in view of the possibility of corrosion of the reinforcement. ② The recommendations of the ACI Committee 224 are summarized in Table 1. However, good engineering judgment must be used in setting limiting values in particular cases. It should be recognized that, because of the random nature of cracking, individual cracks significantly wider than predicted by Eq. (1) are likely. The designer should also keep in mind, however, that Eq. (1) predicts the crack width at the surface of the member, whereas the width of crack is known to be less at the steel-concrete interface. Increasing the concrete cover, even though it increases the surface crack width, may be beneficial in avoiding corrosion.

Cyclic and Sustained Load Effects③

Both cyclic and sustained loading account for increasing crack width④. While there is a large amount of scatter in test data, results of fatigue tests and sustained loading tests indicate that a doubling of crack width can be expected with time. Under most conditions the spacing of cracks does not change with time at constant levels of sustained stress or cyclic stress range. ⑤

Table 1 **Tolerable crack widths for reinforced concrete**

Exposure condition	Tolerable crack width in	Tolerable crack width mm
Dry air or protective membrane	0.016	0.41
Humidity, moist air, soil	0.012	0.30
Deicing chemicals	0.007	0.18
Seawater and seawater spray; wetting and drying	0.006	0.15
Water-retaining structures, excluding nonpressure pipes	0.004	0.10

Notes

①此外，还引入系数 β 来考虑裂缝宽度随着距中性轴的距离而增加。
②在使用中受弯裂缝的允许宽度主要取决于其暴露情况，确定时要考虑钢筋腐蚀的可能性。
③周期荷载与持续荷载的影响。
④周期荷载与持续荷载都是引起裂缝加宽的原因。
⑤在持续应力或周期应力（变化）范围处于恒定水平时，大多数情况下，裂缝间距不随时间而变。

Reading Material B

Creep Effect on Deflections under Sustained Load

The total long-term deflection includes the instantaneous elastic deflection plus the contributions from creep and shrinkage. Creep is inelastic deformation with time under sustained loads at unit stresses within the accepted elastic range (say, below $0.5f'_c$), as shown in Fig 1. This inelastic deformation increases at a decreasing rate during the time of loading. The internal mechanics of creep, or plastic flow, has been the subject of considerable study for many years. Creep deformation is believed to be the result of a combination of the following: (1) closing of internal voids, (2) viscous flow[①] 1 of the cement-water paste, (3) crystalline flow in the aggregate, and (4) the flow of water out of the cement gel[②] due to external load and drying. Factors that affect the magnitude of creep deformation are (1) the constituents—such as the composition and fineness of the cement, the admixtures, and the size, grading, and mineral content of the aggregates; (2) proportions, such as water content and water-cement ratio; (3) curing temperature and humidity; (4) relative humidity during storage; (5) size of the concrete member, particularly the ratio of span length to beam depth; (6) age at loading; (7) duration of loading; and (8) magnitude of stress.

Since, as seen from Fig. 3-2, the result of creep is an increase in strain with constant stress, one of the ways of accounting for it is by the use of a modified modulus of elasticity E ct.[③] An alternative and more recently preferred procedure is to apply a multiplier C_t to the elastic deflection Δ_i.

In order to help understand the qualitative effect of creep on beam deformation, consider the singly reinforced beam of Fig. 3-3. It is noted that the strain at the tension steel is essentially unchanged because the concrete contributes little in taking tension and ordinary deformed steel reinforcement exhibits little creep. Since the neutral axis moves down, two observations may be made: (1) The concrete stress reduces at the compression face (i.e., same compressive force acting and x_{cp} exceeds x_i); and (2) the increase in compressive

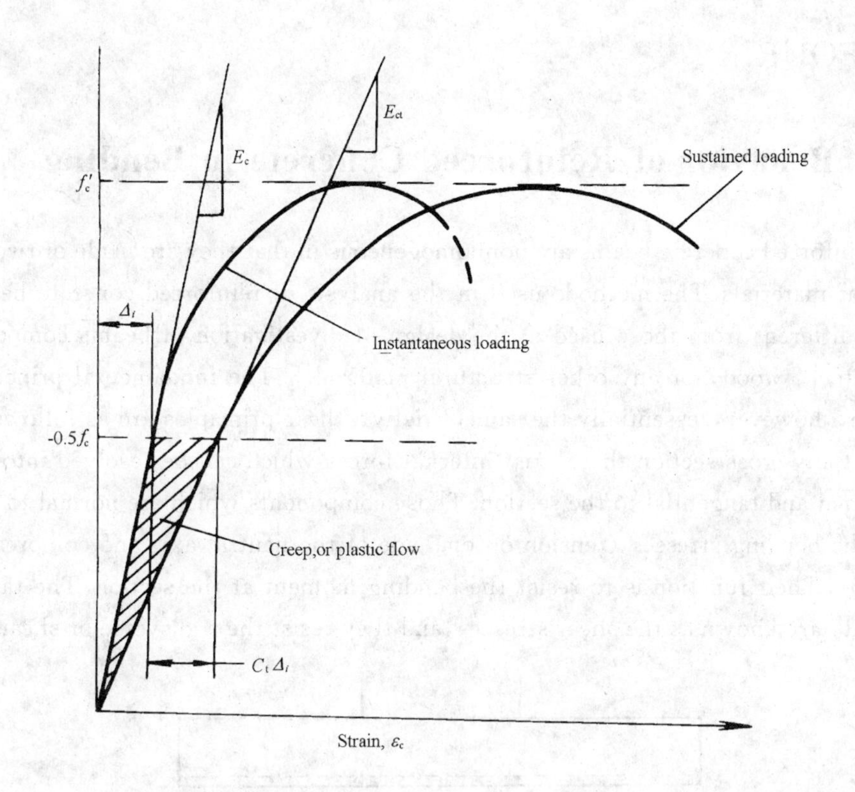

Fig. 3-2 Typical stress-strain curves for instantaneous and long-time loading

strain is much greater than the increase in curvature (ϕ) .

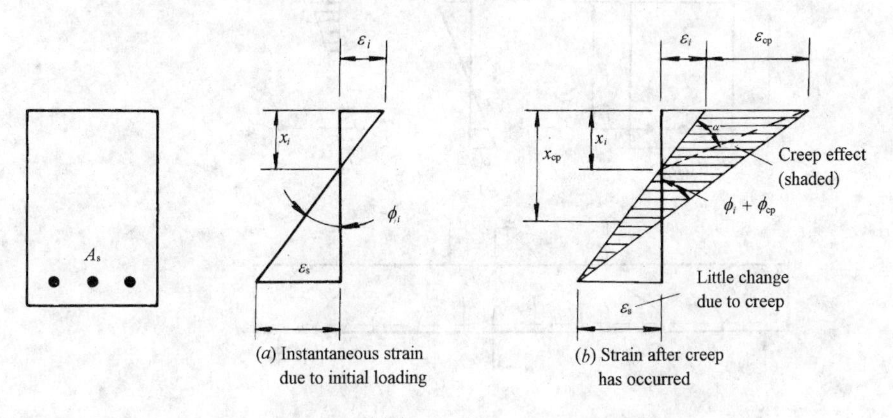

Fig. 3-3 Creep effect on beam curvature

Notes

①viscous flow 粘性流

②gel 水泥凝胶

③如图 3-2 所示，由于徐变而使恒定应力下的应变增加，其解决方法之一就是应用改进的弹性模量 E_{ct}。

UNIT FOUR

Text Behavior of Reinforced Concrete in Bending

[1] Reinforced concrete beams are nonhomogeneous in that they are made of two entirely different materials. The methods used in the analysis of reinforced concrete beams are therefore different from those used in the design of investigation of beams composed entirely of steel, wood, or any other structural material. ① The fundamental principles involved are, however, essentially the same. Briefly, these principles are as follows.

[2] At any cross section there exist internal forces which can be resolved into components normal and tangential to the section. Those components which are normal to the section are the bending stresses (tension on one side of the neutral axis and compression on the other). Their function is to resist the bending moment at the section. The tangential components are known as the shear stresses, and they resist the transverse or shear forces.

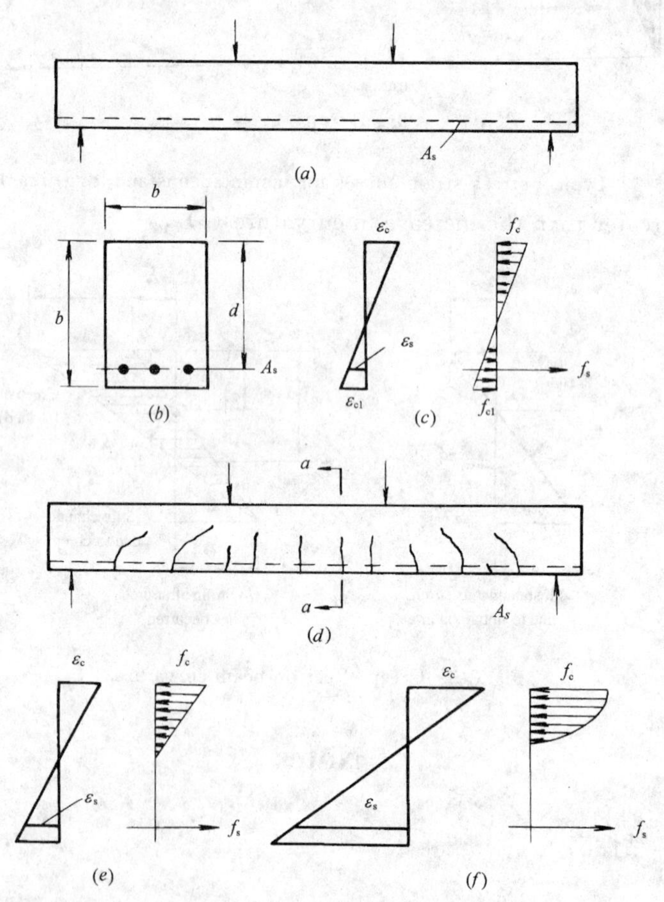

Fig. 4-1 Elastic and inelastic stress distributions in homogeneous beams

[3] Fundamental assumptions relating to flexure and flexural shear are as follows:

1 A cross section which was plane before loading remains plane under load. This means that the unit strains in a beam above and below the neutral axis are proportional to the distance from that axis.

2 The bending stress f at any point depends on the strain at that point in a manner given by the stress-strain diagram of the material. If the beam is made of a homogeneous material whose stress-strain diagram in tension and compression is that of Fig. 4-1*a*, the following holds. ② If the maximum strain at the outer fibers is smaller than the strain ε_p up to which stress and strain are proportional for the given material, then the compression and tension stresses on either side of the axis are proportional to the distance from the axis, as shown in Fig. 4-1*b*. ③ However, if the maximum strain at the outer fibers is larger than ε_p, this is no longer true. The situation which then obtains is shown in Fig. 4-1c; i.e. in the outer portions of the beam, where $\varepsilon > \varepsilon_p$, stresses and strains are no longer proportional. In these regions the magnitude of stress at any level, such as f_2 in Fig. 4-1c, depends on the strain ε_2 at that level in the manner given by the stress-strain diagram of the material. In other words, for a given strain in the beam, the stress at a point is the same as that given by the stress-strain diagram for the same strain.

3 The distribution of the shear stresses v over the depth of the section depends on the shape of the cross section and of the stress-strain diagram. These shear stresses are largest at the neutral axis and equal to zero at the outer fibers. The shear stresses on horizontal and vertical planes through any point are equal.

4 Owing to the combined action of shear stresses (horizontal and vertical) and flexure stresses, at any point in a beam there are inclined stresses of tension and compression, the largest of which form an angle of 90° with each other. ④ The intensity of the inclined maximum or principal stress at any point is given by

$$t = \frac{f}{2} \pm \sqrt{\frac{f^2}{4} + v^2} \tag{1}$$

where f——intensity of normal fiber stress

v——intensity of tangential shearing stress

The inclined stress makes an angle α with the horizontal such that $\tan 2\alpha = 2v/f$.

5 Since the horizontal and vertical shearing stresses are equal and the flexural stresses are zero at the neutral plane, the inclined tensile and compressive stresses at any point in that plane form an angle of 45° with the horizontal, the intensity of each being equal to the unit shear at the point.

6 When the stresses in the outer fibres are smaller than the proportional limit f_p, the beam behaves elastically, as shown in Fig. 1. In this case the following obtains:

①The neutral axis passes through the center of gravity of the cross section.

②The intensity of the bending stress normal to the section increases directly with the distance from the neutral axis and is a maximum at the extreme fibers. The stress at any given point in the cross section is represented by the equation

$$f = \frac{My}{I} \tag{2}$$

where f——bending stress at a distance y from neutral axis

M——external bending moment at section

I——moment of inertia of cross section about neutral axis

[4] The maximum bending stress occurs at the outer fibers and is equal to

$$f_{\max} = \frac{Mc}{I} = \frac{M}{S} \tag{3}$$

where c——distance from neutral axis to outer fiber

S——I/c=section modulus of cross section

③The shear stress (longitudinal equals transverse) v at any point in the cross section is given by

$$v = \frac{VQ}{Ib} \tag{4}$$

where V——total shear at section

Q——statical moment about neutral axis of that portion of cross section lying between a line through point in question parallel to neutral axis and nearest face (upper or lower) of beam⑤

I——moment of inertia of cross section about neutral axis

b——width of beam at given point

④The intensity of shear along a vertical cross section in a rectangular beam varies as the ordinates of a parabola, the intensity being zero at the outer fibers of the beam and a maximum at the neutral axis. ⑥ The maximum is $\frac{3}{2}V/ba$, since at the neutral axis $Q=ba^2/8$ and $I=ba^3/12$ in Eq. (4).

New Words and Expressions

homogeneous * [ˌhɔməˈdʒiːnjəs] a. 均质的，同类的

nonhomogeneous a. 非均质的

tangential * [tænˈdʒenʃəl] a. 切线的，正切的

shear [ʃiə] n. 切力，剪力

assumption * [əˈsʌmpʃən] n. 假定，设想

elastically [iˈlæstikəli] ad. 有弹性地

tan [tæn] n. 正切，切线

inertia * [iˈnəːʃjə] n. 惯性，惯量

longitudinal [ˌlɔndʒiˈtjuːdinl] a. 经度的，纵向的

rectangular * [rekˈtæŋgjulə] a. 矩形的，长方形的

ordinate [ˈɔːdinit] n. 纵标，纵坐标

parabola [pəˈræbələ] n. 抛物线

Notes

①句中 used in the analysis of…used in the design…和 composed entirely of …是过去分词短语作定语。

②句中由 whose 引导的定语从句修饰 material，that 代 stress-strain…compression，holds 是不及物动词，意为有效。

③句中 which 指 ε_p，up to 表示在…范围内。

④the largest of which…中 which 指 stresses of tension and compression。

⑤句中 point in question 意为所求点。

⑥the intensity being 是独立结构。

Exercises ·

Reading Compression

Ⅰ. Choose the best answer.

1. The function of the bending stresses is to ________.

   A. resist the shear forces of the section

   B. resist the tangential force

   C. resist the normal force

   D. resist the bending moment at the section

2. When are the compression and tension stresses on either side of the axis proportional to the distance from the axis?

   A. The maxium strain at the outer fibers is larger than ε_p.

   B. The maxium strain at the outer fibers is equal to ε_p.

   C. The maxium strain at the outer fibers is smaller than ε_p.

   D. None of above.

3. Which of the following statements is not True?

   A. The fundamental principles involved in the reinforced concrete beams are different from those invoved in the beams composed entirely of steel, wood, or any other structural material.

   B. At any point in a beam there are inclined stresses of tension and compression, the largest of which form an angle of 90° with each other.

   C. The horizontal and vertical shearing stresses are equal and the flexural stresses are zero at the neutral plane.

   D. The intensity of the bending stress normal to the section increases directly with the distance from the neutral axis.

4. What does the distribution of the shear stress v over the depth of the section depend on?
   A. It depends on the magnitude of the section and of the stress-strain diagram.
   B. It depends on the depth of the section and of the stress-strain diagram.
   C. It depends on the inclined degree of the section and of the stress-strain diagram.
   D. It depends on the shape of the cross section and of the stress-strain diagram.
5. The intensity of shear along a vertical cross section in a rectangular beam varies as the ordinates of a parabola.
   What does the word ordinates probably mean here?
   A. The crosswise measurement on a graph.
   B. The crosswise strength.
   C. The upward measurement on a graph.
   D. The upward strength.

Ⅱ. Fill in the blanks with the information given in the text.

1. At any cross section there exist internal forces which can be resolved into components ________ and ________ to the section. Those components which are ________ to the section are ________. Their function is to resist the ________ at the section. The ________ components are known as the ________ and they resist the ________.
2. Since the horizontal and vertical shearing stresses are ________ and the flexural stresses are ________ at the neutral plane, the inclined tensile and compressive stresses at ________ in that plane form an angle of 45° with the ________, the intensity of each being ________ to the unit shear at the point.
3. What does the bending stress f at any point depend on?
   It depends on ____.

Vocabulary

Ⅰ. Choose one word or phrase which is the most similar in meaning to the one underlined in the given sentences.

1. They rented the old house on the assumption that the landlord would paint it.
   A. commendation　B. imagination
   C. imitation　D. supposition
2. Life on campus seemed statical, and the students longed for a change.
   A. changeless　B. tedious
   C. hazardous　D. uninteresting
3. Read it through, using the diagram to help you understand it.

A. photo　　　　　　　　B. drawing

C. draft　　　　　　　　D. equation

4. This book is the compression of all his published poetry.

A. shortening　　　　　　B. complimenting

C. attaching　　　　　　D. involving

5. People had been conscious of the problem before, but the new book made them aware of its magnitude.

A. greatness of size　　　　B. greatness of scale

C. greatness of importance　　D. greatness of degree

Ⅱ. Match the words in Column A with their corresponding definitions or explanations in Column B.

A	B
1. modulus	a. a line that divides a regular shape into two equal parts with the same shape
2. equation	b. a curve which is like the line made by a ball when it is thrown in the air and falls to the ground
	c. a measure of the turning power of a force
3. axis	d. straight line touching the edge of a curve but not cutting across it
4. parabola	e. a statement that 2 quantities are equal
5. inertia	f. a standard of measurement esp. as used in building
	g. a figure with 4 straight sides forming 4 right angles
	h. the force which prevents a thing from being moved when it is standing still or prevents it from being stopped when it is moving

Translation

否 定 形 式

在英汉翻译中，对英语否定句需特别注意。英语中有全部否定与部分否定之分，因此必须辨别清楚，才能翻译正确。

例一　（全部否定）

No real structure is absolutely rigid. 实际上没有绝对刚性的结构。

例二　（部分否定）

Every machine here is not imported from abroad. 这里的机器并非每台都是从国外进口的。（错译：“这里的每台机器都不是从国外进口的。”）

Translate the following sentences into Chinese, and pay attention to the words underlined.

1. Not many of the things are of use in form in which they are found.
2. Both of the instruments are not precise.
3. Not much was known of the electronic computer ten years ago.
4. None of the answers are right.
5. All these metals are not good conductors.

Reading Material A

Reinforced Concrete Beam Behavior (1)

Plain concrete beams are inefficient as flexural members because the tension strength in bending is a small fraction of the compression strength. In consequence, such beams fail on the tension side at low loads long before the strength of the concrete on the compression side has been fully utilized. For this reason, steel reinforcing bars are placed on the tension side as close to the extreme tension fiber as is compatible with proper fire and corrosion protection of the steel. In such a reinforced concrete beam the tension which is caused by the bending moments is chiefly resisted by the steel reinforcement, while the concrete alone is usually capable of resisting the corresponding compression. Such joint action of the two materials is assured if relative slip is prevented. This is achieved by using deformed bars with their high bond strength at the steel-concrete interface and, if necessary, by special anchorage of the ends of the bars. ① A simple example of such a beam, with the customary designations for the cross-sectional dimensions, is shown in Fig. 4-2 For simplicity, the discussion which follows will deal with beams of rectangular cross section, even though members of other shapes are very common in most concrete structures.

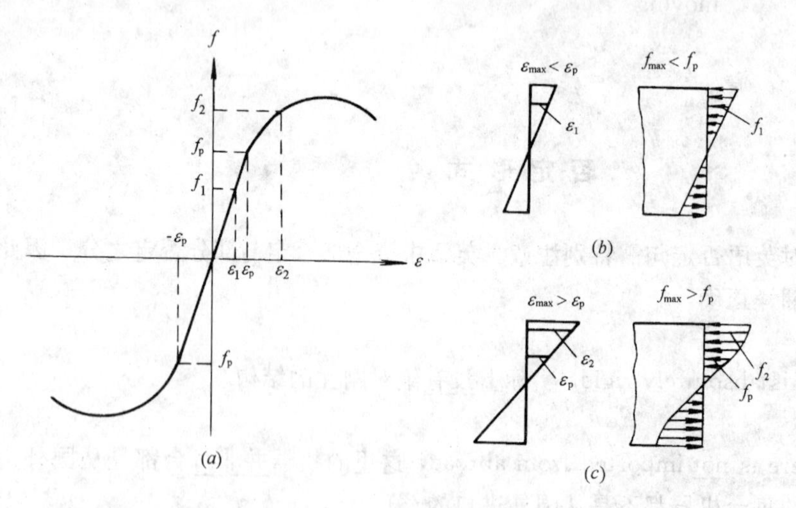

Fig. 4-2 Behavior of reinforced concrete beam under increasing load

When the load on such a beam is gradually increased from zero to that magnitude which will cause the beam to fail, several different stages of behavior can be clearly distinguished. At low loads, as long as the maximum tension stress in the concrete is smaller than the modulus of rupture, the entire concrete is effective in resisting stress, in compression on one side and in tension on the other side of the neutral axis. ② In addition, the reinforcement, deforming the same amount as the adjacent concrete, is also subject to tension stresses. At this stage all stresses in the concrete are of small magnitude and are proportional to trains. The distribution of strains and stresses in concrete and steel over the depth of the section is as shown in Fig. 4-2*c*.

Notes

①这可通过在钢筋混凝土的分界面使用具有强粘结力的变形钢筋，必要的话也可通过在钢筋的端部使用锚具来实现。

②当荷载低时，只要混凝土的最大拉应力小于挠曲模量，整个混凝土仍具有在中性轴一侧抗压在另一侧抗拉的应力。

Reading Material B

Reinforced Concrete Beam Behavior（2）

When the load is further increased, the tension strength of the concrete is soon reached, and at this stage tension cracks develop. These propagate quickly upward to or close to the level of the neutral plane, which in turn shifts upward with progressive cracking. ① The general shape and distribution of these tension cracks is shown in Fig. 4-1*d*. In well-designed beams the width of these cracks is so small (hairline cracks) that they are not objectionable from the viewpoint of either corrosion protection or appearance. Their presence, however, profoundly affects the behavior of the beam under load. Evidently, in a cracked section, i. e., in a cross section located at a crack such as α-α in Fig. 4-1*d*, the concrete does not transmit any tension stresses. Hence, just as in tension members, it is the steel which is called upon to resist the entire tension. At moderate loads, if the concrete stresses do not exceed approximately $f'_c/2$, stresses and strains continue to be closely proportional. The distribution of strains and stresses at or near a cracked section is then that shown in Fig. 4-1*e*. When the load is still further increased, stresses and strains rise correspondingly and are no longer proportional. The ensuing nonlinear relation between stresses and strains is that given by the concrete stress-strain curve. Therefore, just as in homogeneous beams, the distribution of concrete stresses on the compression side of the beam is of the same shape as the stress-strain curve. Fig. 4-1*f* shows the distribution of strains and stresses close to the ultimate load.

Eventually, the carrying capacity of the beam is reached. Failure can be caused in one of two ways. When relatively moderate amounts of reinforcement are employed, at some value of the load the steel will reach its yield point. At that stress the reinforcement yields suddenly and stretches a large amount, and the tensio mn cracks in the concrete widen visibly and propagate upwards, with simultaneous significant deflection of the beam. ② When this happens, the strains in the remaining compression zone of the concrete increase to such a degree that crushing of the concrete, the secondary compression failure, ensues at a load only slightly larger than that which caused the steel to yield. ③ Effectively, therefore, attainment of the yield point in the steel determines the carrying capacity of moderately reinforced beams. Such yield failure is gradual and is preceded by visible signs of distress, such as the widening and lengthening of cracks and the marked increase in deflection.

On the other hand, if large amounts of reinforcement or normal amounts of steel of very high strength are employed, the compression strength of the concrete may be exhausted before the steel starts yielding. Concrete fails by crushing when strains become so large that they disrupt the integrity of the concrete. Exact criteria for this occurrence are not yet known, but it has been observed that rectangular beams fail in compression when the concrete strains reach values of about 0.003 to 0.004. Compression failure through crushing of the concrete is sudden, of an almost explosive nature, and occurs without warning. For this reason it is good practice to dimension beams in such a manner that should they be overloaded, failure would be initiated by yielding of the steel rather than by crushing of the concrete.

The analysis of stresses and strength in the different stages just described will be discussed in the next several sections.

Notes

①这些裂缝迅速向上扩展至或接近中性面水平处，随着不断开裂，中性面逐渐向上移动。

②在那种应力下，钢筋突然屈服并伸长很多，混凝土中的受拉裂缝明显变宽，并且向上扩展，同时梁产生巨大的挠度。

③当这一情况发生时，混凝土剩余受压区的应变增大到使混凝土发生压碎的程度，只要荷载稍大于引起钢筋屈服的荷载，就发生受压破坏。

UNIT FIVE

Text Fundamentals of Flexural Analysis and Design of Beams

[1] The chief task of the structural engineer is the design of structures. By design is meant the determination of the general shape and all specific dimensions of a particular structure so that it will perform the function for which it is created and will safely withstand the influences that will act on it throughout its useful life. ① These influences are primarily the loads and other forces to which it will be subjected, as well as other detrimental agents, such as temperature fluctuations, foundation settlements, and corrosive influences. Structural mechanics is one of the main tools in this process of design. As here understood, it is the body of scientific knowledge that permits one to predict with a good degree of certainty how a structure of given shape and dimensions will behave when acted upon by known forces or other mechanical influences. ② The chief items of behavior that are of practical interest are (1) the strength of the structure, i. e., that magnitude of loads of a given distribution which will cause the structure to fail, and (2) the deformations, such as deflections and extent of cracking, that the structure will undergo when loaded under service conditions.

[2] The fundamental propositions on which the mechanics of reinforced concrete is based are as follows:

1. The internal forces, such as bending moments, shear forces, and normal and shear stresses, at any section of a member are in equilibrium with the effects of the external loads at that section. This proposition is not an assumption but a fact, because any body or any portion thereof can be at rest only if all forces acting on it are in equilibrium.

2. The strain in an embedded reinforcing bar (unit extension or compression) is the same as that of the surrounding concrete. Expressed differently, it is assumed that perfect bonding exists between concrete and steel at the interface, so that no slip can occur between the two materials. Hence, as the one deforms, so must the other. ③ With modern deformed bars a high degree of mechanical interlocking is provided in addition to the natural surface adhesion, so that this assumption is very close to correct.

3. Cross sections which were plane prior to loading continue to be plane in the member under load. Accurate measurements have shown that when a reinforced concrete member is loaded close to failure, this assumption is not absolutely accurate. However, the deviations are usually minor, and the results of theory based on this assumption check well with extensive test information.

4. In view of the fact that the tensile strength of concrete is only a small fraction of its compressive strength, the concrete in that part of a member which is in tension is usually

cracked. While these cracks, in well-designed members, are generally so narrow as to be hardly visible (they are known as hairline cracks), they evidently render the cracked concrete incapable of resisting tension stress. Correspondingly, it is assumed that concrete is not capable of resisting any tension stress whatever. ④ This assumption is evidently a simplification of the actual situation because, in fact, concrete prior to cracking, as well as the concrete located between cracks, does resistance of reinforced concrete beams to shear, it will become apparent that under certain conditions this particular assumption is dispensed with and advantage is taken of the modest tension strength which concrete can develop. ⑤
5. The theory is based on the actual stress-strain relationships and strength properties of the two constituent materials or some reasonable simplifications thereof, rather than on some assumptions of ideal material behavior. This last feature is a relatively new development. It supplants a method of analysis which was based on the assumption that both concrete and steel behave in an elastic manner at all stress levels relevant in calculations. The fact that nonelastic behavior is reflected in modern theory, that concrete is assumed to be ineffective in tension, and that the joint action of the two materials is taken into consideration results in analytical methods which are considerable more complex, and also more challenging, than those which are adequate for members made of a single, substantially elastic material. ⑥

[3]　These five assumptions permit one to predict by calculation the performance of reinforced concrete members only for some simple situations. Actually, the joint action of two materials as dissimilar and complicated as concrete and steel is so complex that it has not yet lent itself to purely analytical treatment. For this reason, methods of design and analysis, while utilizing these assumptions, are very largely based on the results of extensive and continuing experimental research. They are modified and improved as additional test evidence becomes available.

New Words and Expressions

detrimental [ˌdetriˈmentəl]　*a.*　有害的，不利的
fluctuation * [ˌflʌktjuˈeiʃən]　*n.*　变化
certainty * [ˈsəːtənti]　*n.*　肯定，必然
proposition [prɔpəˈziʃən]　*n.*　陈述，定理
thereof [ðεərˈɔv]　*ad.*　它的，其
interface [ˈintəfeis]　*n.*　相交处
interlock [ˌintəˈlɔk]　*vt.*　（使）连接，咬合
adhesion [ədˈhiːʒən]　*n.*　粘着力，附着力
deviation [ˌdi：viˈeiʃən]　*n.*　偏差，偏离
dissimilar [diˈsimilə]　*a.*　不同的，不相似的
compressive force [kəmˈpresiv]　*n.*　压力

hairline crack	*n.*	毛细裂缝
dispense (with) [dis'pens]	*vi.*	(使) 无必要，不用
supplant [sə'plɑːnt]	*vt.*	代替，取代
nonelastic ['nɔni'læstik]	*a.*	无弹性的
ineffective [ˌini'fektive]	*a.*	无效的，不合适的
lend oneself to	*v.*	有助于，适于

Notes

①本句是倒装语序，mean by…意谓，意指。

②…as understood，为 as＋过去分词（短语）。
文中还有类似用法：as shown，as given 等。how 引导一个 predit 的宾语从句。

③so 意为也是如此，也有前面所说的情况，并置于句首，主谓要倒装。此句相当于：…，the other must also deform。

④whatever（用在含有否定词或 any 句中，放在名词后面）任何的（＝at all）。

⑤本句中 advantage is taken of 为被动语态。does resistance…to…对…阻力。

⑥句中…that nonelastic…that concrete…，and that the joint…为 fact 同位语，…results in …为 fact 的谓语。

Exercises

Reading Comprehension

Ⅰ. Choose the best answer.

1. What is meant by design for structural engineers?
   A. They should know the founction of a particular structure.
   B. They should predict the influences that will act on a particular structure.
   C. They should find out exactly the overall shape and every detail demension of a particular structure.
   D. They should apply structural mechanics only in the process of designing a particular structure.

2. Except temperature fluctuations, foundation settlements and corrosive influences, the main influences that a structure will be subjected are ________.
   A. the weight that a structure will support and other forces
   B. the strength that a structure will undergo and other forces
   C. the deformation that a structure will undergo and other forces
   D. the natural disaster that a structure will undergo and other forces

3. If all forces acting on it are in equilibrium, any body or any portion thereof can be

________.

A. in a moving state

B. in a still state

C. in an easy state

D. in a safe state

4. The cracked concrete ________.

A. is not capable of resisting any tension stress whatever

B. can resist as much tension stress as the concrete without cracks

C. is capable of resisting the modest tension strength under certain conditions

D. can resist even more tension stress than the concrete without cracks

5. Modern theory assumes that ________.

A. concrete is ineffective in tension and that the joint action of concrete and steel is taken into consideration

B. both concrete and steel behave in an elastic manner at all stress levels relevant in calculations

C. concrete is effective in tension and that the joint action of concrete and steel is taken into consideration

D. both concrete and steel behave in an nonelastic manner at all stress levels in calculations

Ⅱ. Fill in the table with the information given in the text.

terms	examples
detrimental agents	
structural mechanics	
internal forces	
analytical methods	

Vocabulary

Ⅰ. Choose one word or phrase which is the most similar in meaning to the one underlined in the given sentences.

1. Electric cars may one day <u>supplant</u> petrol-driven ones.

A. take advantage of　　B. take the place of

C. make the most of　　D. get rid of

2. We will have to <u>dispense with</u> a car; we can not afford it.

A. work without　　B. live without

C. do without　　D. go without

3. All the units <u>interlock</u> with one another rigidly.

A. are dealt　　B. are related

C. are mixed　　D. are fastened

4. I had plenty of evidence to support the proposition that man was basically selfish.

A. statement　　B. requirement

C. arrangement　　D. appointment

5. Badly fitting shoes can deform the feet.

A. change the bulk of　　B. change the size of

C. change the volume of　　D. change the shape of

Ⅱ. Match the words in Column A with their correspoding definitions or explanations in Column B.

A	B
1. deviation	a. of harmful and damaging effects
2. embed	b. happenning all the time
3. fluctuation	c. to be the right size or shape
4. constituent	d. being one of the parts that makes a whole
5. detrimental	e. the shaping or developing of something
	f. changing from one state to another
	g. noticeable difference from what is expected
	h. fix firmly and deeply

Translation

词 类 转 换

在英汉翻译中，原文里有些词需在译文中转换词性，才能使译文通顺易懂，自然流畅。

例一　（名词→形容词）

This experiment is an absolute necessity in determining the best processing route.

对确定最佳工艺流程而言，这次实验是绝对必要的。

例二　（副词→动词）

He opens the window to let the fresh air in.

他打开窗户让新鲜空气进来。

例三　（形容词→副词）

Transistors are fairly recent development.

晶体管是最近才发展起来的。

Translate the following sentences into Chinese, and pay attention to the words underlined.

1. An electron or an atom behaves in some ways as though it were a group of waves.
2. They are very familiar with the performance of this type of transistor amplifier.
3. Laser is one of the most sensational developments in recent years, because of its applicability to many fields of science and its adaptability to practical uses.
4. The discovery of rich petroleum resources in China is also inseparable from the oil-worker's efforts to "win honours".

5. The power station here supplies the electric power to the whole city.

Reading Material A

Reinforced Concrete Members Subject to Axial Loads (1)

The behavior of reinforced concrete, through the full range of loading from zero to ultimate, can be introduced most clearly in the context of members subject to simple axial compression or tension. ① Axially loaded members will be discussed briefly in this article, after which flexural behavior and design of beams of various types will be treated.

In members that sustain chiefly or exclusively axial compression loads, such as building columns, it is economical to make the concrete carry most of the load. Still, some steel reinforcement is always provided for various reasons. For one, very few members are truly axially loaded; steel is essential for resisting any bending that may exist. ② For another, if part of the total load is carried by steel with its much greater strength, the cross-sectional dimensions of the member can be reduced-the more so the larger the amount of reinforcement. ③

Here are two chief forms of reinforced concrete columns. In the square column, the four longitudinal bars serve as main reinforcement. ④ They are held in place by transverse small-diameter steel ties which prevent displacement of the main bars during construction operations and counteract any tendency of the compression-loaded bars to buckle out of the concrete by bursting the thin outer cover. ⑤ On the left is showna round column with eight main reinforcing bars. These are surrounded by a closely spaced spiral which serves the same purpose as the more widely spaced ties but also acts to confine the concrete within it, thereby increasing its resistance to axial compression. ⑥ The discussion which follows applies to tied columns. ⑦

When axial load is applied, the compression strain is the same over the entire cross section, and in view of the bonding between concrete and steel, is the same in the two materials. To illustrate the action of such a member as load is applied, one for a concrete with $f_c = 4000$psi (4ksi, 27.6MPa) and the other for a steel with $f_y = 60,000$psi (60kis, 414MPa). ⑧ The curves for the two materials are drawn on the same graph using different vertical stress scales. Curve *b* has the shape which would be obtained in a concrete cylinder test. The rate of loading in most structures is considerably slower than that in a cylinder test, and this affects the shape of the curve. Curve. *c*, therefore, is drawn as being characteristic of the performance of concrete under slow loading. Under these conditions, tests have shown that the maximum reliable compression strength of reinforced concrete is about $0.85f'_c$.

Notes

①钢筋混凝土的性能（从零到极限的荷载全量程）可通过构件在承受轴向压力或轴向拉力的情况下清楚地予以介绍。

②For one，意为 For one reason.

③另一个原因，如果部分总荷载由具有较大强度的钢筋支撑，那么构件的截面尺寸可以减小——截面尺寸减小的越多，钢筋的量就越大。

④Longitudinal bars 纵向钢筋，纵梁

⑤用小直径的箍筋将他们（the four longitudingal bars）固定，以防止主筋在施工中错位，并阻止受压缩荷载的钢筋胀裂混凝土外层薄护面而向外挠曲的倾向。

⑥Closely spaced spiral 密纹螺线

⑦上面的论述适合于系栓。

⑧psi=pounds per square inch 磅/英寸^2

ksi=kilopounds per square inch 千磅/英寸^2

Reading Material B

Reinforced Concrete Members Subject to Axial Loads（2）

At low stresses, up to about $f_c/2$, the concrete is seen to behave nearly elastically, i. e., stresses and strains are quite closely proportional; the straight line d represents this range of behavior with little error for both rates of loading.① For the given concrete the range extends to a strain of about 0.0005. The steel, on the other hand, is seen to be elastic nearly to its yield point°f 60ksi, or to the much greater strain of about 0.002.②

Because the compression strain in the concrete, at any given load, is equal to the compression strain in the steel,

$$\varepsilon_c = \frac{f_c}{E_c} = \varepsilon_s = \frac{f_s}{E_s}$$

from which the relation between the steel stress f_s and the concrete stress f_c is obtained as

$$f_s = \frac{E_s}{E_c} f_c = n f_c \tag{1}$$

where n——E_s/E_c is known as the modular ratio.③

Let A_c——net area of concrete, i. e., gross area minus area occupied by reinforcing bars

A_g——gross area

A_s——area of reinforcing bars

P——axial load

Then

$$P = f_c A_c + f_s A_s = f_c A_c + n f_c A_s$$

or
$$P = f_c (A_c + n A_s) \tag{2}$$

The term $A_c + nA_s$ can be interpreted as the area of a fictitious concrete cross section, the so-called transformed area, which when subjected to the particular concrete stress f_c results in the same axial load P as the actual section composed of both steel and concrete.④ This transformed concrete area is seen to consist of the actual concrete area plus n times the area of the reinforcement. The three bars along each of the two faces are thought of as being removed and replaced, at the same distance from the axis of the section, with added areas of fictitious concrete of total amount nA_s. Alternatively, one can think of the steel bars as replaced with concrete, in which case one has to add to the gross concrete area. A_g so obtained only $(n-1)\ A_s$ in order to obtain the same total transformed area. Therefore, alternatively,

$$P = f_c [A_g + (n-1) A_s] \tag{3}$$

If load and cross-sectional dimensions are known, the concrete stress can be found by solving Eq. (2) or (3) for f_c, and the steel stress can be calculated nearly elastically, i. e., up to about 50 to 60 percent of f_c.⑤ For reasons of safety and serviceability, concrete stresses in structures under normal conditions are kept within this range. Therefore, these relations permit one to calculate service load stresses.

Notes

①在大约 $f_c/2$ 以下的低应力时，混凝土呈弹性，即应力与应完全接近正比。直线 d 几乎没有误差地表示出两种加载速率的特性范围。

②yield point 屈服点

③…at any given load, ……在任何给定荷载下

…from which…is obtained as…从上式中得出钢筋的应力 f_s 和混凝土的应力 f_c 之间的关系为…

where $n=E_s/E_c$ is known as the modular ratio…式中 $n=E_s/E_c$ 称之为模量比。

④transformed area 换算面积

⑤这些关系限制了混凝土呈弹性的范围，即最大为大约 50%～60% f'_c.

UNIT SIX

Text Longtime Deflections

[1] Longtime deflectios are caused by shrinkage and by creep (chiefly the later). It was pointed out that creep deformations of concrete are directly proportional to the compression stress. They increase asymptotically with time and, for the same stress, are larger for low than for high-strength concrete. Correspondingly longtime deflections caused by sustained loads can be estimated by replacing E_c with an equivalent sustained modulus· This modulus must also be used in determining n when calculating I_{ut} or I_{et}.

[2] In this same investigation at Cornell University it was shown from many tests that the following simplified method leads to an adequate estimate of longtime deflections, including the effect of normal shrinkage: (1) Calculate the instantaneous deflection due to the sustained load. (2) Multiply this short-time deflection by a coefficient λ; the resulting value is the additional longtime deflection caused by creep and normal shrinkage. That is, Additional longtime deflection $=\lambda\times$ instantaneous deflection.

[3] The coefficient λ depends on the duration of the sustained load. It also depends on whether the flexural member carries only reinforcement of amount A_s on the tension side or whether additional longitudinal reinforcement A'_s is provided on the compression side. ① In the latter case, the longtime deflections are much reduced. This is so because when no compression reinforcement is provided, the compression concrete is subject to unrestrained creep and shrinkage. ② On the other hand, since steel is not subject to creep, if additional bars are located close to the compression face, they will resist, and thereby reduce, the amount of creep and shrinkage and the corresponding deflection. Compression reinforcement may be included for this reason alone. The appropriate coefficient can be read from Table6-1.

[4] On the basis of experimental information such as in Table6-1 the ACI Code gives a curve-fitting expression for the multiplier for longtime deflections as follws:

$$\lambda = 2 - 1.2\frac{A'_s}{A_s} \geqslant 0.6 \qquad (a)$$

which gives values very close to those in the last line of Table6-1. For continuous beams, in which different values of λ will ordinarily be obtained at positive-and negative-bending regions, an average value may be used.

[5] More recent research indicates that the compression-steel ratio $\rho' = A'_s/bd$ may be a somewhat more accurate parameter than A'_s/A_s for representing the effect of compression steel in restraining creep and shrinkage and thereby reducing longtime deflections. This holds particularly for members with low tensile-steel ratios A_s/bd. ③ The equation which has been proposed in this connection is

$$\lambda = \frac{2.5}{1 + 50\rho'} \qquad (b)$$

However, the 1977 Code continues the use of Eq. (*a*) as a satisfactory means of estimating longtime deflections.

[6] If a beam carries a certain sustained load P_{sus} (e. g. , the dead load plus the average traffic load on a bridge) and is subjected to a short-time peak load P_{sh} (e. g. , the weight of an unusually heavy-vehicle combination), the maximum deflection under this short-time is obtained as follows:

1. Calculate the instantaneous deflection $\delta_{i,su}$ caused by the sustained load P_{sus}.

Table6-1 Multiplier λ for additional longtime deflections

Duration of loading	A_s only	$A_s = \frac{A_s}{2}$	$A'_s = A_s$
1 month	0.6	0.4	0.3
6 months	1.2	1.0	0.7
1 year	1.4	1.1	0.8
3 years and more	2.0	1.2	0.8

2. Calculate the additional longtime deflection caused by P_{sus}, that is, $\delta_{i,sus} = \lambda\delta_{i,sus}$.

3. Then the total deflection caused by the sustained part of the load is

$$\delta_{sum} = \delta_{i,sus} + \delta_{t,sus}$$

4. In calculating the additional instantaneous deflection caused by the shorttime load P_{sl}, account must be taken of the fact that the load-deflection relation after cracking is non-linear. [4] Hence,

$$\delta_{i,sh} = \delta_{i,tot} - \delta_{i,su}$$

where $\delta_{i,tot}$ is the total instantaneous deflection which would obtain if $P_{sus} + P_{sh}$ were applied simultaneously, calculated by using I_e determined for the moment caused by $P + P_{sh}$.

5. Then the total deflection under the sustained and the heavy short-time load is

$$\delta_{tot} = \delta_{sus} + \delta_{i,sh}$$

[7] In calculating deflections, careful attention must be paid to the time sequence, as well as the relative magnitudes, of the applied loads. [5] To illustrate with reference to the beam just described, if the short-time peak load had been applied early in the life of the member, before time-dependent deformations occurred, the sustained-load deflection δ_{sus} of step 3 should be calculated using I_c based on the total load-moment diagram (sustained plus peak load) because the cracking which would result from that load would permanently reduce the stiffness of the member. If the peak load were reapplied at a later time, the total deflections δ_{tot} of step 5 would be larger than before.

[8] It will be realized from this discussion that the magnitude of the deflections in reinforced-concrete structures depends on so many influences that no precise calculation is possible. On the other hand, great precision is generally not necessary. From extensive experimental information it can be said that the methods presented here permit deflections to be

estimated with an accuracy of about ± 25 percent, which is adequate for most purposes of design. More accurate but also more elaborate procedures are available in the literature.

[9] To ensure satisfactory deflection characteristics, the ACI Code imposes certain limits of deflections computed according to the above procedures. These limits are given in Table6-2.

Table6-2 Maximum allowable computed deflections

<table>
<tr><th>Type of member</th><th>Deflection to be considered</th><th>Deflection limitation</th></tr>
<tr><td>Flat roofs not supporting or attachcd to nonstructural elements likely to be damaged by large deflections</td><td>Immediate deflection due to the live load L</td><td>$\frac{1}{180}$</td></tr>
<tr><td>Floors not supporting or attached to nonstructural elements likely to be damaged by large deflections</td><td>Immediate deflection due to the live load L</td><td>$\frac{1}{360}$</td></tr>
<tr><td>Roof or floor construction supporting or attached to nonstructural elements likely to be damaged by large deflections</td><td rowspan="2">That part of the total deflection which occurs after attachment of the nonstructural elements, the sum of the longtime deflection due to all sustained loads, and the immediate deflection due to any additional live load</td><td>$\frac{1}{480}$</td></tr>
<tr><td>Roof or floor construction supporting or attached to nonstructural elements not likely to be damaged by large deflections</td><td>$\frac{1}{240}$</td></tr>
</table>

The last two limits given may be exceeded under special conditions.

Table6-3 Minimum thickness of beams or one-way slabs unless deflections are computed

<table>
<tr><th rowspan="3">Member</th><th colspan="4">Minimum thickness, h</th></tr>
<tr><th>Simply supported</th><th>One end continuous</th><th>Both ends continuous</th><th>Cantilever</th></tr>
<tr><td colspan="4">Members not supporting or attached to partitions or other construction likely to be damaged by large deflections</td></tr>
<tr><td>Solid one-way slabs</td><td>1/20</td><td>1/24</td><td>1/28</td><td>1/10</td></tr>
<tr><td>Beams or ribbed one-way slabs</td><td>1/16</td><td>1/18.5</td><td>1/21</td><td>1/8</td></tr>
</table>

[10] In lieu of explicit calculation of deflections, for members of lesser importance it is satisfactory to control deflection indirectly by limiting the span-depth ratio. According to the Code, beams and one-way slabs must not have thicknesses less than those specified by Table6-3 unless deflections are calculated. For members using lightweight concrete, having unit weight in the range from 90 to 120 pcf, the values of Table6-3 should be multiplied by $(1.65-0.005w)\geqslant 1.09$, where w is the unit weight in pcf. [6] For yield strengths other than 60 ksi, the values that are given in Table6-3 should be multiplied by $(0.4+f_y/100,000)$,

where f_y is expressed in psi.

New Words and Expressions

longtime [ˈlɔŋtaim] *a.* 长期的
asymptotically [əsimpˈtəutikəli] *ad.* 逐渐地
sustained [sʌˈsteind] *a.* 持续不断的
instantaneous * [instənˈteinjəs] *a.* 瞬息的，即刻的
coefficient [ˌkəuifiˈʃənt] *n.* 系数，常数
parameter * [pəˈræmitə] *n.* 参数
curve-fitting [ˈkəːvˈfitiŋ] *a.* 曲线配合的
short-time [ˈʃɔːttaim] *a.* 短期的
simultaneously [siməlˈteinjəsli] *ad.* 同时发生地，同时存在地
attachment * [əˈtætʃmənt] *n.* 附件，辅助机构
nonstructural * [nɔnˈstrʌktʃərəl] *a.* 非结构的，不用于结构上的
cantilever * [ˈkæntiliːvə] *n.* 臂悬（梁）
partition * [pɑːˈtiʃən] *n.* 隔墙，隔板
in lieu of 作为……的替代
explicit * [iksˈplisit] *a.* 明确的，清晰的

Notes

①It depends on 后接两个宾语从句：whether…carries…or whether…is provided….
②句中 so 指代上句。
③句中 hold 意为，站得住，有效。
④此处 account must be taken of 为 take account of 的被动语态。
⑤…of the applied loads 修饰 careful attention。
⑥pcf＝pounds per cubic foot 磅/英尺^3。

Exercises

Reading Comprehension

Ⅰ. Choose the best answer.

1. What is the main cause of longtime deflections?

   A. Shrinkage.

   B. Creep.

   C. Compression stress.

D. Sustained loads.

2. The longtime deflections are reduced when ________ .

A. the flexural member carries only reinforcement of amount A_s on the tension side

B. no compression reinforcement is provided

C. additional longitudinal reinforcement A_s is provided on the compression side

D. the duration of the sustained load is known.

3. The sentence 'Compression reinforcement may be included for this reason alone' means ________ .

A. compression reinforcement may be provided to reduce the amount of creep and shrinkage and deflection

B. because steel is not subject to creep, compression reinforcement may be provided

C. compression may be included for calculating the deflections

D. close to the compression face, compression reinforcements may be used

4. In most design, the magnitude of the deflection ________ .

A. can't be calculated

B. must be calculated as accurately as possible

C. is not necessary to be calculated

D. doesn't need precise calculation

5. Which of the following statements is True?

A. Thickness of a beam must be greater than specified.

B. It is satisfactory to use less important members.

C. Usually it is a good method to control deflection indirectly by limiting the span-depth ratio.

D. It is not used under any conditions to limit the span-depth ratio to control deflection

Ⅱ. Fill in the blanks with the information given in the text.

1. What do you know about the quality of creep deformations of concrete?

a. Creep deformations of concrete ________________ .

b. They ________________
________________ .

2. To what must careful attention be paid in calculating deflections?

Careful attention must be paid to ________________
________________ .

Vocabulary

Ⅰ. Choose one word or phrase that is the most similar in meaning to the one underlined in the given sentences.

1. We should <u>present</u> some suggestions which would lessen the existing tension.

A. give away B. put forward

C. introduce into D. show to

2. He gave explicit directions about the matter.

A. definite B. explanatory

C. firm D. limit

3. His tastes are quite other than mine.

A. except for B. in addition to

C. different from D. not anything but

4. The book was a work of such magnitude that it took 10 years to write.

A. greatness of importance B. the degree of brightness

C. the degree of importance D. greatness of size

5. A scientist must be precise in making tests.

A. charply clear B. very particular

C. careful and correct D. careful and fussy

Ⅱ. Match the words in Column A with their corresponding definitions or explanations in Column B.

A	B
1. instantaneous	a. kept in continuance
2. coefficient	b. a standard of measurement used in building
3. longitudinal	c. going from end to end not across
4. unrestrained	d. of or in line
5. sustained	e. a number written before and multiplying another number
	f. not held back or reduced
	g. happening at once
	h. in the long distance

Translation

成 分 转 换

英汉翻译时，为使译文明确、通顺，往往需要将原文中某一语法成分在译文中转译成另一种语法成分，这就是成分转换。

例一 （谓语→主语）

Gold weighs about twenty times as much as water. 金子的重量约为水重的二十倍。

例二 （主语转译为谓语）

Attempts were made to develop a new technique for polymerization. 曾试图研究出一种新的聚合技术。

例三 （谓语转译为状语）

In the long run, most experts agree, we'll have to start building factories, offices and homes with robots in mind. 大多数专家一致认为，从长远看，今后在开始建造工厂、办公楼和住宅时必须考虑到机器人。

Translate the following sentences into Chinese, and pay attention to the words underlined.

1. Disputations about this problem within the engineering circle has lasted many years.
2. These reactors had an internal diameter of 140mm.
3. The rotor is a well-designed structure.
4. The number of molecules in any object we can see is unimaginably large.
5. Test results of pure W have been included for comparison.

Reading Material A

Deflections at Service Loads

In order to serve its intended purpose, a structure must be (1) safe and (2) serviceable. A structure is safe if it is able to resist, without distress and with some margin to spare, all forces which foreseeably will act on it during its lifetime. Serviceability implies, among other things, that deflections and other distortions under load will be unobjectionably small. For example, excessive beam and slab deflections can lead to objectionable cracking of partitions, ill-fitting doors and windows, poor drainage, misalignment of sensitive machinery or other equipment, excessive vibrations, etc. It becomes important, therefore, to be able to predict deflections with reasonable accuracy, so that members can be dimensioned to ensure both adequate strength and appropriately small deflections.

The deflections of interest are those which occur under normal service conditions. In service, a structure sustains the full dead load plus some fraction or all of the maximum design live load. The usual safety factors provide that under service loading the steel and concrete are not stressed beyond their respective elastic ranges. For this reason the deflections which occur immediately upon application of the load, the so-called instantaneous deflections, can be calculated by methods based on the elastic behavior of flexural members.

It was pointed out that, in addition to those concrete deformations which occur immediately upon load application, other deformations and volume changes take place gradually and over long intervals of time. ① These are chiefly creep deforma tions and shrinkage. In consequence, def lections of reinforced-concrete members continue to increase for some time after load application, at a decreasing rate, and the longtime deflections may exceed the instantaneous deflections by a large amount. For this reason, methods for estimating both the instantaneous and the longtime deflections are essential.

Instantaneous deflections Elastic deflections can be expressed in the general form

$$\delta = \frac{F(\text{loads}, \text{spans})}{EI}$$

where EI is the flexural rigidity and F (loads, spans) is a function of the particular load-and-span arrangement. For instance, the deflection of a uniformly loaded simple beam is $5wL^4/384$Ei, so that $F=5wL^4/384$. Similar deflection equations have been tabulated or can easily be computed for many other loadings and span arrangements, simple, fixed, or continuous, and the corresponding functions F can be determined. The particular problem in reinforced-concrete structures is therefore the determination of the appropriate flexural rigidity EI for a member consisting of two materials with properties and behavior as widely different as steel and concrete. ②

If the maximum moment in a flexural member is so small that the tension stress in the concrete does not exceed the flexural tensile strength (modulus of rupture), no flexural tension cracks will occur. The full, uncracked section is then available for resisting stress and providing rigidity. The effective moment of inertia for the range of low loads is that of the uncracked, transformed section I_{ut}, and E is the modulus of concrete E_c. Correspondingly, for this load range,

$$\delta_{iu} = \frac{F}{E_c I_{ut}} \tag{a}$$

At higher loads flexural tension cracks are formed; in addition, if shear stresses exceed v_{cr} and web reinforcement is employed to resist them, diagonal tension cracks can exist at service loads. In the region of flexural cracks the position of the neutral axis varies: directly at each crack it is located at the level calculated for the cracked, transformed section; midway between cracks it dips to location closer to that calculated for the uncracked, transformed section. Correspondingly, flexural tension cracking causes the effective moment of inertia to be that of the cracked, transformed section in the immediate neighborhood of flexural tension cracks and closer to that of the uncracked, transformed section midway between cracks, with a gradual transition between these extremes. ③

It is seen that the value of the local moment of inertia varies in those portions of the beam in which the bending moment exceeds the cracking moment of the section

$$M_{cr} = \frac{f_1 I_{ut}}{y_t} \tag{b}$$

where y_t is the distance from the neutral axis to the tension fiber and f_r is the modulus of rupture. The exact variation of I depends on the shape of the moment diagram and on crack pattern and is difficult to determine. This makes an exact deflection calculation tedious, if not impossible. It was found, however, that the deflections δ_{ic} occurring in a beam after the maximum moment M_{max} has reached and exceeded the cracking moment M_{cr} can be calculated by utilizing an effective moment of inertia I_e; that is,

$$\delta_{ic} = \frac{F}{E_e I_e} \tag{c}$$

where

$$I_e = \left(\frac{M_{er}}{M_{max}}\right)^3 I_{at} + \left[1 - \left(\frac{M_{cr}}{M_{max}}\right)\right]^3 I_{ct} \tag{d}$$

where I_{et} is the moment of inertia of the cracked, transformed section. It is seen that $I_{ut} >$

$I_e > I_{et}$ and that I_e approaches closer to I_{et} the more M_{max} exceeds M_{er}.

Notes

①已明确指出，除了在施加荷载时立刻出现混凝土变形外，在长期使用过程中会渐渐地产生其他变形及体积的变化。

②因此，钢筋混凝土结构的一个特别的问题就是确定由钢和混凝土这两种性能及特点完全不同的材料组成的构件的适当的抗弯刚度 EI。

③与此相应，弯曲受拉开裂使得有效惯性矩变为在紧挨着裂缝的开裂后的折算截面惯性矩与裂缝中间未开裂的折算截面惯性矩两个极端之间逐渐变化。

Reading Material B

Strength and Deformation of Concrete in Compression

Short-time loading

Performance of a structure under load depends to a large degree on the stress-strain relationship of the material from which it is made, under the type of stress to which the material is subjected in the structure.[①] Since concrete is used mostly in compression, its compressive stress-strain curve is of primary interest. Such a curve is obtained by appropriate strain measurements in cylinder tests or on the compression side in beams. Figure 1 shows a typical set of such curves, obtained at normal, moderate testing speeds on concretes 28 days old, for various cylinder strengths f'_c.

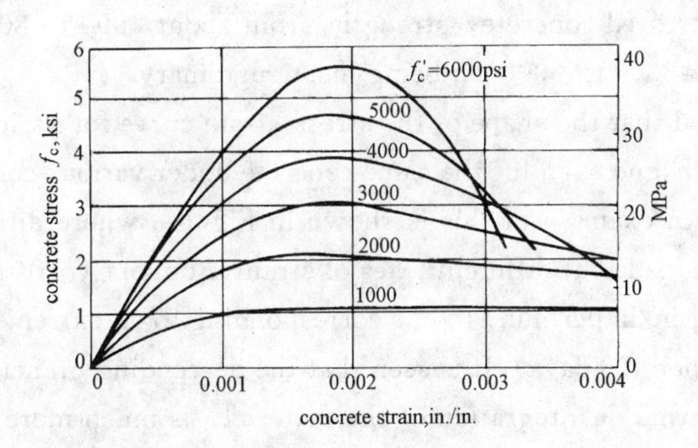

Fig. 6-1 Typical concrete stress-strain curves (1000 psi = 6.895MPa)

All the curves have somewhat similar character. They consist of an initial relatively straight elastic portion in which stress and strain are closely proportional, then begin to curve to the horizontal, reaching the maximum stress, i. e., the compressive strength, at a strain of approximately 0.002 in/in, and finally show a descending branch. It is also seen that concretes of lower strength are less brittle, i.e., fracture at a larger maximum strain, than high-strength concretes.

The modulus of elasticity E_c (in psi units), i.e., the slope of the initial straight portion of the stress-strain curve, is seen to be larger the higher the strength of the concrete. ② It can be computed with reasonable accuracy from the empirical equation

$$E_s = 33w^{3/2}\sqrt{f_c} \qquad (a)$$

where w is the unit weight of the hardened concrete in pcf and f'_c its cylinder strength in psi. Equation (*a*) has been obtained by testing structural concretes with values of w from 90 to 155 pcf. For normal sand-and-stone concretes, with $w=145$ pcf, one obtains

$$E_c = 57,000\sqrt{f_c} \qquad (b)$$

Information on concrete strength properties such as those discussed is usually obtained through tests made 28 days after pouring. However, cement continues to hydrate, and consequently concrete continues to harden, long after this age, at a decreasing rate. Figure 2 shows a typical curve of the gain of concrete strength with age.

In present practice, 28-day cylinder strengths in the range of

$$f'_c = 2500 \text{ to } 6000 \text{ psi} (17.2 \text{ to } 42 \text{ MPa})$$

are usually specified for reinforced-concrete structures, values between 3000 and 4000 being the most common.

However, for special situations such as lower-story columns in high-rise buildings, high-strength concretes with f'_c up to 10,000 psi (69 MPa) are coming into use. They require special approaches and care in production. Current design methods were developed chiefly in connection with concretes with $f'_c = 3000$ to 5000 psi. To what extent these methods may need modification when applied to such high-strength concretes with their greater brittleness and differently shaped stress-strain curves is a matter of investigation at this time. ③ For prestressed concrete, strengths from about 4000 to 8000 psi (23.5 to 55 MPa) are used, $f'_c=5000$ to 6000 psi being most customary.

It should be noted that the shape of the stress-strain curve for various concretes of the same cylinder strength, and even for the same concrete under various conditions of loading, varies considerably. An example of this is shown in Fig. 6-3 where different specimens of the same concrete are loaded at different rates of strain, from one corresponding to relatively fast loading (0.001 in/in per min) to one corresponding to an extremely slow application of load (0.001 in/in per 100 days). It is seen that the descending branch of the curve probably indicative of internal disintegration of the material, is much more pronounced at fast than at slow rates of loading. It is also seen that the peaks of the curves, i.e., the maximum strength reached, is somewhat smaller at slower rates of strain.

When compressed in one direction, concrete, like other materials, expands in the direction transverse to that of the applied stress. The ratio of the transverse to the longitudinal strain is known as Poission's ratio and depends on composition and other factors. At stress-

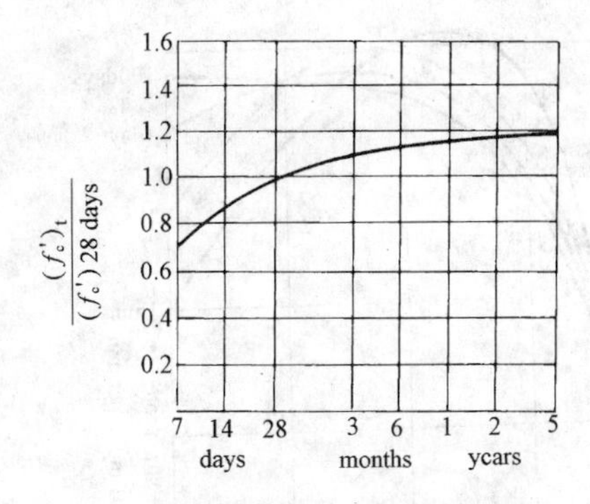

Fig. 6-2 Effect of age on compression strength f'_c

es lower than about 0.7 f'_c, Possion's ratio for concrete falls within the limits of 0.15 and 0.20 with 0.17 the most representative value.

Longtime loading

In some engineering materials, such as steel, strength and the stress-strain relationship are independent of rate and duration of loading, at least within the usual ranges of rate of stress, temperature, and other variables. In contrast, Fig. 6-3 illustrates the fact that the influence of time, in this case of rate of loading, on the behavior of concrete under load is pronounced. ④ The main reason for this is that concrete creeps under load, while steel does not exhibit creep under conditions prevailing in buildings, bridges, and similar structures.

Creep is the property of many materials by which they continue deforming over considerable lengths of time at constant stress or load. The nature of the creep process is shown schematically in Fig. 6-4. This particular concrete was loaded at age 28 days with resulting instantaneous strain ε_{inst}. The load was then maintained for 230 days, during which time creep is seen to have increased that total deformation to almost 3 times its instantaneous value. If the load were maintained, the deformation would follow the solid curve. If the load is removed, as shown by the dashed curve, the elastic instantaneous strain ε_{inst} is of course recovered, and some creep recovery is seen to occur. If the concrete is reloaded at some later date, instantaneous and creep deformations develop again, as shown.

Creep deformations for a given concrete 2are practically proportional to the magnitude of the applied stress; at any given stress, high-strength concretes show less creep than lower-strength concretes. As seen in Fig. 6-4 with elapsing time creep proceeds at a decreasing rate and ceases after 2 to 5 years at a final value which, depending on concrete strength and other factors, attains 1.5 to 3 times the magnitude of the instantaneous strain. If, instead of being applied quickly and thereafter kept constant, the load is increased slowly and gradually, as is the case in many structures during and after construction, instantaneous and creep deformations proceed simultaneously. The effect is that shown in Fig. 6-3; that is, the previously discussed difference in the shape of the stress-strain curve for various rates of loading is chiefly the result of the creep deformations of concrete.

For stresses not exceeding about one-half of the cylinder strength, creep strains are di-

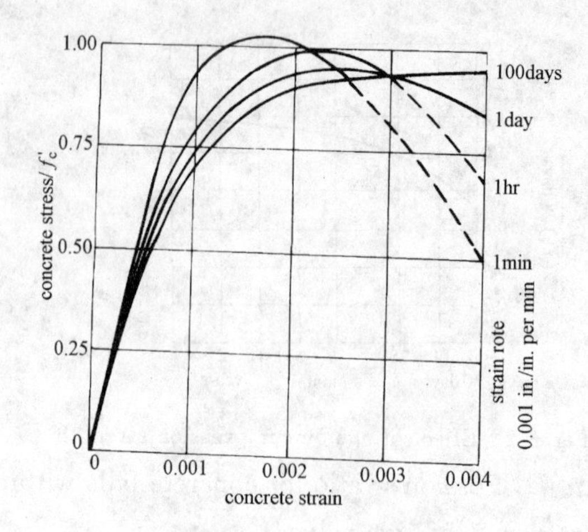

Fig. 6-3 Stress-strain curves at various strain rates, concentric compression

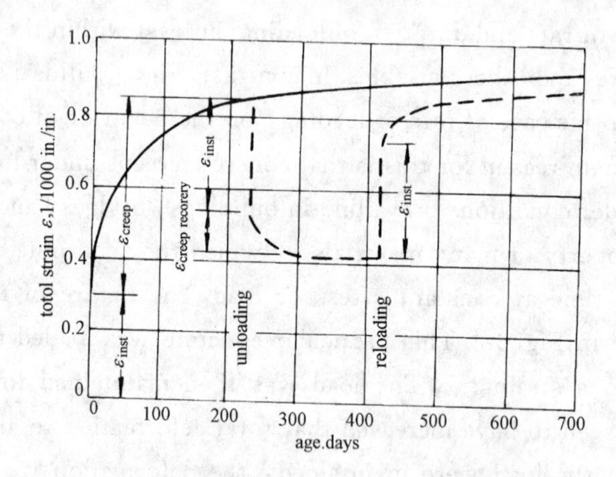

Fig. 6-4 Typical creep curve (concrete loaded to 600 psi at age 28 days)

rectly proportional to stress. Creep also depends on the average ambient relative humidity, being about twice as large for 50 percent as for 100 percent humidity. This is so because part of the reduction in volume under sustained load is caused by an outward migration of free pore water, which evaporates into the surrounding atmosphere. Other things being equal, creep is larger for low-strength than for high-strength concretes. Table6-4 refers to average humidity conditions. If ε'_{creep} is the final asymptotic value of the creep strain $\varepsilon_{creep}$and ε_{inst} the initial, instantaneous strain (Fig. 6-4), the specific creep is ε'_{creep} per psi and the creep coefficient $C_c=\varepsilon'_{creep}\varepsilon_{inst}$.

Table 6-4 **Typical creep parameters**

Compressive strength		Specific creep		Creep coefficient
psi	MPa	$10^{-6}psi^{-1}$	$10^{-4}MPa^{-1}$	C_c
3000	20.7	1.0	1.45	3.1
24000	27.6	0.80	1.16	2.9
6000	41.4	0.55	0.80	2.4
8000	55.2	0.40	0.58	2.0

Notes

① 荷载下的结构性能在很大程度上取决于其所用材料的应力-应变关系，以及结构中材料受的压力状态。

②看得出混凝土的强度越高，弹性模量 E_c（磅/英寸²），即应力-应变曲线的初直线部分斜度就越大。

③这些方法当应用于具有较高强度，和不同应力-应变曲线的这样高强度混凝土时，需要作什么程度的修改，目前还是个有待调查的问题。

④相比之下，图 6-3 表明，在这种加载速率的情况下，时间对荷载下混凝土性能的影响是明显的。

UNIT SEVEN

Text Shear and Diagonal Tension

[1] It was pointed out that when the material is elastic (stresses proportional to strains), shear stresses

$$v=\frac{VQ}{Ib} \tag{1}$$

act in any section in addition to the bending stresses

$$f=\frac{My}{I} \tag{2}$$

except for those locations at which the shear force V happens to be zero.

[2] The role of shear stresses is easily visualized by the performance under load of the laminated beam of Fig7-1; it consists of two rectangular pieces bonded together along their contact surface. If the adhesive is strong enough, the member will deform as one single beam, as shown in Fig. 1a. On the other hand, if the adhesive is weak, the two pieces will separate and slide relative to each other, as shown in Fig7-1*b*. Evidently, then, when the adhesive is effective, there are forces or stresses acting in it which prevent this sliding or shearing. ① These horizontal shear stresses are shown in Fig7-1*c* as they act, separately, on the top and bottom pieces. The same stresses occur in horizontal planes in single-piece beams; they are different in intensity at different distances from the neutral axis.

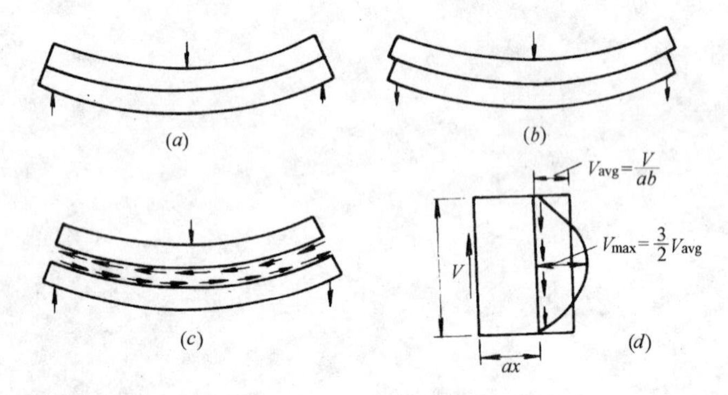

Fig. 7-1 Shear in homogeneous rectangular beam

[3] Fig. 7-1*d* shows a differential length of a single-piece rectangular beam acted upon by a shear force of magnitude *V*. Upward translation is prevented, i. e. , vertical equilibrium is provided, by the vertical shear stresses *v*. Their average value is equal to the shear force divided by the cross-sectional area, $v_{av}=V/ab$, but their intensity varies over the depth of the section. As is easily computed from Eq. 1, the shear stress is zero at the outer fibers and has a maximum of 1.5 v_{av} at the neutral axis, the variation being parabolic as shown. Other

values and distributions are found for other shapes of the cross section, the shear stress always being zero at the outer fibers and of maximum value at the neutral axis.

[4] If a small square element located at the neutral axis of such a beam is isolated as in Fig. 7-2*b*, the vertical shear stresses on it, equal and opposite on the two faces for reasons of equilibrium, act as shown.② However, if these were the only stresses present, the element would not be in equilibrium ; it would spin. Therefore, on the two horizontal faces there exist equilibrating horizontal shear stresses of the same magnitude. That is, at any point in the beam, the horizontal shear stresses of Fig. 7-2*b* are equal in magnitude to the vertical shear stresses of Fig. 7-2*d*.

[5] It is proved in any strength-of-materials text that on an element cut at 45° these shear stresses combine in such a manner that their effect is as shown in Fig. 7-2*c*. That is, the action of the two pairs of shear stresses on the vertical and horizontal faces is the same as that of two pairs of normal stresses, one tension and one compression, acting on the 45° faces and of numerical value equal to that of the shear stresses. If an element of the beam is considered which is located neither at the neutral axis nor at the outer edges, its vertical faces are subject not only to the shear stresses but also to the familiar bending stresses whose magnitude is given by Eq. 2 (Fig. 7-2*d*).③ The six stresses which now act on the element can again be combined into a pair of inclined compression stresses and a pair of inclined tension stresses which act at right angles to each other. They are known as principal stresses (Fig. 7-2*e*). Their value is given by and their inclination α by $\tan 2\alpha = 2v/f$.

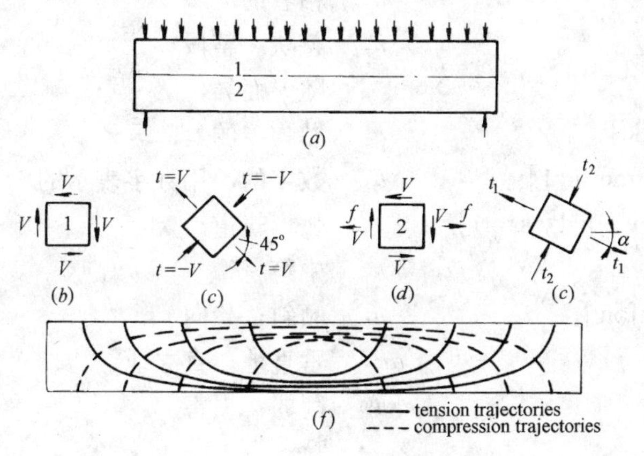

Fig. 7-2 Stress trajectories in homogeneous rectangular beam

$$t = \frac{f}{2} \pm \sqrt{\frac{f^2}{4} + v^2} \tag{3}$$

[6] Since the magnitudes of the shear stresses v and the bending stresses f change both along the beam and vertically with distance from the neutral axis, the inclinations as well as the magnitudes of the resulting principal stresses t also vary from one place to anoth-

er. Fig. 7-2f shows the inclinations of these principal stresses for a rectangular beam uniformly loaded. That is, these stress trajectories are lines which, at any point, are drawn in that direction in which the particular principal stress, tension or compression, acts at that point. It is seen that at the neutral axis the principal stresses in a beam are always inclined at 45° to the axis. In the vicinity of the outer fibers they are horizontal near midspan.

[7] An important point follows from this discussion. Tension stresses, which are of particular concern in view of the low tensile strength of the concrete, are not confined to the horizontal bending stresses f, which are caused by bending alone. ④ Tension stresses of various inclinations and magnitudes, resulting from shear alone (at the neutral axis) or from the combined action of shear and bending, exist in all parts of a beam and can impair its integrity if not adequately provided for. ⑤ It is for this reason that the inclined tension stresses, known as diagonal tension, must be carefully considered in reinforced-concrete design.

New Words and Expressions

diagonal * [dai'ægənl]	*a.*	对角线的
visualize ['vizjuəlaiz]	*vt.*	想像
lamineit ['læmineit]	*v.*	把…分成 薄片，用薄片叠成
adhesive [əd'hi:siv]	*n.*	胶粘剂
	a.	粘着的
single-piece ['siŋglpi:s]	*n.*	整块，整段
vary over		随…而异
parabolic * [pærə'bɔlik]	*a.*	抛物线的
numerical * [nju (:) 'merikəl]	*a.*	数字的，用数字表示的
trajectory ['trædʒiktəri: trə'dʒektəri]	*n.*	弧形轨道
midspan ['midspæn]	*n.*	中跨
inclination * [inklin'eiʃən]	*n.*	倾斜；趋向
vertically ['və:tikəli]	*ad.*	垂直地；直立地
impair * [im'pεə]	*vt.*	削弱，损害

Notes

①… acting in it… 为分词短语，修饰 forces or stresses，which 引导一个定词从句。

②…for reason of… 根据……原理，act 的主语为 shear stresses

③… which is located neither…nor…为定语从句修饰 an element of the beam。

④句中两个 which 引导的是非限定性定语从句，分别对 tension stresses 和 bending stresses 加以补充说明。

⑤exist 的主语是 tension stress…，resulting from…or from…and bending 修饰 tension stress，…if not…provided for 中省略了 it is。

Exercises

Reading Comprehension

Ⅰ. Choose the best answer.

1. If the adhesive of the two pieces is weak, ________ .
   A. one of the piece will deform and slide toward the other
   B. both of the pieces will deform and slide together
   C. the two pieces will set apart and slide relative to each other
   D. the member will deform as one single beam
2. The intensity of the shear stresses changes because ________ .
   A. the depth of the section is different
   B. the depth of the section is same
   C. the depth of the section is maximum
   D. the depth of the section is minimum
3. In order to keep a beam in equilibrium, ________ .
   A. the vertical shear stresses on it should be equal and opposite on the two faces
   B. the vertical shear stresses should be the only stresses present
   C. the horizontal shear stresses on it should be equal and opposite on the two faces
   D. the horizontal shear stresses should be equal in magnitude to the vertical shear stresses at any point in the beam
4. The principal stresses at the neutral axis in a beam ________ .
   A. are always inclined at 45° in the vicinity of the outer fibers
   B. are always inclined at 45° to the axis
   C. are horizontal near midspan
   D. vary from one place to another
5. The inclined tension stresses, known as diagonal tension, must be carefully considered in reinforced-concrete design, because if not adequately provided for, it can ______ .
   A. impair the integrity of a beam
   B. weaken the strength of a beam
   C. cause the bending of a beam
   D. cause the inclination of a beam

Ⅱ. Fill in the blanks with the information given in the text.

1. What is the performance under load of the laminated beam?
   A. If the adhesive is strong enough, the member ____________________ .
   B. If the adhesive is weak, the two pieces ____________________ .
2. What will happen to the principal stresses in a beam at the neutral axis?

A. They are always inclined ________________ .

B. In the vicinity of outer fibers they are ________________ .

Vocabulary

Ⅰ. Choose one word or phrase which is the most similar in meaning to the one underlined in the given sentences.

1. Life depends on the equilibrium between the heat received from the sun and the heat lost to cooler surroundings.

   A. contrast　　B. relationship

   C. exchange　　D. balance

2. Communication is one of the most important bonds that hold cultural systems together.

   A. obligations　　B. qualities

   C. links　　D. needs

3. Several villages in the north has been isolated by heavy snowfalls.

   A. divided　　B. separated

   C. parted　　D. decomposed

4. He has an inclination to stoutness.

   A. a tendency　　B. a desire

   C. an apperance　　D. a symptom

5. His digestion had been impaired by his recent illness.

   A. spoiled　　B. reduced

   C. damaged　　D. decreased

Ⅱ. Match the words in Column A with their corresponding definitions or explanations in Column B.

A	B
1. homogeneous	a. make or become more intense
2. vicinity	b. with the desires or attentions directed towards
3. intensity	c. of the same kind
4. integrity	d. nearness or closeness of relationship
5. edge	e. strength and depth
	f. state or condition of being complete
	g. outer limit or boundary of a surface
	h. narrow border

Translation

Translate the following sentences into Chinese, and pay attention to the words underlined.

1. They made up a bed on the sofa for the unexpected visitor. （词义选择）
2. We have to drive fast to make up the hour we lost in Boston. （词义选择）
3. The shortest distance between raw material and a finished part is precision casting. （词义引伸）
4. The sun gives us warmth and light. （增词）
5. The atom is the samllest particle of an element. （减词）
6. This material is nowhere to be had. （否定形式）
7. There is no material but will deform more or less under the action of force. （否定形式）
8. No other changes occur upon mixing the two compounds. （词类转换）
9. These materials are highly variable in nature. （成分转换）
10. Their fundamentally different chemical compositions are of great importance. （成分转换）

Reading Material A

Design for Shear and Diagonal Tension (1)

In addition to meeting flexural requirements, beams must be safe against premature failure due to diagonal tension in the concrete, resulting from combined shear and longitudinal flexural stress. ①

Most concrete beams are provided with shear reinforcement in regions of high shear, in the form of vertical U-shaped stirrups or bent-up longitudinal steel or both. Shear reinforcement increases member strength against diagonal tension failure not only by direct transfer of shear forces by the web steel but also through improvement of aggregate interlock in the concrete and dowel action of the main steel; in addition it helps maintain the integrity of the concrete compression zone. ② Furthermore, it improves member ductility by restraining the growth of inclined cracks, thus providing warning of impending failure.

Shear reinforcement may be omitted in members where shear stresses are well below the value corresponding to diagonal cracking. This is normally the case for edge-supported slabs and for footings and may be so for some beams. ③

According to ACI Code procedures, the design of cross sections subject to shear is to be based on the relation

$$V_u \leqslant \phi V_n \tag{1}$$

where V_u is the total shear force applied to the section due to factored loads and V_n is the nominal shear strength, equal to the sum of the contributions of the concrete and the web steel if present. ④ The strength-reduction factor ϕ is to be taken equal to 0.85 for shear. The slight additional conservatism, compared with the value of $\phi=0.90$ for flexure, reflects both the sudden nature of diagonal tension failure and the still imperfect understanding of that failure mode. Because of the beneficial effect of vertical compression due to support reactions, sections located less than a distance d from the face of a support may normally be designed for the same shear V_u as that computed at a distance d.⑤

Notes

①梁除了要满足抗弯要求外，还必须防止由于剪应力和纵向的弯曲应力共同作用的结果而在混凝土中产生斜向拉力而引起的过早破坏。

②抗剪钢筋提高了构件抵抗斜拉破坏的强度，这不仅是因为腹筋传递剪力，还因为改善了混凝土内骨料的咬合作用和主筋的销栓作用。另外，抗剪钢筋还有助于保持混凝土受压区的整体性。

③边缘支承板和基础都属于这种情况，某些梁也可能属于此种情况。

④…，等于混凝土和腹筋（如已配置）所起作用之和。

⑤由于支座反力产生竖向压力的有利作用，在与支座边缘距离 d 以内的各截面通常可按距离支座 d 截面所计算出来的相同剪力 V_u 进行设计。

Reading Material B

Design for Shear and diagonal Tension (2)

Beams with no web reinforcement For beams which are reinforced only for flexural tension, the nominal shear strength is equal to that provided by the concrete, i. e.,

$$V_n = V_c \tag{2}$$

V_c in turn, is equal to the cracking shear V_{cr} Thus

$$V_c = \left(1.9\sqrt{f'_c} + 2500\rho_w \frac{V_u d}{M_u}\right) b_w d \leqslant 3.5\sqrt{f'_c} b_u d \tag{3a}$$

where b_w——web width for T sections or beam width for rectangular sections, in

d——effective depth to tensile steel, in

ρ_w——longitudinal tensile-steel ratio $A_s/b_w d$ or, A_s/bd

V_u——shear force at section at factored loads, Ib or kips

M_u——moment at section at factored loads, in. Ib or in. kips

f'_c——specified compressive strength of the concrete, psi

The resulting shear strength V_c is expressed in pounds. In computing V_c by Eq. 3a, the quantity $V_u d/M_u$ is not to be taken greater than 1.0.

As an alternative to Eq. 3a the Code provisions allow use of the simpler, more conservative, but less accurate equation

$$V_c = 2\sqrt{f'_c} b_w d \tag{3b}$$

which is adequate for most design purposes. If V_u, the shear force at factored loads, is no larger than ϕ times V_c, calculated by Eq 3*a* or alternatively by Eq. 3*b*, then theoretically no web reinforcement is required. ① Even in such a case, however, the Code requires provision of at least a minimum area of web reinforcement equal to

$$A_v = 50\frac{b_w s}{f_y} \tag{4}$$

where s——longitudinal spacing of web reinforcement, in

f_y——yield strength of web steel, psi

A_v——total cross-sectional area of web steel within distances, in^2

This provision holds unless V_u is less than one-half of the design shear strength ϕV_c provided by the concrete. ② Specific exceptions to this requirement for minimum web steel are made for slabs and footings, for concrete-joist floor construction, and for beams with total depth not greater than 10 in, 2 ½ times the thickness of the flange, or one-half the web width (whichever is greater). ③ These members are excluded because of their capacity to redistribute internal forces before diagonal tension failure, as confirmed both by tests and successful design experience. ④

Reginon in which web reinforcement is required If the required shear strength V_u is greater than the design shear strength ϕV_c provided by the concrete in any portion of a beam, there is a theoretical requirement for web reinforcement. Elsewhere in the span, web steel at least equal to the amount given by Eq. 4 must be provided, unless he calculated shear force is less than $\frac{1}{2}\phi V_c$.

The portion of any span through which web reinforcement is theoretically necessary can be found by drawing the shear diagram for the span and superimposing a plot of the design shear strength of the concrete. ⑤ Where the shear force V_u exceeds ϕV, shear reinforcement must provide for the excess. The additional length through which at least the minimum web steel is needed can be found by superimposing a plot of $\phi V_c/2$. ⑥

At a section where web reinforcement is needed, the total nominal shear resistance is the sum of that provided by the concrete and that provided by the steel:

$$V_n = V_c + V_s \tag{5}$$

and the design strength is equal to ϕV_n as usual.

The concrete contribution to shear strength, after diagonal cracking, includes the contributions of aggregate interlock, dowel action, and the shear resistance of the uncracked concrete in the compression zone above the neutral axis. ⑦ The sum of these three contributions can be taken equal to the shear force which caused the diagonal crack to initiate in the beam web. ⑧ thus V_c is given by Eq. 3*a* or its alternative Eq. 3*b*.

Notes

①如果计算荷载作用下的剪力 V_u 不大于 ϕ 乘以用方程（3*a*）或（3*b*）计算出来的 V_c，从理

论上讲，不需要腹筋。

②除非 V_u 小于混凝土设计抗剪强度 ϕV_c 的一半，否则均需遵守这项规定。

③但对板、基础、混凝土密肋楼板结构，和总高不超过 10 英寸，或不超过 2.5 倍翼缘板厚或腹板宽度一半的梁（取上述三数中较大者）均属特殊例外，无需满足最小腹筋面积的要求。

④这是因为上述构件能在斜拉破坏前重新分布内力，这一点已由试验和成功的设计经验所证实。

⑤把任一跨内的剪力图和混凝土的剪切抗力图重叠，即可求出该跨内理论上需要配筋的部分。

⑥此外，尚需延伸一定长度配置最低限度的腹筋，这一长度由 $\phi V_c/2$ 处水平线与剪力图交叠定出。

⑦在发生斜裂缝后混凝土对抗剪强度的贡献包括以下几部分：
骨料的咬合作用、销栓作用以及中性轴以上受压区未开裂混凝土的抗剪作用。

⑧取这三部分抗剪作用之和等于使腹板开始出现斜向裂缝时的剪力。

UNIT EIGHT

Text Two-Way Column-Supported Slabs

[1] When two-way slabs are supported by relatively shallow, flexible beams, or if column-line beams are omitted altogether, as for flat plates or flat slabs, several new considerations are introduced. Fig. 8-1*a* shows a portion of a floor system in which a rectangular slab panel is supported by relatively shallow beams on four sides. The beams, in turn, are supported by columns at the intersections of their centerlines. If a surface load w is applied, that load is shared between imaginary slab strips S in the short direction and L in the long direction, as before. Note that the portion of the load that is carried by the long strips L is delivered to the beams B spanning in the short direction of the panel. This portion carried by the beams B plus that carried directly in the short direction by the slab strips S sums up to 100 percent of the load applied to the panel. Similarly, the short-direction slab strips S deliver a part of the load to long-direction girders G. That load plus load carried directly in the long direction by the slab includes 100 percent of the applied load. It is clearly a requirement of statics that for column-supported construction 100 percent of the applied load must be carried in each direction, jointly by the slab and its supporting beams. ①

[2] A similar situation is obtained in the flat-plate floor shown in Fig. 8-1*b*. In this case beams are omitted. However, broad strips of the slab centered on the column lines in each direction serve the same function as the beams of Fig. 8-1*a*; for this case, also, the full load must be carried in each direction. The presence of dropped panels or column capitals in the double-hatched zone near the columns does not modify this requirement of statics.

[3] Fig. 8-2*a* shows a flat-plate floor supported by columns at A, B, C, and D. Fig. 8-2*b* shows the moment diagram for the direction of span l_1. In this direction, the slab may be considered as a broad, flat beam of width l_2. Accordingly, the load per foot of span is wl_2. In any span of a continuous beam, the sum of the midspan positive moment and the average of the negative moments at adjacent supports is equal to the midspan positive moment of a corresponding simply supported beam. In terms of the slab, this requirement of statics may be written

$$\frac{1}{2}(M_{ab} + M_{cd}) + M_{ef} = \frac{1}{8}wl_2l_1^2 \qquad (a)$$

A similar requirement exists in the perpendicular direction, leading to the relation

$$\frac{1}{2}(M_{ac} + M_{bd}) + M_{gh} = \frac{1}{8}wl_1l_2^2 \qquad (b)$$

[4] These results disclose nothing about the relative magnitudes of the support moments and span moments. The proportion of the total static moment which exists at each critical section can be found from an elastic analysis which considers the relative span lengths in adjacent panels, the loading pattern, and the relative stiffness of the supporting

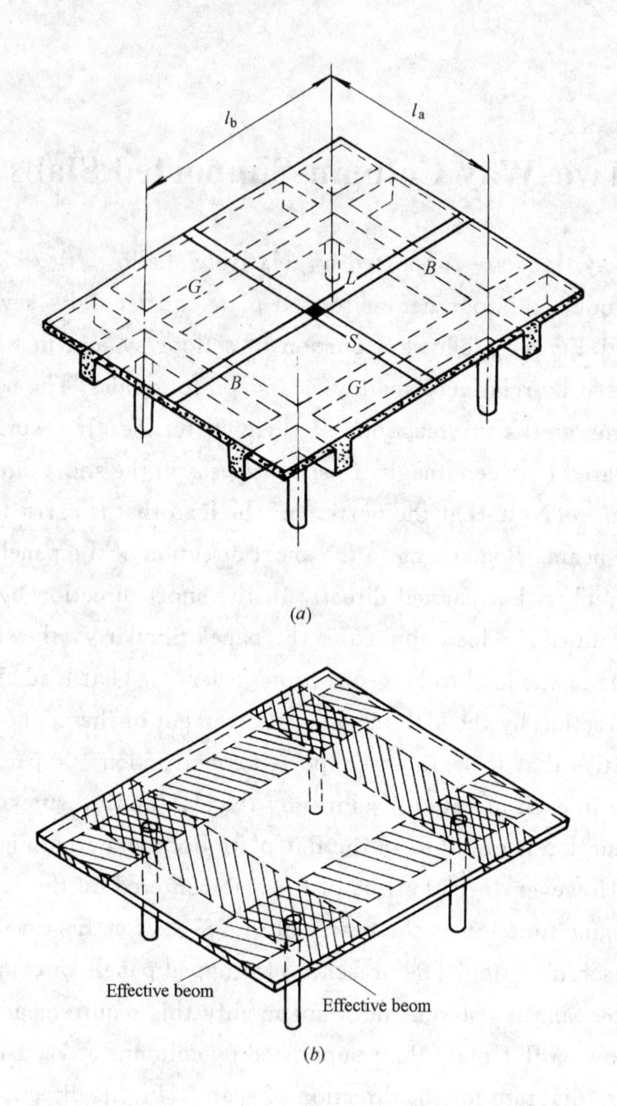

Fig. 8-1 Column-supported two-way slabs

(*a*) two-way slab with beams and columns

(*b*) two-way slab without beams

beams, if any, and that of the columns. ② Alternatively, empirical methods which have been found to be reliable under restricted conditions may be adopted.

[5] The moments across the width of critical sections such as *AB* or *EF* are not constant but vary as shown qualitatively in Fig. 8-2*c*. The exact variation depends on the presence or absence of beams on the column lines, the existence of dropped panels and column capitals, as well as on the intensity of the load. ③ For design purposes it is convenient to divide each panel as shown in Fig. 8-2*c* into column strips, having a width of one-fourth the panel width, on each side of the column centerlines, and middle strips in the one-half panel width between two column strips. Moments may be considered constant within the bounds

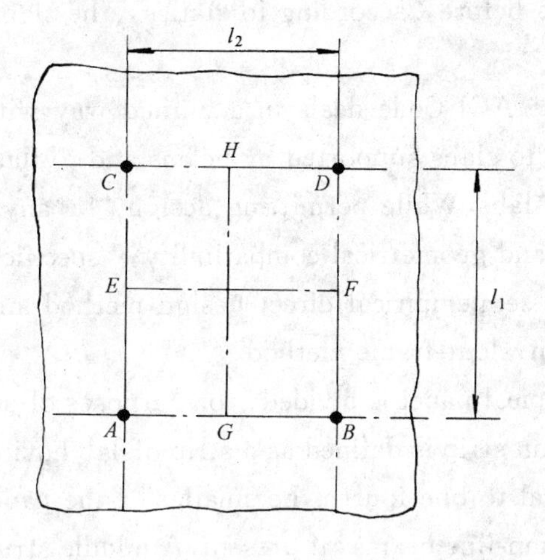

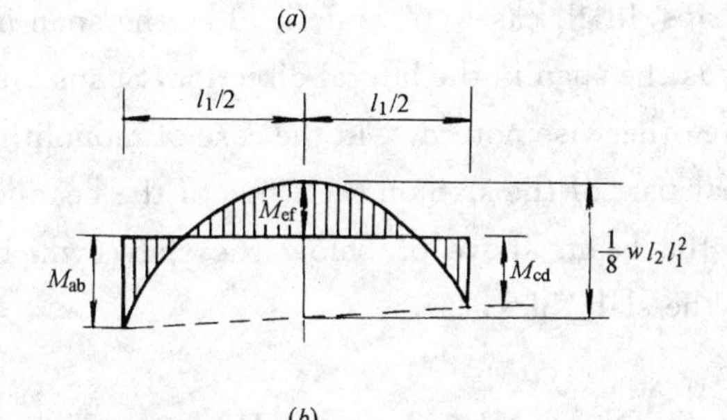

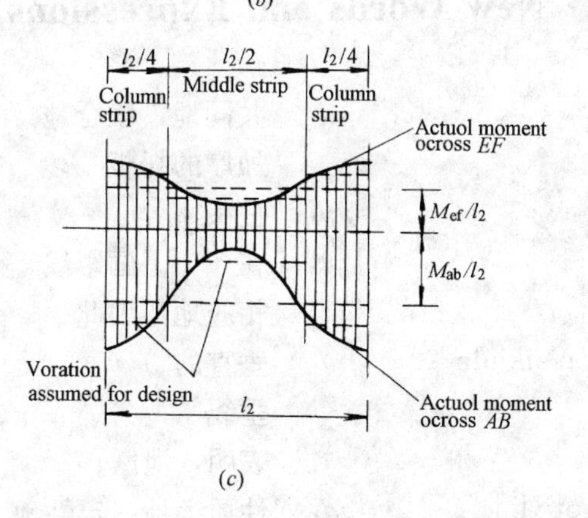

Fig. 8-2 Moment variation in column-supported two-way slabs

(*a*) moment sections;

(*b*) moment variation along span;

(*c*) moment variation across width of critical sections

of a middle strip or column strip, as shown, unless beams are present on the column lines. In the latter case, while the beam must have the same curvature as the adjacent slab strip, the beam moment will be larger in proportion to its greater stiffness, producing a discontinuity in the moment-variation curve at the lateral face of the beam. Since the total moment must be the same as before, according to statics, the slab moments must be correspondingly less.

[6] Chapter 13 of the ACI Code deals in a unified way with all such two-way systems. Its provisions apply to slabs supported by beams and to flat slabs and flat plates, as well as to two-way grid slabs. While permitting design "by any procedure satisfying the conditions of equilibrium and geometrical compatibility," specific reference is made to two alternative approaches: a semiempirical direct design method and an approximate elastic analysis known as the equivalent-frame method.

[7] In either case a typical panel is divided, for purposes of design, into column strips and middle strips. A column strip is defined as a strip ofslab having a width on each side of the column centerline equal to one-fourth the smaller of the panel dimensions l_1 and l_2.④ Such a strip includes column-line beams, if present. A middle strip is a design strip bounded by two column strips. In all cases, l_1 is defined as the span in the direction of the moment analysis, and l_2 as the span in the lateral direction. Spans are measured to column centerlines, except where otherwise notecd.⑤ In the case of monolithic construction, beams are defined to include that part of the slab on each side of the beam extending a distance equal to the projection of the beam above or below the slab (whichever is greater) but not greater than 4 times the slab thickness.

New Words and Expressions

jointly [ˈdʒɔintli]	*ad*.	共同地，联合地
droped pannels		加厚的托板
capital [ˈkæpitl]	*n*.	柱头
hatch [hætʃ]	*vt*.	在……上画影线
accordingly [əˈkɔːdiŋli]	*ad*.	相应地，因此
perpendicular * [ˌpəːpənˈdikjulə]	*a*.	垂直的
	n.	垂线
disclose * [disˈkləuz]	*vt*.	表明，泄露
qualitatively * [ˈkwɔlitətivli]	*ad*.	性质上地，定性地
curvature * [ˈkəːvətʃə]	*n*.	曲率，弯曲
discontinuity * [ˈdiskɔntiˈnju(ː)iti]	*n*.	不连续性，不连续点
unified [ˈjuːnifaid]	*a*.	统一的
code [kəud]	*n*.	规范
provision [prəˈviʒən]	*n*.	规定，条款
grid [grid]	*n*.	格子，窗格
eguilibrium [ˌiːkwiˈlibriəm]	*n*.	平衡，均衡
compatibility [kəmˌpætəˈbiliti]	*n*.	相容性
projection [prəˈdʒekʃən]	*n*.	突出物，突出

Notes

①that 引导主语从句，jointly by…是状语，修饰 be carried。

②if any=if there are any supporting beams，that 代前面的 the relative stiffness。

③句中 the presence or absence of…, the existence of…, the intensity of…是三个并列成分作 depend on 的宾语。

④ 句中 having a width…作 slab 的定语，on each side…和 equal to…作 width 的定语，smaller of…作 one -fourth 的定语。

⑤ 句中 where…引导的句子省略了 it is，作介词 except 的宾语。

Exercises

Reading Comprehension

I. Choose the best answer.

1. The portion of the load that is carried by the long strip L is equal to ________.

   A. the load carried by the slab strips *S*

   B. 100%

   C. the load carried by the beams *B*

   D. the load carried by the long-direction girders

2. What does Para. 1 mainly talk about?

   A. When two-way slabs are supported by relatively shallow, flexible beams, or if colum-line beams are omitted together, several new considerations are introduced.

   B. If a surface load *W* is applied, that load is shared between imaginary slab strips *S* in the short direction and *L* in the long direction.

   C. The short-direction slab strips *S* deliver a part of the load to long-direction girders.

   D. For column-supported construction 100 percent of the applied load must be carried in each direction, jointly by the slab and its supporting beams.

3. Which of the following statements is True?

   A. The sum of the midspan positive moment plus the average of the negative moment at adjacent supports is zero.

   B. The sum of the midspan positive moment is equal to the midspan positive moment of a corresponding simply supported beam.

   C. The average of the negative moments at adjacent supports plus the midspan positive moment of a corresponding simply supported beam is zero.

   D. The sum of the midspan positive moment and the average of the negative moments at adjacent supports is equal to the midspan positive moment of a corresponding simply supported beam.

4. Why is a typical panel divided into column strips and middle strips?

A. For purpose of calculating.

B. For purpose of designing.

C. For purpose of understanding.

D. For purpose of building.

5. In the case of monolithic construction, beams are defined to include that part of the slab.

What does the word monolithic probably mean here?

A. partial B. independent C. complete D. integral

Ⅱ. Fill in the blanks with the information given in the text.

1. The moment across the width of ____________ are not constant. The exact variation depends on ____________ or ____________ of beams on the ____________, the existence of ____________ and ____________, as well as on the ____________ of the load.

2. Moments may be considered ____________ within ____________ or ____________, as shown, unless beams are present on ____________.

3. The provisions of Chapter 13 of the ACI Code apply to ____________ and to ____________, as well as to ____________.

Vocabulary

Ⅰ. Choose one word or phrase which is the most similar in meaning to the one underlined in the given sentences.

1. We must ascertain the actual conditions and arrange accordingly.

A. alterablly B. alternately

C. correspondingly D. independently

2. The plumb line is always perpendicular to the horizontal plane.

A. vertical B. parallel

C. precipitous D. crossed

3. A cone resting on its base will remain in equilibrium.

A. unstanding B. equalizing

C. uprising D. balancing

4. According to the provision of the agreement the money must be paid back in monthly amounts.

A. qualification B. specification

C. restriction D. stipulation

5. The two families live in adjacent street.

A. touching B. conjoining

C. adjoining D. connecting

Ⅱ. Match the words in Column A with their corresponding definitions or explanations in Column B.

A	B
1. girder	a. guided only by practical experience rather than by scientific ideas out of books
2. curvature	b. of, at, from, or towards the side
3. compatibility	c. the degree to which something is curved
4. span	d. the length of a bridge, arch, etc. between supports
5. grid	e. a strong beam, usu. of iron or steel, which supports the smaller beams in a floor or roof
	f. a set of bars set across each other in a frame
	g. a breaking or space between
	h. the state of existing or working in agreement together or with another

Translation

被动语态：（1）译成汉语主动句

英语被动语态结构运用的非常广泛。汉语也有被动结构，但使用范围狭窄的多。因此，英译汉时在很多情况下，都可以译成主动句。

例一

The experiment will be finished in a week. 这项实验将在一周后完成。

例二

The material must be tested to determine its suitability before application. 使用前须对材料进行试验，以确定其适用性。（利用“对”字结构，将原主语改译为“对”字的宾语）

Translate the following sentences into Chinese, and pay attention to the words underlined.

1. The whole country was armed in a few days.
2. The discovery is highly appreciated in the circle of science.
3. It would be astonishing if that loss were not keenly felt.
4. It is said that numerical control is the operation of machine tools by numbers.
5. Solution to the problem was ultimately found.

Reading Material A

Two-Way Edge-Supported Slabs (1)

The slabs discussed in Arts. 5.2 to 5.4 deform under load into a cylindrical surface. The main structural action is one-way in such cases, in the direction normal to supports on two opposite edges of a rectangular panel. ① In many cases, however, rectangular slabs are of such proportions and are supported in such a way that two-way action results. When loaded, such slabs bend into a dished surface rather than a cylindrical one. This means that at any point the slab is curved in both principal directions, and since bending moments are proportional to curvatures, moments also exist in both directions. To resist these moments, the slab must be reinforced in both directions, by two layers of bars perpendicular, respectively, to two pairs of edges. The slab must be designed to take a proportionate share of the load in each direction.

Types of reinforced-concrete construction which are characterized by two-way action include slabs supported by walls or beams on all sides, flat plates, flat slabs, and grid slabs.

The simplest type of two-way slab action is where the slab, or slab panel, is supported along its four edges by relatively deep, stiff, monolithic concrete beams or by walls or steel girders. If the concrete edge beams are shallow or are omitted altogether, as for flat plates and flat slabs, deformation of the floor system along the column lines significantly alters the distribution of moments in the slab panel itself. Two-way systems of this type are considered separately. The present discussion pertains to the former type, in which edge supports are stiff enough to be considered unyielding.

Such a slab is shown in Fig. 8-3*a*. To visualize its flexural performance it is convenient to think of it as consisting of two sets of parallel strips, in each of the two directions, intersecting each other. ② Evidently, part of the load is carried by one set and transmitted to one pair of edge supports, and the remainder by the other.

Fig. 8-3*a* shows the two center strips of a rectangular plate with short span l_a and long span l_b. If the uniform load is w per square foot of slab, each of the two strips acts approximately like a simple beam uniformly loaded by its share of w. Because these imaginary strips actually are part of the same monolithic slab, their deflections at the intersection point must be the same. Equating the center deflections of the short and long strips gives

$$\frac{5w_a l_a^4}{384EI} = \frac{5w_b l_b^4}{384EI} \qquad (a)$$

where w_a is the share of the load w carried in the short direction and w_b is the share of the load w carried in the long direction. Consequently,

$$\frac{w_a}{w_b} = \frac{l_b^4}{l_a^4} \tag{b}$$

One sees that the larger share of the load is carried in the short direction, the ratio of the two portions of the total load being inversely proportional to the fourth power of the ratio of the spans.

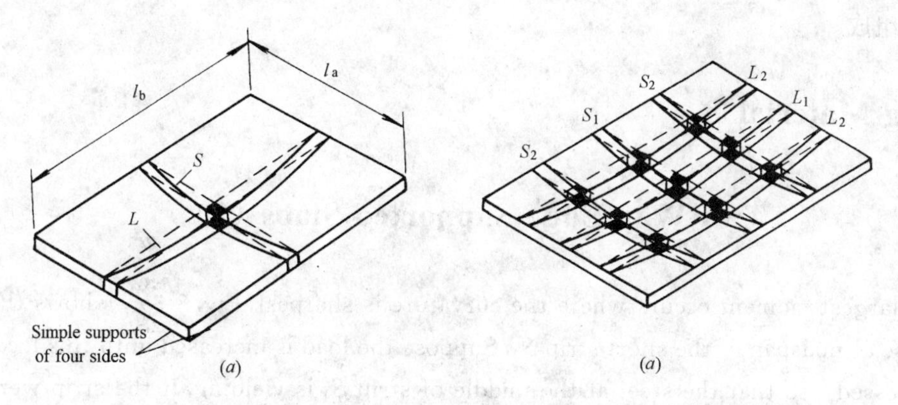

Fig. 8-3 Two-way slab on simple edge supports.
(a) Bending of center strips of slab (b) Grid model of slab

This result is approximate because the actual behavior of a slab is more complex than that of the two intersecting strips. An understanding of the behavior of the slab itself can be gained from Fig. 8-3b, which shows a slab model consisting of two sets of three strips each. It is seen that the two central strips S_1 and L_1 bend in a manner similar to that of Fig. 8-3a. The outer strips S_2 and L_2, however, are not only bent but also twisted. Consider, for instance, one of the intersections of S_2 with L_2. It is seen that at the intersection the exterior edge of strip L_2 is at a higher elevation than the interior edge, while at the nearby and of strip L_2 both edges are at the same elevation; the strip is twisted. This twisting results in torsional stresses and torsional moments which are seen to be most pronounced near the corners. Consequently, the total load on the slab is carried not only by the bending moments in two directions but also by the twisting moments. For this reason bending moments in elastic slabs are smaller than would be computed for sets of unconnected strips loaded by w_a and w_b. For instance, for a simply supported square slab, $w_a = w_b = w/2$. If only bending were present, the maximum moment in each strip would be

$$\frac{(w/2)l^2}{8} = 0.0625wl^2 \tag{c}$$

The exact theory of bending of elastic plates shows that, actually, the maximum moment in such a square slab is only $0.048wl^2$, so that in this case the twisting moments relieve the bending moments by about 25 percent.

Notes

①这种情况下，其主要的结构作用是单向的，它垂直于矩形板两相对的支承边。

②为想象它的弯曲受力状况方便起见，我们可把板看作是由两组方向不同，相互交叉的平行板条组成。

Reading Material B

Two-Way Edge-Supported Slabs （2）

The largest moment occurs where the curvature is sharpest. Fig. 8-3*b* shows this to be the case at midspan of the short strip S_1. Suppose the load is increased until this location is overstressed, so that the steel at the middle of strip S_1 is yielding. If the strip were an isolated beam, it would now fail. Considering the slab as a whole, however, one sees that no immediate failure will occur. The neighboring strips (those parallel as well as those perpendicular to S_1), being actually monolithic with it, will take over that share of any additional load which strip S_1 can no longer carry until they in turn start yielding.[①] This inelastic redistribution will continue until in a rather large area in the central portion of the slab all the steel in both directions is yielding. Only then will the entire slab fail. From this reasoning, which is confirmed by tests, it follows that slabs need not be designed for the absolute maximum moment in each of the two directions (such as $0.048wl^2$ in the example of the previous paragraph) but only for a smaller average moment in each of the two directions in the central portion of the slab. For instance, one of the several analytical methods in general use permits the above square slab to be designed for a moment of $0.036wl^2$. By comparison with the actual elastic maximum moment $0.048wl^2$, it is seen that, owing to inelastic redistribution, a moment reduction of 25 percent is provided.

The largest moment in the slab occurs at midspan of the short strip S_1 of Fig. 8-3*b*. It is evident that the curvature, hence the moment, in the short strip S_2 is less than at the corresponding location of strip S_1.[②] Consequently, a variation of short-span moment occurs in the long direction of the span. This variation is shown qualitatively in Fig. 8-4. The short-span-moment diagram in Fig. 8-4*a* is valid only along the center strip at 1-1. Elsewhere the maximum-moment value is less, as shown in Fig. 8-4*b*; all other moment ordinates are reduced proportionately. Similarly, the long-span-moment diagram in Fig. 8-4*c* applies only at the longitudinal centerline of the slab; elsewhere ordinates are reduced according to the variation shown in Fig. 8-4*d*. These variations in maximum moment across the width and length of a rectangular slab are accounted for in an approximate way in most practical design methods by designing for a reduced moment in the outer quarters of the slab span in each direction. [③]

It should be noted that only slabs with side ratios less than about 2 need be treated as two-way slabs. From Eq. (*b*) above it is seen that for a slab of this proportion the share of the load carried in the long direction is only of the order of one-sixteenth that in the short direction. Such a slab acts almost as if it were spanning in the short direction only. Consequently, rectangular slab panels with aspect ratio of 2 or more may be reinforced for one-way action, with the main steel perpendicular to the long edges. Shrinkage and temperature steel should be provided in the long direction, of course, and auxiliary reinforcement should be provided over, and perpendicular to, the short support beams and at the slab corners to control cracking. [④]

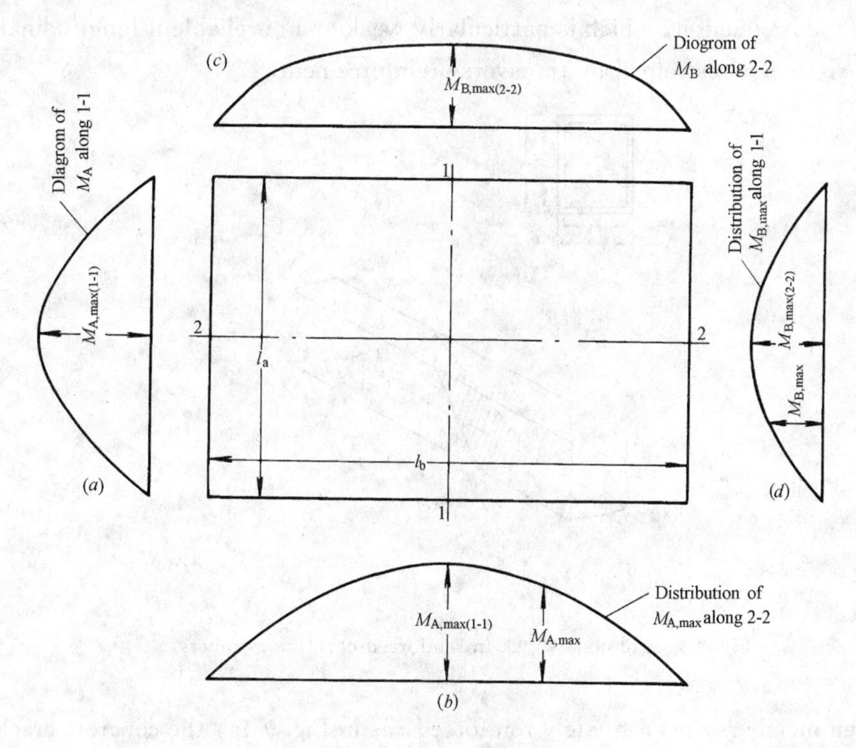

Fig. 8-4 Moments in uniformly loaded, simply supported slab.

Notes

①实际上与它是一个整体的相邻板条(那些平行于或垂直于 S_1 的板条)将分担 S_1 不能承担的附加荷载直到它们开始屈服。

②显然短向板条 S_2 上的曲率和力矩都小于相应位置的板条 S_1 上的曲率和力矩。

③沿矩形板宽度和长度的最大力矩的变化在绝大多数实用设计方法中，是取每个板跨方向上侧边 1/4 处降低了的弯矩进行设计，以简化的方式来计算的。

④在（板的）长向应设置收缩和温度钢筋，当然，为控制开裂，在垂直于短跨支承梁方向上部及板角上部还应设置附加钢筋。

UNIT NINE

Text Torsion in Reinforced Concrete Members

[1] To resist torsion, reinforcement must consist of closely spaced stirrups and of longitudinal bars. ① Tests have shown that longitudinal bars alone hardly increase the torsional strength, test results showing an improvement of at most 15 percent. ② This is understandable because the only way in which longitudinal steel alone can contribute to torsional strength is by dowel action, which is particularly weak and unreliable if longitudinal splitting along bars is not restrained by transverse reinforcement. ③

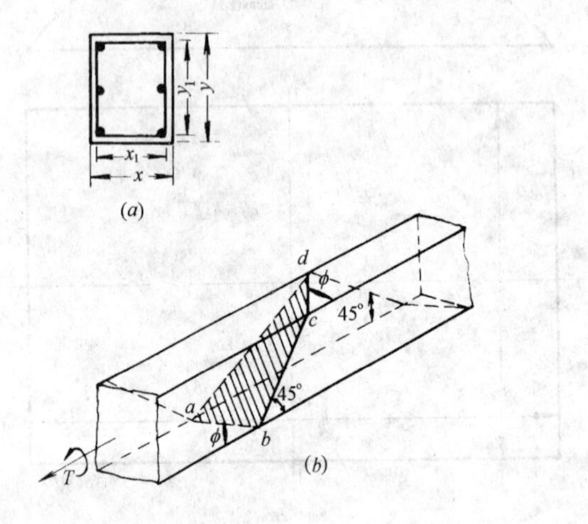

Fig. 9-1 Torsional crack in reinforced-concrete members.

[2] When members are adequately reinforced, as in Fig. 9-1a, the concrete cracks at a torque equal to or only somewhat larger than in an unreinforced member. ④ The cracks form a spiral pattern. In actuality, a great number of such spiral cracks develop at close spacing. Upon cracking, the torsional resistance of the concrete drops to about half of that of the uncracked member, the remainder being now resisted by reinforcement. ⑤ This redistribution of internal resistance is reflected in the torque-twist curve (Fig. 9-2), which at the cracking torque shows continued twist at constant torque until the reinforcement has picked up the portion of the torque no longer carried by concrete. Any further increase of applied torque must then be carried by the reinforcement. Failure occurs when somewhere along the member the concrete crushes along a line such as *a-d* in Fig. 9-1. In a well-designed member such crushing occurs only after the stirrups have started to yield.

[3] The torsional strength can be analyzed by considering the equilibrium of the internal

forces which are transmitted across the potential failure surface, shown shaded in Fig. 9-1. This surface is seen to be bounded by a 45° tension crack across one wider face, two cracks across the narrower faces of inclination ϕ, an angle generally between 45° and 90°, and the zone of concrete crushing along line a-d. ⑥ The failure is basically flexural, as for plain beams, with a concrete compression zone developing adjacent to *a-d*.

[4] Figure 3 shows the partially cracked failure surface, including the compression zone of concrete (shaded) and the horizontal and vertical stirrup forces S_a and S_v of all the stirrups intersecting the failure surface, except for those located in the compression zone. The number of horizontal stirrup legs, top or bottom, crossing the surface is seen to be $n_h=(x_1 \cot\phi)/s$, and the number of vertical legs opposite the compression zone, $n_v=y_1/s$. It is known from tests that at failure the vertical stirrup legs yield while the horizontal legs are generally not stressed to yielding. Correspondingly, the twisting couple produced by the horizontal stirrup forces is

$$T_h = n_h S_h y_1 = \frac{x_1 \cot\phi}{S} A_l f_{sh} y_1 = k_h \frac{x_1 y_1}{S} A_l f_y \qquad (a)$$

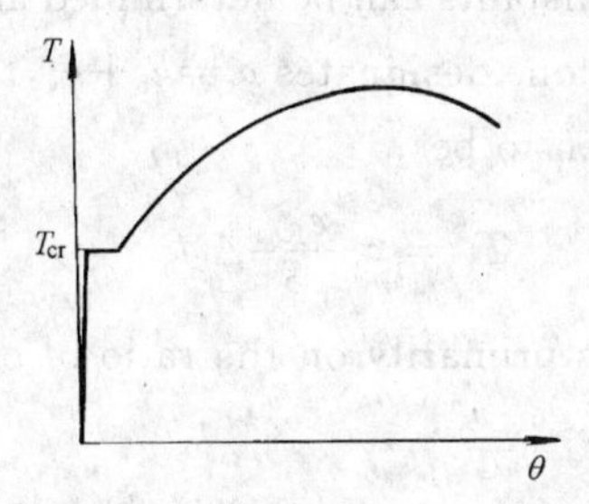

Fig. 9-2 Torque-twist curve in reinforced concrete

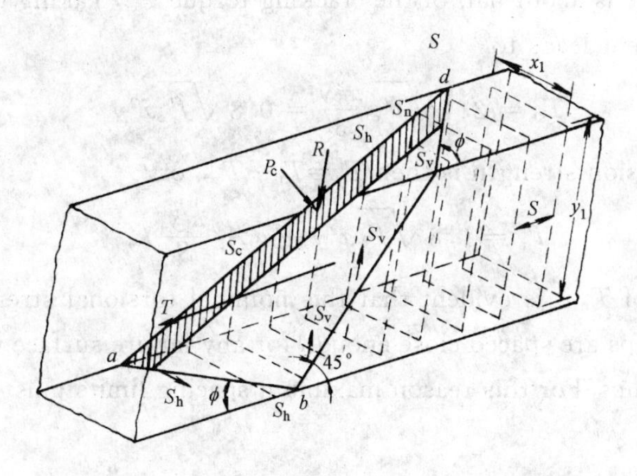

Fig. 9-3

Where A_l——area of one stirrup leg

f_{sh}——tension stress in horizontal stirrup leg

f_y——yield point

k_h——$\cot\phi \ (f_{sh}/f_y)$

[5] To analyze the torque produced by the vertical stirrup forces near the front face, one must note, first, that the equilibrating forces near the rear face, in the compression zone, are fairly indeterminate. They consist, at the least, of a shear force S_c and a compression force P_c in the concrete and forces in the stirrup legs located in that zone. It is clear, however, that because of equilibrium, all these forces must have a resultant R equal and opposite to the sum of the vertical stirrup forces S_c. Correspondingly, the torque produced by the vertical stirrup forces can be written

$$T_v = n_v S_v x_v = \frac{y_1}{S} A_l f_y k_v x_1 = k_v \frac{x_1 y_1}{S} A_l f_y \qquad (b)$$

where x_v is the lever arm of the internal forces S_v and R, and $k_v = x_v / x_1$.

[6] It is seen that Eqs. (a) and (b) are identical except for k_h and k_v. At the present stage of knowledge, neither of these constants can be determined analytically, and recourse must be had to extensive tests.[7] When one designates $\alpha_t = k_h + k_v$, the total torque contributed by the stirrups, $T_s = T_v + T_h$, is seen to be

$$T_s = \alpha_t \frac{x_1 y_1}{S} A_l f_y \qquad (1)$$

Tests have shown that α_t depends primarily on the ratio of cross-sectional dimensions and can be taken as

$$\alpha_t = 0.66 + 0.33 \frac{y_1}{x_1} \leqslant 1.50 \qquad (2)$$

[7] It was mentioned previously that after cracking, the torque T_0 contributed by the concrete compression zone is about half of the cracking torque T_{cr}. Taking the fraction conservatively to be 40 percent leads to[8]

$$T_0 = 2.4\sqrt{f'_c} \frac{x^2 y}{3} = 0.8\sqrt{f'_c} x^2 y \qquad (3)$$

The total nominal torsion strength is then $T_n = T_0 + T_s$, or

$$T_n = 0.8\sqrt{f'_c} x^2 y + \alpha_t A_l \frac{x_1 y_1}{S} f_y \qquad (4)$$

From the derivation of T_n it is evident that this nominal torsional strength will be developed only if the stirrups are spaced close enough for any failure surface to intersect an adequate number of stirrups. For this reason maximum spacing limits must be set for the stirrups.

New Words and Expressions

stirrup ['stirəp]　　*n.* 箍筋，钢箍

torsional * [ˈtɔːʃənl] *a.* 扭转的
dowel [ˈdauəl] *n.* 销栓
understandable [ˌʌndəˈstændəbl] *a.* 能领会的，可被了解的
unreliable [ʌnriˈlaiəbl] *a.* 不可靠的，不可信赖的
spiral * [ˈspaiərəl] *a.* 螺旋的
unreinforced [ʌnriːnˈfɔːst] *a.* 无钢筋的，不加固的
actuality [æktjuˈæliti] *n.* 现实，实际
in actuality 实际上
remainder * [riˈmeində] *n.* 剩余部分
redistribution [ˌridistriˈbjuːʃən] *n.* 重新分布，再分配
plain [plein] *a.* 素的，不配筋的
analytically [ænəˈlitikəli] *ad.* 分析地，解析地
recourse * [riˈkɔːs] *n.* 依赖（靠），救助
have recourse to 依靠，借助于
designate * [ˈdezigneit] *vt.* 指明，选定
intersect * [ˌintə（:）ˈsekt] *v.* 相交，交叉；横切

Notes

①…，reinforcement must consist of closely spaced stirrups and of longitudinal bars.
两个 of 并列，均为短语动语 consist of 的一部分。

②…，test results showing an improvement of at most 15 percent. 为分词独立结构，作状语；an improvement 指 an increase of the torsional strength。

③…in which …to torsional strength 在 because 引导的状语从句中作定语，修饰 the only way；逗号后面的 which 引导的非限定性定语从句修饰 action。

④cracks 是主句中的谓语动词；equal to or larger than 至句尾为形容词短语作后置定语，修饰 a torque，其中 than 后面省略了一个指代比较对象的 that。

⑤…，the remainder being now resisted by reinforcement. 这是分词独立结构作状语。

⑥…to be bounded by 后面有三个宾语，分别是 a 45° tention crack…，two cracks…，and the zone of concrete；an angle generally between 45° and 90°是 inclination ϕ 的同位语。

⑦recourse must be had to 为 have recourse to 的被动式用法，意为：必须借助于大量的试验。

⑧Taking…to be 40 percent 是句子的主语，谓语动词是 leads to ；the fraction 指的是 40 percent。

Exercises

Reading Comprehension

Ⅰ. Choose the best answer.

1. In order to resist torsion, what measures should be taken?
   A. Closely spaced stirrups and longitudinal bars should be used in reinforcement.
   B. Longitudinal bars should be closely spaced.
   C. Horizontal stirrups should be closely placed.
   D. Verticle stirrups can be neglected.
2. What will happen to the torsional resistance of the concrete upon cracking?
   A. It remains unchanged.
   B. It increases by about 15 percent.
   C. It drops to about half of that of the uncracked member.
   D. It is resisted by reinforcement.
3. What will happen when members are adequately reinforced?
   A. The concrete cracks at a torque which is equal to that in an unreinforced member.
   B. The concrete cracks at a torque larger than that in an unreinforced member.
   C. The torsional resistance of the concrete will increase by half of the unreinforced member.
   D. Both A and B.
4. Why must people have recourse to extensive tests to determine some constants?
   A. Tests can be easily carried out.
   B. Because man's knowledge is limited at present.
   C. It is not safe to do so by analysis.
   D. It is the most economical way.
5. Which of the following statements is True according to the passage?
   A. Longitudinal steel alone can increase the torsional strength.
   B. The role of the longitudinal reinforcement in providing torsional strength is clearly understood.
   C. When members are adequately reinforced, the concrete will not crack.
   D. Only by dowel action can longitudinal bars help increase torsional strength.

Ⅱ. Fill in the blanks with the information given in the text.

1. We learn from tests that at failure the vertical stirrup legs __________ while the horizontal legs ____________________.
2. To analyze the torque produced by the verticle stirrup forces near the front face, we should note, first, __________________, in the compression zone, __________________. They consist, __________, of __________ and

________ in the concrete and ________________ in that zone.

3. From the derivation of T_n it is evident that ________________ only if ________. For this reason ________________ for the stirrups.

Vocabulary

Ⅰ. Choose one word or phrase that is the most similar in meaning to the one underlined in the given sentences.

1. The sick man <u>had recourse to</u> drugs to lessen his pain.

A. depended on	B. turned into
C. sought help from	D. took up

2. I'll pay you a hundred dollars deposite and the <u>remainder</u> on delivery.

A. ticket	B. rest
C. former	D. receipt

3. Red lines <u>designate</u> main railways on this map.

A. mark	B. point
C. stand	D. lead

4. Officially he is in charge, but <u>in actuality</u> his secretary does all the work.

A. in name	B. in contrast
C. in form	D. in fact

5. They enjoy music, but they don't listen to it <u>analytically</u>.

A. in public	B. with critical examination
C. now and then	D. at random

Ⅱ. Match the words in Column A with their corresponding definitions or explanations in Column B.

A	B
1. bound	a. (of lines) cut or cross each other
2. constant	b. advancing in continuous curve
3. torsion	c. jump or spring up and down
4. intersect	d. the act of twisting or turning
5. spiral	e. number or quantity that does not change
	f. usual or average
	g. keep within a certain space
	h. the amount of force stretching something

Translation

被动语态：(2) 译成汉语被动句

汉语也有用被动形式来表达的情况。这类句子都着重被动的动作。汉语常用“被”、

"受"、"由"、"给"等来表示。

例一

Our foreign policy is supported by the people all over the world.

我们的对外政策受到全世界人民的支持。

例二

They should be severely criticized for their production plan was not completed in time.

他们没有按时完成生产计划，应当给他们以严厉批评。

Translate the following sentences into Chinese, and pay attention to the words underlined.

1. Its use is therefore restricted to articles in which lightness is a prime essential.
2. Last year the region was visited by the worst drought in 60 years.
3. Other processes will be discussed briefly.
4. Part or all of the light may be reflected, absorbed or transmitted by the thing or object that comes into its way.
5. Running water has long been used to turn the wheels of industry.

Reading Material A

Tension Strength

While concrete is best employed in a manner which utilizes its favorable compression strength, its tension strength is also of consequence in a variety of connections. ① Thus, the shear and torsion resistance of reinforced-concrete beams appears to depend primarily on the tension strength of the concrete. Also, the conditions under which cracks form and propagate on the tension side of reinforced-concrete flexural members depend strongly on the tension strength. ②

There are considerable experimental difficulties in determining true tensile strengths for concrete. In direct tension tests, minor misalignments and stress concentrations in the gripping devices are apt to mar the results. ③ For many years, tension properties have been measured in terms of the modulus of rupture, i. e., that computed flexural tension stress M_c/I at which a test beam of plain concrete would fracture. Because this nominal stress is computed on the assumption that concrete is an elastic material, and because this bending stress is localized in the outermost fibers, it is apt to be larger than the strength of concrete in uniform axial tension. ④ It is thus a measure of, but not identical with, the real axial tension strength.

More recently the result of the so-called split-cylinder test has established itself as a measure of the tensile strength of concrete. A 6- ×12-in concrete cylinder, the same type as is used for compression tests, is inserted in a compression-testing machine in the horizontal position, so that compression is applied uniformly along two opposite generatrices. Plywood pads are inserted between the compression platens of the machine and the cylinder in order to equalize and distribute the pressure. It can be shown that in an elastic cylinder so loaded, a nearly uniform tensile stress of magnitude $2P/\pi dL$ exists at right angles to the plane of load application. ⑤ Correspondingly, such cylinders, when tested, split into two halves along that plane, at a stress which can be computed from the above expression. P is the applied compression load at failure, and d and L are the diameter and length of the cylinder. Because of local stress conditions at the load lines and the presence of stresses at right angles to the aforementioned tension stresses, the results of the split-cylinder tests likewise are not identical with (but are believed to be a good measure of) the true axial tensile strength. ⑥ The results of all types of tensile tests show considerably more scatter than those of compression tests.

Tensile strength, however determined, does not correlate well with the compression strength f'_c. It appears that for sand-and-gravel concrete the tensile strength depends primarily on the strength of bond between hardened cement paste and aggregate, whereas for lightweight concretes it depends largely on the tensile strength of the porous aggregate. ⑦ The compression strength, on the other hand, is much less determined by these particular characteristics.

Notes

①利用混凝土有利的抗拉强度，会使其得到最佳的利用。而其抗拉强度也在各种联结中举足轻重。

②而且，钢筋混凝土弯曲构件拉面裂缝的形成及扩展主要取决于抗拉强度。

③在直接拉力试验中，夹具中微小的对准误差及应力集中都极易将试验结果弄糟。

④由于这种名义应力是以假定混凝土是一种弹性材料进行计算的，还由于挠曲应力仅限于最外层纤维，所以它往往大于混凝土的均匀轴向抗拉强度。

⑤可以证明，在上述荷载下，弹性圆柱体中，在垂直于施加荷载的平面上，有一个数量为 $2P/\pi dL$ 近乎均匀的拉应力。

⑥由于荷载线上局部应力状态和垂直于上述拉应力处出现的应力，劈裂圆柱体试验结果同样与实际轴向抗拉强度不相等（但被认为是一种很好的实际轴向抗拉强度的测量方法）。

⑦看起来，对于砂砾石混凝土，抗拉强度主要取决于硬结的水泥浆与骨料间的粘结强度。而对于轻混凝土，则主要取决于多孔集料的抗拉强度。

Reading Material B

Torsion and Torsion Plus Shear

Reinforced-concrete members are rarely designed to resist torsion alone. However, in many situations beams and other members are subject to torsion in addition to shear and bending, and in some cases, to axial compression or tension. [1] Typical situations are spandrel beams or any edge beams of slabs, where the torsional rigidity of the beam provides rotational edge restraint to the slab. [2] This causes corresponding flexural restraining moments in the slab, which in turn are balanced by torsional moments in the beam. Another frequent example is edge members of shells. To understand the behavior of members subject to such combinations of load effects, it is first necessary to discuss the effects of simple torsion on reinforced-concrete members. For simplicity the discussion will be restricted initially to rectangular members. **a. Torsion in plain concrete members.** Fig. 9-4 shows a portion of a prismatic member subject to equal and opposite torques T at both ends. If the material is elastic, St. Venant's classical torsion theory indicates that torsional shear stresses are distributed over the cross section as shown in Fig. 9-4*b*. The largest shear stresses occur at the middle of the wide faces and are equal to

$$T_{max} = \frac{T}{\alpha x^2 y} \tag{1}$$

where α is a shape factor approximately equal to 1/4 and x and y are, respectively, the shorter and longer sides of the rectangle, as shown. If the material is inelastic, the stress distribution is similar, as shown by dashed lines, and the maximum shear stress is still given by Eq. (1) except that α assumes a larger value.

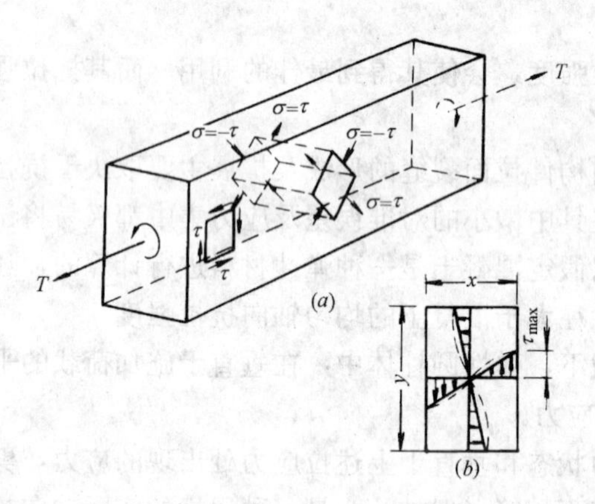

Fig. 9-4 Stresses caused by torsion

Shear stresses in pairs act on an element at or near the wide surface, as shown in Fig. 9-4*a*. As shown in strength of materials, this state of stress corresponds to equal tension and compression stresses on the faces of an element at 45° to the direction of shear. [3] These inclined tension stresses are of the same kind as those caused by transverse shear. However, in the case of torsion, since the torsional shear stresses are of opposite signs in the two halves of the member (Fig. 9-4*b*) the corresponding diagonal tension stresses in the two halves are at right angles to each other (Fig. 9-4*a*). [4]

When the diagonal tension stresses exceed the tension resistance of the concrete, a crack forms at some accidentally weaker location and spreads immediately across the beam, as shown in Fig. 9-5. Observation shows that the tension crack (on the near face on Fig. 9-5*b*) forms at practically 45°, that is, perpendicular to the diagonal tension stresses. The cracks on the two narrow faces, where diagonal tension stresses are smaller, are of more indefinite inclination, as shown, and the fracture line on the far face connects the cracks at the short faces. [5] This completes the formation of an entire fracture surface across the beam which fails the member.

For purposes of analysis this somewhat warped fracture surface can be replaced by a plane section inclined at 45° to the axis, as in Fig. 9-5*b*. Test observation shows that on such a plane, failure is more nearly by bending than by twisting. As shown in Fig. 9-5*b* and c, the applied torque T can be resolved into a component T_b which causes bending about the axis *a-a* of the failure plane and a component T_t which causes twisting. [6] It is seen that

$$T_b = T\cos 45°$$

The section modulus of the failure plane about *a-a* is

$$Z = \frac{x^2 y \csc 45°}{6}$$

Then the maximum bending (tension) stress in the concrete is

$$f_{tb} = \frac{T_b}{Z} = T\sin 45° \cos 45° \frac{6}{x^2 y}$$

or

$$f_{tb} = \frac{3T}{x^2 y} \tag{2}$$

It is seen that the tension stress so calculated is identical with the St. Venant shear stress τ_{max} [Eq. (1)] or with the corresponding diagonal tension stress σ (Fig. 9-4) for $\alpha = 1/3$. If f_{tb} were the only stress acting, cracking should occur when $f_{tb} = f_r$ the modulus of rupture of concrete, which can be taken as $f_r = 7.5\sqrt{f'_c}$ for normal-density concrete. However, at right angles to the tension stress f_{tb} there exists a compression stress f_{cb} of equal magnitude (see Fig. 9-4*a* and 9-5*a*). For this state of biaxial stress, tests show that the presence of equal perpendicular compression reduces the tension strength of concrete by about 15 percent. Consequently, a crack forms and the member fails approximately when $f_{tb} = 0.85 f_r = 6\sqrt{f'_c}$. Let this value of f_{tb} be designed as the cracking stress

$$f_{cr} = \tau_{cr} = 6\sqrt{f_c} \tag{3}$$

Then, upon substitution of f_{cr} for f_{tb} in Eq. (2), one obtains the magnitude of the torque which will crack and fail a plain rectangular concrete member.

$$T_{cr} = 6\sqrt{f'_c}\,\frac{x^2 y}{3} \tag{4}$$

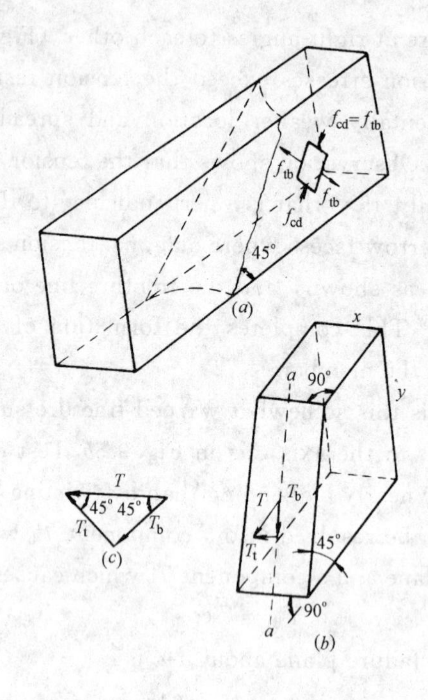

Fig. 9-5 Torsional crack in plain concrete member

Notes

①但是，在很多情况下，梁和其他构件除了受到剪力和弯矩外，还要经受扭矩；在有些情况下，还要经受轴向压力或拉力。

②典型的情况就是外墙托梁或楼板边梁。在此处，梁的扭转刚度对楼板提供了边缘转动约束。

③正如材料力学中所指出的，这种应力状态和构件表面上与剪力方向成45°角的等拉应力和等压应力相一致。

④但是，就扭矩而言，由于扭剪应力在构件的两侧符号相反，因此，两侧对应的斜拉应力相互垂直。

⑤在斜拉应力较小的两个窄面上，裂缝的倾斜更不明确（如图所示）。远的一面上的断裂线与短面上的裂缝相连。

⑥如图 9-5*b* 和 *c* 所示，作用扭矩 T 可以被分解为在破坏面上绕轴 *a-a* 弯矩分量 T_b 和形成扭矩的分量 T_t。

UNIT TEN

Text Strength under Combined Stress

[1] In many structural situations concrete is subjected simultaneously to various stresses acting in various directions. For instance, in beams much of the concrete is subject simultaneously to compression and shear stresses and in slabs and footings to compression in two perpendicular directions plus shear. ① By methods well known in the study of strength of materials, any state of combined stress, no matter how complex, can be reduced to three principal stresses acting at right angles to each other on an appropriately oriented elementary cube in the material. Any or all of the principal stresses can be either tension or compression. If one of them is zero, a state of biaxial stress is said to exist; if two of them are zero, the state of stress is uniaxial, either simple compression or simple tension. In most cases only the uniaxial strength properties of a material are known from simple tests, such as the cylinder strength f'_c and the tensile strength f'_t. For predicting the strengths of structures in which concrete is subject to biaxial or triaxial stress, it would be desirable to be able to calculate the strength of concrete in such states of stress, knowing from tests only either f'_c or f'_c and f'_t.

[2] In spite of extensive and continuing research, no general theory of the strength of concrete under combined stress has yet emerged. Modifications of various strength theories, such as the maximum-tension stress, the Mohr-Coulomb, and the octahedral-stress theories, all of which are discussed in strength-of-materials texts, have been adapted with varying partial success to concrete. Current experimental evidence indicates that limiting tensile strain, which is a function of mean normal stress, may be a failure criterion which is generally applicable. At present none of these theories has been generally accepted, and many have obvious internal contradictions. The main difficulty in developing an adequate general strength theory lies in the highly nonhomogeneous nature of concrete and in the degree to which its behavior at high stresses and at fracture is influenced by microcracking and other discontinuity phenomena. ②

[3] However, the strength of concrete has been well established by tests at least for the biaxial state. Results may be presented in the form of an interaction diagram such as Fig. 10-1 which shows the strength in direction 1 as a function of the stress applied in direction 2. All stresses are nondimensionalized in terms of the uniaxial compressive strength f'_c. It is seen that in the quadrant representing biaxial compression a strength increase as great as about 20 percent over the uniaxial compressive strength is attained, the amount of increase depending upon the ratio of f_2 to f_1. ③ In the biaxial tension-stress state, the strength in direction 1 is independent of tension in direction 2. When tension in direction 2 is combined with compression in direction 1, the compressive strength is reduced almost

linearly. For example, lateral tension of about half the uniaxial tensile strength will reduce the compressive strength by half compared with the uniaxial compressive strength. This fact is of the greatest importance in predicting cracking in deep beams or shear walls, for example.

[4] Experimental investigations into the triaxial strength of concrete have been few, due mainly to the practical difficulty of applying load in three directions simultaneously without introducing significant restraint from the loading equipment. From information now available the following tentative conclusions can be drawn relative to the triaxial strength of concrete: ④ (1) in a state of equal triaxial compression, concrete strength may be an order of magnitude larger⑤ than the uniaxial compressive strength; (2) for equal biaxial compression combined with a smaller value of compression in the third direction, a strength increase greater than 20 percent can be expected; and (3) for stress states including compression combined with tension in at least one other direction, the intermediate principal stress is of little consequence, ⑥ and the compressive strength can be predicted safely based on Fig. 10-1.

[5] The Mohr-Coulomb theory can be used to describe in an approximate way the influence of triaxiality on strength. ⑦It represents a special form of the Mohr theory and defines a failure envelope such that any Mohr stress circle which is tangent to the envelope represents a combination of stresses that will cause failure of the material. ⑧For Mohr's stress circle as used here, the two endpoints of the horizontal diameter are defined by the largest and smallest of the three principal stresses, so that the size and location of the circle is not influenced by the intermediate principal stress. In Fig. 10-2 Circle 1 represents failure in simple tension at a stress f'_t and Circle 2 failure in compression⑨ at a stress f'_c. The failure envelope can be approximated by two straight lines as shown. From experimental studies the slope of the line tangent to Circle 2 on the compression side has an inclination of 37°. On the tension side, the line is laid from the intercept, tangent to Circle 1.

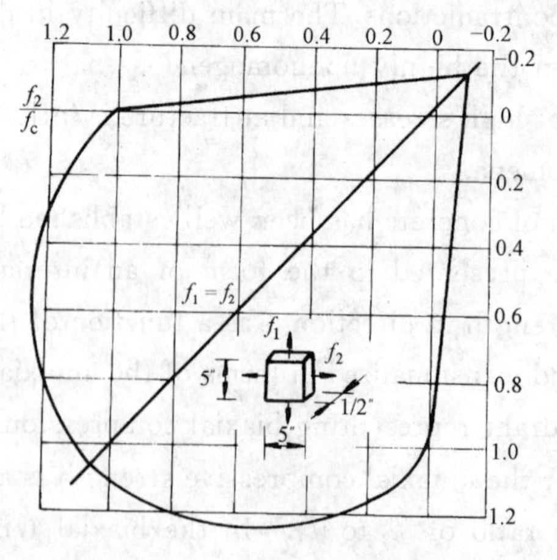

Fig. 10-1 Strength of concrete in biaxial stress

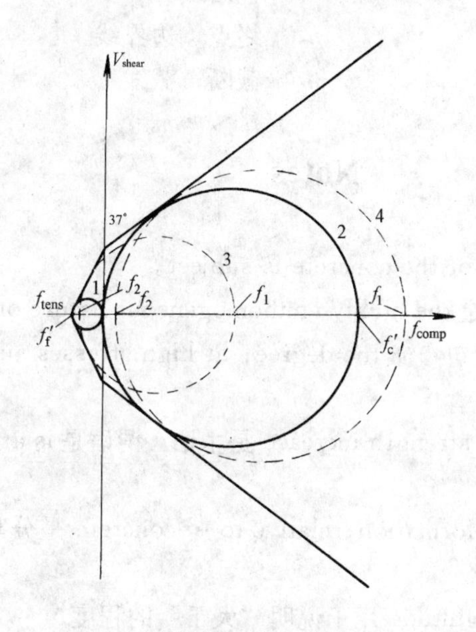

Fig. 10-2　Strength of concrete under combined stress

New Words and Expressions

footing [ˈfutiŋ]	*n.*	基础，立足点
appropriately [əˈprəupriitli]	*ad.*	适合地，正确地
orient * [ˈɔːriənt]	*v.*	定向，定位
biaxial [baiˈæksiəl]	*a.*	双轴的
uniaxial [juːniˈæksiəl]	*a.*	单轴的
cylinder * [ˈsilində]	*n.*	圆柱体，圆筒
tensile [ˈtensail]	*a.*	张力的，拉力的
triaxial [traiˈæksiəl]	*a.*	三轴的
modification * [ˌmɔdifiˈkeiʃən]	*n.*	更改，修正
octahedral [ɔktəˈhedrəl]	*a.*	八面体的，八面的
criterion * [kraiˈtiəriən]	*n.*	
criteria [kraiˈtiəriə]	(*pl.*)	准则，标准
microcrack * [ˈmaikrəukræk]	*n.*	微裂缝
nondimensionalize [nɔndiˈmenʃənəlaiz]	*vt.*	使无量纲化
quadrant [ˈkwɔdrənt]	*n.*	象限，扇形体
linearly [ˈliniəli]	*ad.*	呈直线地，线性地
tentative [tentətiv]	*a.*	试验性的，初步的
triaxiality [traiæksiˈæliti]	*n.*	三轴性，三维
tangent * [ˈtændʒənt]	*n.*	正切，切线
	a.	切线的，相切的

envelope [ˈenviləup]	n.	包络线
endpoint [ˈendpɔint]	n.	终点，边界线
intercept * [intəˈsept]	v./n.	截断；截线

Notes

①在 footings 后面省略了 much of the concrete is subject。

②lie5 in 后面接两个宾语，分别是 the highly nonhomogeneous nature of concrete 和 the degree；to which 引导的定语从句修饰 the degree；at high stresses and at fracture 是 behavior 的定语。

③在 that 引导的主语从句中，a strength increase 是主语，谓语是 is attained；逗号后面的部分为分词独立结构。

④now available 作定语，修饰 information；relative to … concrete 是分割定语，修饰 conclusions。

⑤order：等级，an order of magnitude 用于说明"大于"的程度。

⑥of little consequence 意为：无足轻重

⑦句中不定式 to describe 的逻辑宾语是 the influence of triaxiality on strength；方式状语 in an approximate way 被提到了宾语之前。

⑧it 指代前一句中的 the Mohr-Coulomb theory，such that 引导的是状语从句。

⑨在 Circle 2 后面省略了动词 represents。

Exercises

Reading Comprehension

Ⅰ. Choose the best answer.

1. According to Para. 2, what is part of the main difficulty in developing an adequate general strength theory?

   A. No extensive research has been made yet.

   B. The highly nonhomogeneous nature of concrete.

   C. Many theories have internal contradictions.

   D. Current experimental evidence shows that limiting tensile strain is an inapplicable failure criterion.

2. Which of the following statements is True according to the passage?

   A. In most cases, the uniaxial strength properties of a material can only be known from complex tests.

   B. Because of extensive and continuing research a general theory of the strength of concrete has been developed.

C. Experimental investigations into the biaxial strength of concrete have been few.

D. In many structural situations concrete is subjected to different stresses acting in different directions at the same time.

3. It seems safe to say that ________ .

A. the influence of the triaxiality on strength can be described by the Mohr-Coulomb theory in detail

B. modifications of various strength theories have been adapted to concrete successfully

C. the strength of concrete has been well established for the biaxial state by tests

D. the maximum-tension stress theory will be discussed further

4. By methods known in the study of strength of materials, ________ .

A. any state of combined stress can be reduced to three principal stresses acting to each other at right angles

B. none of the principal stresses can be tension

C. only some complex states of combined stress can be reduced

D. any principal stresses can be compression

5. What can the Mohr-Coulomb theory be used to do?

A. To define the cause of a failure envelope.

B. To describe a combined stress on materials.

C. To represent failure in simple tension.

D. To describe the influence of triaxiality on strength approximately.

Ⅱ. Fill in the blanks with the information given in the text.

1. According to Para. 1,

a. any or all of the principal stresses can be either ________ or ________;

b. if one of them is zero, ________ is said to exist;

c. if two of them are zero, the state of stress is ________, either ________ or ________ .

2. From information now available, the following tentative conclusions relative to the triaxial strength of concrete can be drawn:

a. in a state of equal triaxial compression, ________;

b. for equal biaxial compression ________ of compression in the third direction, ________ can be expected;

c. for stress states including ________ in at least one other direction, the intermediate principal stress ________ .

Vocabulary

Ⅰ. Choose one word or phrase that is the most similar in meaning to the one underlined in the given sentences.

1. The footing for the foundation of a house extends below ground which might be affected by frost.

A. place B. situation

C. root D. base

2. Each individual is required to state the criteria on which his judgements are based.

A. reasons B. standards

C. facts D. evidence

3. We have made tentative plans for a holiday but haven' t decided anything certain yet.

A. perfect B. experimental

C. satisfactory D. careful

4. It is difficult to play the piano and sing simultaneously.

A. one by one B. at the same pace

C. in turn D. at the same time

5. Plain, simple clothes fit the students appropriately.

A. properly B. regularly

C. respectively D. appreciatively

Ⅱ. Match the words in Column A with their corresponding definitions or explanations in Column B.

A	B
1. orient	a. from or towards the side
2. fracture	b. cause to begin
3. magnitude	c. the act of changing
4. lateral	d. of the present day
5. modification	e. greatness of size or importance
	f. a crack or break
	g. give direction or guidance to
	h. in a fashionable way

Translation

增加量译法

英语中表示数量的增加有许多不同方式，翻译时应注意与汉语的对应关系。

例一 “[by] *n*+（单位）”：表示净增量。

The production has increased [by] 36%. 产量已增加了36%。

例二 “by *n* times (by *n*00%)”：表示净增的倍数。

The steel output has increased by two times (by twice). 钢产量已增加了两倍（增加了200%）。

例三 “*n* times + 比较级+than”：表示增加到*n*倍，可译为“比……大（长、宽……）*n*

一1 倍（是……的 *n* 倍）"。

This capacity was <u>two to three times greater than</u> silica gel treated at 300℃。此容量比在 300℃下处理过的硅胶［的容量］大<u>1～2 倍</u>。（是……2～3 倍）。

例四 "*n* times as 十形容词或副词＋as"：表示"是……的 *n* 倍"（增加 *n*−1 倍）。

A is twice (two times) <u>as heavy as</u> *B*. *A* 的重量为 *B* 的<u>两倍</u>。（或"*A* 比 *B* 重一倍。"）

Translate the following sentences into Chinese, and pay attention to the words underlined.

1. The output <u>went up</u> 56, 000 tons.
2. Chromium masks last <u>10 to 100 times longer than</u> the emulsion masks.
3. China′ s coal output in 1984 was <u>ten times more than</u> that in 1959.
4. The laboratory building is <u>3 times as tall as</u> the dormitory.
5. The production of machine tools has been <u>increased by</u> 6 times since 1965.

Reading Material A

Strength under Combined Stress (continued)

This theory suffers from the same defect as the general Mohr theory in implying that the intermediate of the three principal stresses has no effect on strength. ①In particular, for the frequent case of biaxial stress, it predicts that if both principal stresses are of the same sign, there is no effect of biaxiality on strength. In contrast, Fig. 10-2 shows that the strength in biaxial compression is larger than in uniaxial compression by about 8 to 23 percent, depending on the ratio f_1/f_2.

Information of the type presented in Figs. 10-1 and 10-2 permits one to visualize correctly the effects of bi-and triaxial stresses qualitatively and to obtain reasonable quantitative approximations in simple situations. However, the fact that the strength of concrete under combined stress cannot yet be calculated rationally and , equally important, that in many situations in concrete structures it is nearly impossible to calculate all the acting stresses and their directions are two of the main reasons for continued reliance on tests. ② Because of this, the design of reinforced-concrete structures continues to be based more on extensive experimental information than on consistent analytical theory, particularly in the many situations where combined stresses occur. ③

Volume changes: shrinkage, temperature

The deformations discussed earlier were induced by stresses caused by external loads. Influences of a different nature cause concrete, even when free of any external loading, to undergo deformations and volume changes. ④ The most important of these are shrinkage and the effects of temperature variations.

Any workable concrete mix contains more water than is needed for hydration. If the concrete is exposed to air, the larger part of this free water evaporates in time, the rate and completeness of drying depending on ambient temperature and humidity conditions⑤. As the concrete dries, it shrinks in volume, probably due to the capillary tension which develops in the water remaining in the concrete. ⑥Conversely, if dry concrete is immersed in water, it expands, regaining much of the volume loss from prior shrinkage. ⑦Shrinkage, which continues at a decreasing rate for several months, depending on the configuration of the member, is a detrimental property of concrete in several respects. ⑧When not adequately controlled, it will cause unsightly and often deleterious cracks, as in slabs, walls, etc. In structures which are statically indeterminate (and most concrete structures are), it can cause large and harmful stresses. In prestressed concrete it leads to partial loss of initial prestress. For these reasons it is essential that shrinkage be minimized and controlled.

As is clear from the nature of the process, the chief factor which determines the amount of final shrinkage is the unit water content of the fresh concrete. This is clearly illustrated in Fig. 10-3, which shows the amount of shrinkage in units of 0.001 in/in for varying amounts of mixing water. The same aggregates were used for all tests, but in addition to and independently of water content, the amount of cement was also varied, from 4 to 11 sacks per cubic yard of concrete. ⑨This very large variation of cement content had only very minor effects on the amount of shrinkage, compared with the effect of water content; this is evident from the narrowness of the band which comprises the test results for the widely varying cement contents. ⑩It is evident from this that the chief means of reducing shrinkage is to reduce the water content of the fresh concrete to the minimum compatible with the required workability. In addition, prolonged and careful curing is beneficial for shrinkage control.

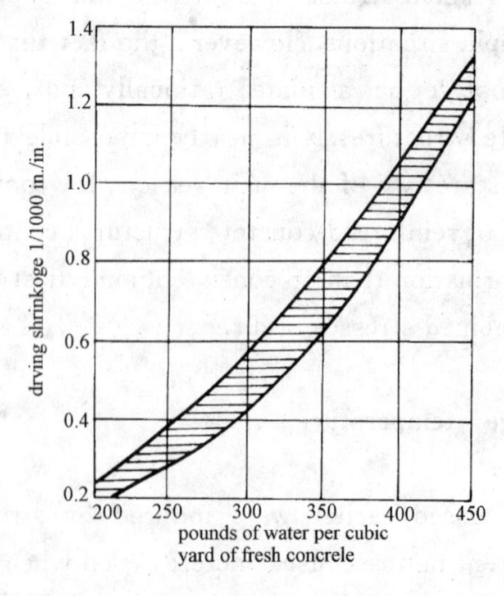

Fig. 10-3 Effect of water content on drying shrinkage

Values of final shrinkage for ordinary concretes are generally of the order of 0.0002 to 0.0007 in/in depending on initial water content, ambient temperature and humidity conditions, and the nature of the aggregate. Highly absorptive aggregates, such as some sandstones and slates, result in shrinkage values 2 and more times those obtained with less absorptive materials, such as granites and some limestones. [11]Some lightweight aggregates, in view of their great porosity, easily result in much larger shrinkage values than ordinary concretes.

Notes

①这一理论与通用的莫尔理论具有同样的缺点，认为三个主应力的中间值对（混凝土）强度没有影响。

②然而，在复合应力作用下混凝土的强度尚无法进行合理的计算。在很多情况下，几乎无法计算出混凝土结构中所有作用的应力及其方向。这两个同样重要的事实是必须继续依赖试验的两个主要原因。

③因此，在钢筋混凝土结构设计中，尤其在出现复合应力的很多情况下，仍然更多地依赖从广泛试验中获取的信息，而不是始终如一地应用分析理论。

④即使在没有外荷载的时候，不同自然条件的影响也使混凝土变形和改变体积。

⑤… the rate and completeness of drying depending on ambient temperature and humidity conditions. 该部分为分词独立结构作状语，表示补充说明，意为：干硬速度及程度取决于周围温度及湿度条件。

⑥随着混凝土的干硬，其体积收缩。这很可能是由于滞留在混凝土中的水产生的毛细张力所致。

⑦相反，如果把干硬的混凝土浸入水中，它便会膨胀，重新获得先前收缩时所丧失的大部分体积。

⑧收缩，要持续好几个月，而且收缩率越来越小，这取决于构件的外形。从好几方面来看，收缩是混凝土的一个缺点。

⑨所有试验都使用同样的骨料，但是用水量不同，水泥用量也不同，从每立方码混凝土四至十一袋不等。

⑩与用水量的影响相比，这种水泥含量的巨大差异对收缩量的影响很小。水泥用量差异很大，而试验结果都集中在很窄的带状范围内，这一点可以明显地看出。

⑪高吸水率的骨料（像某些砂子和板岩）其收缩值为低吸水率的骨料（像花岗岩和某些石灰岩）的二倍或更多。

Reading Material B

Reinforced-concrete Beams without Shear Reinforcement

The discussion of shear in a homogeneous elastic beam applies very closely to a plain concrete beam without reinforcement. ①As the load is increased in such a beam, a tension crack will form where the tension stresses are largest and will immediately cause the beam to fail. Except for beams of very unusual proportions, the largest tension stresses are those caused at the outer fiber by bending alone, at the section of maximum bending moment. In this case, shear has little, if any, influence on the strength of a beam.

However, when tension reinforcement is provided, the situation is quite different. Even though tension cracks form in the concrete, the required flexural tension strength is furnished by the steel, and much higher loads can be carried. Shear stresses increase proportionally to the loads. In consequence, diagonal tension stresses of significant intensity are created in regions of high shear forces, chiefly close to the supports. ②The longitudinal tension reinforcement has been so calculated and placed that it is chiefly effective in resisting longitudinal tension near the tension face. It does not reinforce the tensionally weak concrete against those diagonal tension stresses which occur elsewhere, caused by shear alone or by the combined effect of shear and flexure. ③Eventually, these stresses attain magnitudes sufficient to open additional tension cracks in a direction perpendicular to the local tension stress. These are known as diagonal cracks, in distinction to the vertical flexural cracks. The latter occur in regions of large moments, the former in regions in which the shear forces are high. In beams in which no reinforcement is provided to counteract the formation of large diagonal tension cracks, their appearance has far-reaching and generally detrimental effects. For this reason methods of predicting the loads at which these cracks will form are desired.

Notes

①对均质弹性梁剪力的讨论非常适用于没有加固物的混凝土梁。
②因此，在高剪力区（主要在支柱附近）产生了极强的斜拉力。
③纵筋不能帮助混凝土承受在别处出现的由剪力或剪力与弯曲共同作用而产生的斜拉应力。

UNIT ELEVEN

Text Yield Line Theory of Slabs

[1] Reinforced concrete design methods under the present ACI Code are based on the results of an elastic analysis of the structure as a whole, when subjected to the action of factored loads such as $1.4D+1.7L$ where D and L refer to service dead and live loads. ① Actually the behavior of a statically indeterminate structure is such that after the ultimate moment capacities at one or more points have been reached, discontinuities develop in the elastic curve at those points and the results of an elastic analysis are no longer valid. If there is sufficient ductility, redistribution of bending moments will occur until a sufficient number of sections of discontinuity, commonly called "plastic hinges", form to change the structure into a mechanism, at which time the structure collapses or fails. ②The term "ultimate load analysis", as opposed to "elastic analysis", relates to the use of the bending moment diagram at the verge of collapse as the basis for design. ③Other than the provisions for redistribution of moments at the supports of continuous flexural members the present ACI Code has as yet made no allowance for ultimate load analysis.

[2] The chief concern of this chapter is to develop the yield line theory for two-way slabs. Although not yet adopted by the ACI Code, slab analysis by yield line theory may be useful in providing the needed information for understanding the behavior of irregular or single-panel slabs with various boundary conditions.

[3] Although the study of flexural behavior of plates up to the ultimate load may date back to the 1920s, the fundamental concept of the yield line theory for the ultimate load design of slabs has been expanded considerably by K. W. Johansen. In this theory the strength of a slab is assumed to be governed by flexure alone; other effects such as shear and deflection are to be separately considered. The reinforcing steel is assumed to be fully yielded along the yield lines at collapse and the bending and twisting moments are assumed to be uniformly distributed along the yield lines.

[4] Yield line theory for one-way slabs is not much different from the limit analysis of continuous beams. On a continuous beam the achievement of flexural strength at one location, say in the negative-moment region over a support, does not necessarily constitute reaching the ultimate load on the beam. If the section having reached its flexural strength can continue to provide a constant resistance while undergoing further rotation, then the flexural strength may be reached at additional locations. Complete failure theoretically can not occur until yielding has occurred at several locations (or along several lines in case of one-way slabs) so that a mechanism forms giving a condition of unstable equilibrium. ④

[5] Consider for example, the one-way slab of finite width shown in Fig. 11-1. A uniform loading on the slab will cause uniform maximum negative bending moment along AB

and EF and uniform positive bending moment along CD, which is parallel to the supports. When the uniform load is increased until the moments along AB, CD, and EF reach their respective ultimate moment capacities, rotation of the slab segments will occur with the yield lines acting as axes of rotation. Once the ultimate moment capacity is achieved, angle change can occur without additional resisting moment being developed. Thus, under the limiting condition with the slab segments able to rotate with no change in resisting moment, the slab system is geometrically unstable. ⑤This condition is known as a "collapse mechanism."

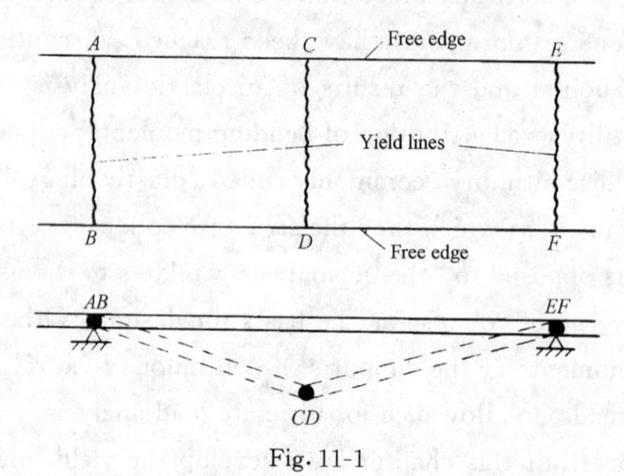

Fig. 11-1

[6] Yield line theory for two-way slabs requires a different treatment from limit analysis of continuous beams, because in this case the yield lines will not in general be parallel to each other but instead form a yield line pattern. The entire slab area will be divided into several segments which can rotate along the yield lines as rigid bodies at the condition of collapse or unstable equilibrium.

[7] The slab of Fig. 11-2*a* has nonparallel supports. At the collapse condition this slab will break into two segments; one segment will have an edge rotating about Ⅰ and the other will have an edge rotating about Ⅱ. The positive moment yield line must then intersect lines Ⅰ and Ⅱ at their intersection, point 0. The exact position of yield line Ⅲ will depend on the reinforcement amount and direction, both in the positive and negative moment regions.

[8] For the case of Fig. 11-2*b* where a rectangular panel is either simply supported or continuous over four linear supports, the collapse mechanism consists of four slab segments. ⑥The exact locations of points a and b will depend on the moment capacities at the supports and the positive moment reinforcement in each direction.

[9] The slab in Fig. 11-2*c* is supported along two edges and in addition is supported by two isolated columns. The rotational axes for the slab segments at collapse must occur along the supports (lines Ⅰ and Ⅱ), and additional rotational axes must pass through the isolated columns. The critical position of the positive moment yield lines *a*, *b*, *c*, *d*, and *e* is a function of the reinforcement amount and direction; in the meantime compatibility of

deflection along the yield lines must be maintained during the rigid body rotations of the slab segments.

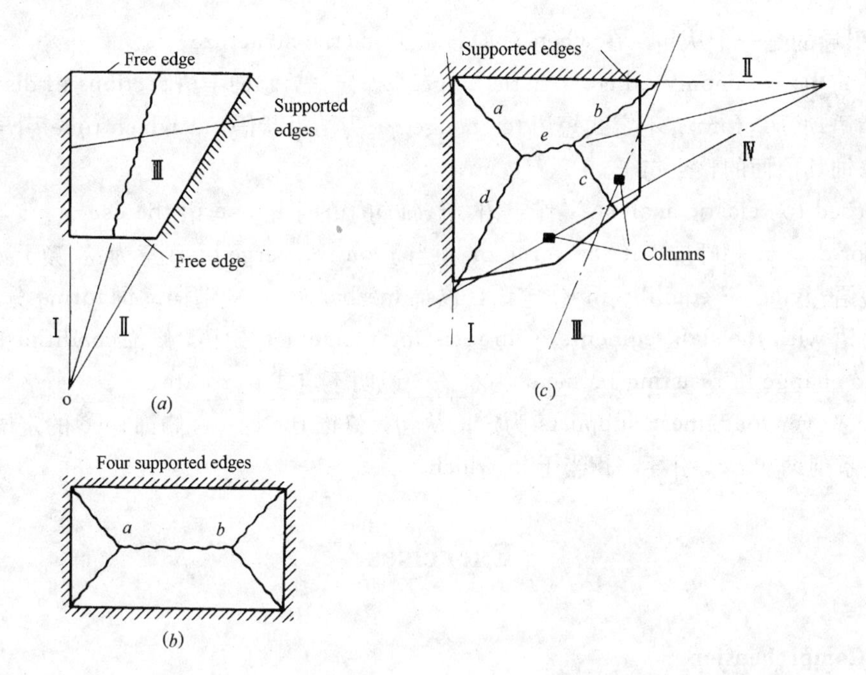

Fig. 11-2

New Words and Expressions

factored [ˈfæktəd] *a.* 乘系数的
ductility * [dʌkˈtiliti] *n.* 延性，延度
hinge [hindʒ] *n.* 铰（链）
as opposed to 与……相反（相对立）
verge [vəːdʒ] *n.* 边缘，边际
as yet 到目前为止（仍）
make allowance (s) for 允许，考虑到
segment * [ˈsegmənt] *n.* 一部分，段
geometrically [dʒiəˈmetrikəli] *ad.* 几何学上
mechanism * [ˈmekənizəm] *n.* 机构，机械
rotational [rəuˈteiʃənl] *a.* 旋转的，转动的
nonparallel [nɔnˈpærəlel] *a.* 不平行的

Notes

①when 引导的是一个从句，在 when 后面省略了 it (the structure) is。

②在该从句中，commonly called "plastic hinges" 作定语，修饰主语 sections of discontinuity，谓语动词是 form；不定式短语 to change … 为结果状语；at which time 引导的定语从句修饰其前面的整个句子。

③as opposed to "elastic analysis" 作定语，修饰句子的主语；宾语 the use of … 与 as the basis for design 相呼应；at the verge of 相当于 on the verge of，意为："濒于，即将"。

④分词短语 giving … equilibrium 作定语，修饰 mechanism，被谓语动词 forms 分割开了。

⑤介词短语 with the slab segments … in resisting moment 作定语，修饰 condition；其中的 with no change in resisting moment 为状语，说明不定式 to rotate。

⑥where … over four linear supports 为定语从句，修饰 the case。修饰 case 的定语从句常常由关系副词 where 引导，相当于 in which。

Exercises

Reading Comprehension

Ⅰ. Choose the best answer.

1. According to the passage, redistribution of bending moments will occur ________.
   A. at intervals
   B. if enough discontinuous sections form
   C. when the structure changes into a mechanism
   D. when there is enough ductility
2. Which of the following statements is True according to the passage?
   A. Ultimate load analysis has not been allowed by the ACI code so far.
   B. Slab analysis by yield line theory has been adopted by the ACI code.
   C. Elastic analysis is no longer effective.
   D. The study of flexural behavior of plates up to the ultimate load began in 1920.
3. What can be concluded about the yield line theory for the ultimate load design of slabs?
   A. K. W. Johansen has founded it.
   B. The theory was originated in 1920.
   C. Flexure alone is supposed to govern the strength of a slab according to the theory.
   D. Shear and deflection effects will be chiefly considered.
4. What will be mainly discussed in this chapter?

A. The substitution for the elastic analysis.

B. The development of the yield line theory for two-way slabs.

C. The adoption of ultimate load analysis by the ACI Code.

D. The design of two-way slab systems.

5. In which figure is the slab supported along two edges and by two isolated columns?

A. Fig. 11-2 (*a*)　　B. Fig. 11-2 (*b*)

C. Fig. 11-2 (*c*)　　D. None of them

Ⅱ. Fill in the blanks with the information given in the text.

1. Yield line theory for one-way slabs is ________________ the limit analysis of continuous beams.

2. If the section ________________ can continue to provide ____________ while __________, then ____________ may be reached __________.

3. A uniform loading on the slab will cause ____________ along *AB* and EF and __________ along *CD*, which __________ the supports.

4. Once __________ is achieved, angle change can occur ________________.

5. Yield line theory for two-way slabs __________ limit analysis of continuous beams, because __________ the yield lines will not __________ each other but __________ form a yield line pattern.

Vocabulary

Ⅰ. Choose one word or phrase that is the most similar in meaning to the one underlined in the given sentences.

1. In drawing up a plan it is always advisable to <u>make allowance for</u> unforeseen circumstances.

A. make room for　　B. give space to

C. take into consideration　　D. give regards to

2. The city's housing scheme is still at an <u>indeterminate</u> stage as some of the funds are not available.

A. ultimate　　B. uncertain

C. imaginable　　D. incredible

3. She tried to hide her grief but she was on the <u>verge</u> of tears.

A. edge　　B. line

C. occasion　　D. stage

4. Owing to the depression in British coal industry, all business here is off the <u>hinges</u>.

A. way　　B. orbit

C. edge　　D. joints

5. There has been <u>discontinuity</u> in the boy's education because of his health.

A. destruction　　B. interruption

C. discrimination　　　　　　　　D. determination

Ⅱ. Match the words in Column A with their corresponding definitions or explanations in Column B.

A	B
1. finite	a. divide by cutting or passing across
2. segment	b. the amount that something can produce
3. intersect	c. have an effect on each other
4. deflection	d. having an end or limit
5. mechanism	e. turning aside
	f. section or division
	g. principles of justice
	h. structure or mechanical operation

Translation

减量翻译法

英语中表示数量的减少和增加类似，也有许多不同的表达方式。

例一　by n 表净减量。

The loss of metal was reduced by 40%. 金属损耗减少了40%。

例二　(by) n times。

译时须换算成分数，译为"减少到$1/n$"或"减少了$\frac{n-1}{n}$"。

The operating cost decreased three times. 操作费用减少了三分之二。(减少到三分之一)。

例三　"n　times＋比较级＋than…"

译为"减少了$\frac{n}{n+1}$"或"为……的$\frac{1}{n+1}$"。

This kind of film is twice thinner than ordinary paper. 这种薄膜的厚度只及普通纸的三分之一。

Translate the following sentences into Chinese, and pay attention to the words underlined.

1. This process used 22 percent less fuel.
2. *A* is twice less than *B*.
3. The loss of metal was reduced to 15%.
4. Switching time of the new-type transistor is shortened 2 times.
5. The total enthalpy of the gas to be cooled would also be three to four times smaller.

Reading Material A

Fundamental Assumptions

In applying the yield line theory to the ultimate load analysis of reinforced concrete slabs, the following fundamental assumptions are made:

1. The reinforcing steel is fully yielded along the yield lines at failure. In the usual case, when the slab reinforcement is well below that in the balanced condition, the moment-curvature relationship [4] is as shown in Fig. 11-3. ①

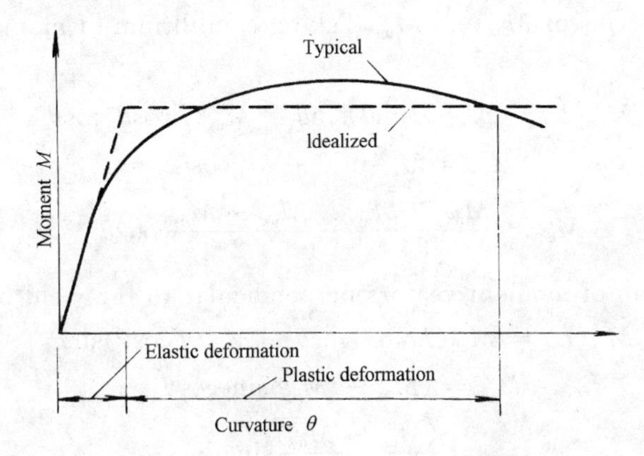

Fig. 11-3 Typical and idealized M-ϕ relationship for reinforced concrete slab

2. The slab deforms plastically at failure and is separated into segments by the yield lines.
3. The bending and twisting moments are uniformly distributed along the yield line and they are the maximum values provided by the ultimate moment capacities in two orthogonal directions (for two-way slabs). ②
4. The elastic deformations are negligible compared with the plastic deformations; thus the slab parts rotate as plane segments in the collapse condition.

Assumption No. 3 may be considered to be the yield criterion of orthotropic reinforced concrete slabs. It means that along a yield line as shown in Fig. 11-4, the bending moment M_{ub} and twisting moment M_{ut}, each per unit distance along the yield line, are exactly equal to what can be provided by the ultimate moment capacities M_{ux} and M_{uy} per unit distance in the y and x directions, respectively. It may be noted that M_{ux} is resisted by the reinforcement in the x direction, and M_{uy} is resisted by the reinforcement in the y direction. ③Also the sign convention is that the bending moments M_{ux}, M_{uy}, and M_{ub} are positive for tension in the lower portion of the slab and the twisting moment M_{ut} is positive if its vector is directed away from the free body on which it acts. ④

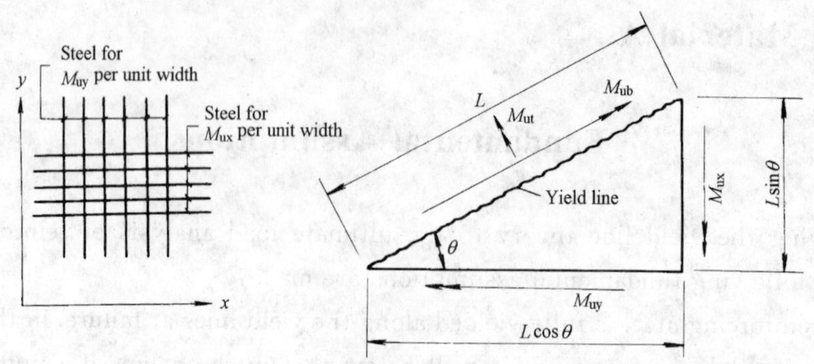

Fig. 11-4 Bending and twisting moments on yield line

The bending moment M_{ub} and twisting moment M_{ut} along the yield line in Fig. 11-4 may be expressed in terms of M_{ux} and M_{uy}. Taking equilibrium of moment vectors parallel to the yield line,

$$M_{ub}(L) = M_{ux}(L\sin\theta)\sin\theta + M_{uy}(L\cos\theta)\cos\theta$$

$$M_{ub} = M_{ux}\sin^2\theta + M_{uy}\cos^2\theta$$

$$M_{ub} = \frac{M_{ux} + M_{uy}}{2} - \frac{M_{ux} - M_{uy}}{2}\cos 2\theta \qquad (1)$$

and, taking equilibrium of moment vectors perpendicular to the yield line,

$$M_{ut}(L) = M_{ux}(L\sin\theta)\cos\theta - M_{uy}(L\cos\theta)\sin\theta$$

$$M_{ut} = (M_{ux} - M_{uy})\sin\theta\cos\theta$$

$$= \frac{(M_{ux} - M_{uy})}{2}\sin 2\theta \qquad (2)$$

In using Eqs (1) and (2), it is important to note that θ is the counterclockwise angle measured from the positive x axis to the yield line. ⑤

Notes

①通常情况下，当板的配筋低于平衡状态时，力矩-曲率关系就如图 11-3 所示。

②弯矩和扭矩沿屈服线均匀分布，而且它们是由（双向板）两个正交方向的极限力矩提供的最大值。

③可以看到，M_{ux}由 x 方向的钢筋抵抗，M_{uy}由 y 方向钢筋抵抗。

④符号的惯例是板的下部受拉，弯矩 M_{ux}，M_{uy}和 M_{yb}为正量，扭矩向量指向其作用的自由体外，M_{ut}为正。

⑤在利用以上两等式时，注意 θ 是从 x 轴正向至屈服线所测得的逆时针方向夹角。这一点很重要。

Reading Material B

Methods of Analysis

There are two methods of yield line analysis of slabs: the virtual-work method and the equilibrium method. ① Based on the same fundamental assumptions, the two methods should give exactly the same results. In either method, a yield line pattern must be first assumed so that a collapse mechanism is produced. ②For a collapse mechanism, rigid body movements of the slab segments are possible by rotation along the yield lines while maintaining deflection compatibility at the yield lines between slab segments. ③There may be more than one possible yield line pattern, in which case solutions to all possible yield line patterns must be sought and the one giving the smallest ultimate load would actually happen and thus should be used in design. ④For instance the failure pattern of the simply supported rectangular slab subjected to uniform load may be that shown either in Fig. 11-5*a* or in Fig. 11-5*b*, depending on the aspect ratio of the rectangular panel and the moment capacities M_{ux} and M_{uy}.

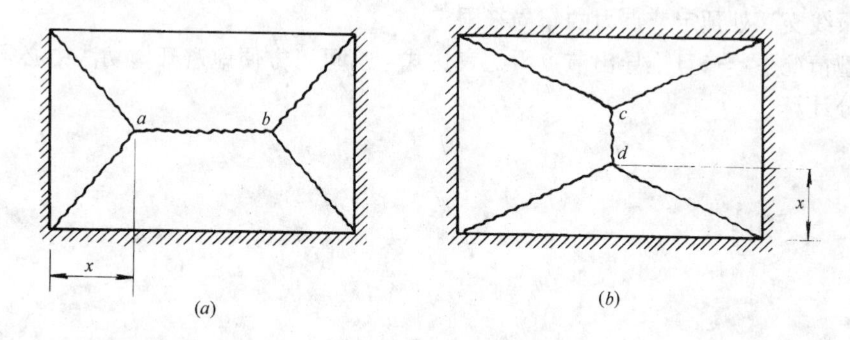

Fig. 11-5 Yield-line patterns of a simply supported rectangular slab

After the yield line pattern has been assumed, the next step is to determine the position of the yield lines, such as defined by the unknown x in Fig. 11-5*a* or *b*. It is at this point that one may choose to use the virtual-work method or the equilibrium method. In the virtual-work method, an equation containing the unknown x is established by equating the total positive work done by the ultimate load during simultaneous rigid body rotations of the slab segments (while maintaining deflection compatibility) to the total negative work done by the bending and twisting moments on all the yield lines. ⑤Then that value of x which gives the smallest ultimate load is found by means of differential calculus. ⑥In the equilibrium method, the value of x is obtained by applying the usual equations of statical equilibrium to the slab segments, but the optimal position x is defined by the placement of predetermined nodal forces at the intersection of yield lines. ⑦Expressions for the nodal forces in typical situations, once derived, can be conveniently used to avoid the necessity of mathematical differentiation as required in the virtual-work method.[⑧]

In the following sections, yield line analysis for one-way slabs is dealt with first in a manner similar to limit analysis of continuous beams. Then both the virtual-work method and the equilibrium method are presented and illustrated for two-way slabs.

Notes

①板的屈服线分析方法有两种：虚功法和平衡法。

②无论使用哪种方法，必须首先假定屈服线模式，才能形成破坏机构。

③对于破坏机构，既要保持屈服线两侧板块的挠度协调，又要使板块沿屈服线可以作刚体运动。

④或许屈服线图形不止一种，这样就必须探寻各种可能的屈服线图形，设计中应采用极限荷载最小的屈服线图形，这种屈服线才会实际形成。

⑤在虚功法中，让各板块作刚体旋转（且保持挠度协调）时，极限荷载所作的全部正功等于弯矩和扭矩在各屈服线处所作的负功，则含有未知数 x 的等式就成立。

⑥然后给出最小极限荷载的 x 的值就可以用微分计算得到。

⑦在平衡法中，x 的值是通过把通常的静力平衡方程用于各板块而获得。而 x 的最佳位置是由屈服线交叉处预定节点力的布局来限定。

⑧在典型情况下，一旦推导出节点力的表达式，就可以方便地避开虚功法中必须使用的数学微分计算。

UNIT TWELVE

Text Prestressed Concrete

[1] Modern structural engineering tends to progress toward more economic structures through gradually improved methods of design and the use of higher strength materials. This results in a reduction of cross-sectional dimensions and consequent weight savings. Such developments are particularly important in the field of reinforced concrete, where the dead load represents a substantial part of the total design load. Also, in multistory buildings, any saving in depth of members, multiplied by the number of stories, can represent a substantial saving in total height, load on foundations, length of heating and electrical ducts, plumbing risers, and wall and partition surfaces.

[2] Significant savings can be achieved by the use of high strength concrete and steel in conjunction with present-day design methods, which permit an accurate appraisal of member strength. However, there are limitations to this development, due mainly to the interrelated problems of cracking and deflection at service loads. The efficient use of high strength steel is limited by the fact that the amount of cracking (width and number of cracks) is proportional to the strain, and therefore the stress, in the steel. Although a moderate amount of cracking is normally not objectionable in structural concrete, excessive cracking is undesirable in that it exposes the reinforcement to corrosion, it may be visually offensive, and it may trigger a premature failure by diagonal tension. ① The use of high strength materials is further limited by deflection considerations, particularly when refined analysis is used. The slender members which result may permit deflections which are functionally or visually unacceptable. ② This is further aggravated by cracking, which reduces the flexural stiffness of members.

[3] These undesirable characteristics of ordinary reinforced concrete have been largely overcome by the development of prestressed concrete. A prestressed concrete member can be defined as one in which there have been introduced internal stresses of such magnitude and distribution that the stresses resulting from the given external loading are counteracted to a desired degree. ③ Concrete is basically a compressive material, with its strength in tension a low and unreliable value. Prestressing applies a precompression to the member which reduces or eliminates undesirable tensile stresses that would otherwise be present. Cracking under service loads can be minimized or even avoided entirely. Deflections may be limited to an acceptable value; in fact, members can be designed to have zero deflection under the combined effects of service load and prestress force. Deflection and crack control, achieved through prestressing, permit the engineer to make use of efficient and economical high strength steels in the form of strands, wires, or bars, in conjunction with concretes of much higher strength than normal. Thus prestressing results in overall im-

provement in performance of structural concrete used for ordinary loads and spans, and extends the range of application far beyond old limits, leading not only to much longer spans than previously thought possible, but permitting innovative new structural forms to be employed. ④

[4] The first suggestions for prestressing seem to have been made between 1886 and 1908 by the Americans P. H. Jackson and G. R. Steiner, the Austrian J. Mandl, and German J. Koenen. The use of high-strength steel was first suggested by the Austrian F. von Emperger in 1923, while at about the same time, the American R. H. Dill proposed "full prestressing" to eliminate cracks completely. These proposals remained mainly on paper; the practical development of prestressed-reinforced-concrete structures is chiefly due to E. Freyssinet and Y. Guyon (France), E. Hoyer (Germany), and G. Magnel (Belgium). Circular prestressing of cylindrical tanks and pipes, originated by W. H. Hewitt in 1923, was the first important application of the principles of prestressing in the United States. Important contributions have been made by T. Y. Lin in the design of many types of prestressed concrete structures in the United States since 1950. ⑤

[5] It is interesting to contrast the development of prestressed concrete in Europe, where a high ratio of material to labor cost prevails, with that in the United States, where the ratio is reversed. ⑥ In Europe, many sophisticated designs have been executed which minimize the material used but require a great amount of highly qualified labor to build and to prestress. Long-span bridges, two-dimensional floor systems, shells, and even space trusses have resulted. In the United States, development has been in the direction of relatively small precast building components, well suited to mass production. A few types of standardized precast members have accounted for the bulk of prestressed concrete construction in the United States over the past 20 years. This difference is less apparent now than previously. European industry now produces standardized precast building components, utility poles, railroad ties, and other items using techniques perfected in the United States, while engineers here have made use of European experience in the design of special structures of major span.

New Words and Expressions

prestressed [ˌpriːˈstrest]	*a.*	预应力的
multistory [ˌmʌltiˈstɔːri]	*a.*	多层的，高层的
in conjunction with		共同，一起
appraisal [əˈpreizəl]	*n.*	鉴定，评价
interrelated [intəriˈleitid]	*a.*	相关的
objectionable * [əbˈdʒekʃənəbl]	*a.*	令人不愉快的，令人厌恶的
undesirable * [ʌndiˈzaiərəbl]	*a.*	不合乎需要的，不希望有的
offensive [əˈfensiv]	*a.*	冒犯的，令人不快的，讨厌的

trigger [ˈtrigə] *v.* 引发，导致
premature [preməˈtjuə] *a.* 过早的，不成熟的
functionally [ˈfʌŋkʃənli] *ad.* 功能上，从使用的观点设计地
unacceptable * [ˈʌnəkˈseptəbl] *a.* 不能接受的，不中意的
counteract * [ˌkauntəˈrækt] *v.* 消除，抵消
precompression [ˈpriːkəmpreʃən] *n.* 预先压缩，预压力
strand * [strænd] *n.* 股线，绞合线
innovative * [inəˈvitiv] *a.* 创新的
cylindrical * [siˈlindrikəl] *a.* 圆柱形的
standardize [ˈstændədaiz] *v.* 标准化

Notes

①句中 in that 意为 because 因为。
②句中 which result 为定语从句，修饰 The slender members；which are … unacceptable 为定语从句，修饰 deflections。
③句中 one 为代词，指代 member；such … that 引起结果状语从句。
④句中 … leading not only to…，but permitting…为分词短语作状语；…longer spans than previously thought possible，中省略 it was，possible 为补足语。
⑤T. Y. Lin 林同炎（美籍华人，建筑工程师）。
⑥句中 …contrast … with that… 结构中 that 指代 the development of prestressed concrete；两个 where … 从句分别修饰 Europe 和 the United States。

Exercises

Reading Comprehension

Ⅰ. Choose the best answer.

1. The advantage of improved methods of design and using higher strength materials is that ____________.
   A. buildings can go higher
   B. buildings will become strong
   C. the structural engineering will become more economic
   D. designs are made with present-day methods.
2. Structural concrete permits ____________.
   A. a moderate amount of cracking
   B. excessive cracking
   C. corrosion

D. visual offensiveness

3. Which of the following is True?

A. High strength steel can be used without limitations.

B. When high strength materials are used, deflections should be taken into account.

C. The slender members can allow deflections.

D. The use of high strength concrete can achieve savings.

4. One way to control deflections and cracks is to ________.

A. use much more steel

B. use structural concrete

C. use modern design methods

D. apply prestressing

5. What's the main idea of the last paragraph?

A. The definition of a prestressed concrete member.

B. How the designers make use of high strength steel.

C. The application of prestressing and its effects.

D. How to use prestressed concrete.

Ⅱ. Fill in the blanks with the information given in the text.

1. What can a prestressed concrete member be defined as?

A prestressed concrete member can be defined as one ____________
____________ such ____________ that ____________
____________ to a desired degree.

2. What examples are given by the author to contrast the development of prestressed concrete in Europe with that in the United States?

In Europe, ____________________________
____
____________________ trusses have resulted.

In the United States, ____________________________
____
____________________ the past 20 years.

Vocabulary

Ⅰ. Choose one word or phrase that is the most similar in meaning to the one underlined in the given sentences.

1. The army is acting <u>in conjunction with</u> the police to hunt and find terrorists.

A. together with　　　　B. to connect with

C. in the same way as　　　　D. as well as

2. I'm in a slightly awkward position, <u>in that</u> he's not arriving until the 10th.

A. so　　　　B. because

C. if　　　　　　　　　　　　D. unless

3. Large price increases will trigger demands for even larger wage increases.

A. make　　　　　　　　　　　B. begin

C. cause　　　　　　　　　　D. result

4. The drug should counteract the snake′ s poison.

A. move in opposition　　　　　B. make of no value

C. return attacks　　　　　　　D. oppose the effect by opposit action

5. We have made an objective appraisal of his work.

A. expression of admiration　　　B. working out the quality, value

C. speaking favourably　　　　　D. finding fault with

Ⅱ. Match the words in Column A with their corresponding definitions or explanations in Column B.

A	B
1. precast	a. having several levels or floors
2. multistory	b. any straight line which runs in a slopping direction
3. partition	c. form blocks ready for use in buildings
4. diagonal	d. the act of working out the value of something
5. offensive	e. something that divides a thin wall inside
	f. too much, too great
	g. unpleasant
	h. relating to

Translation

定 语 从 句

定语从句一般由关系代词that、which、who、as等和关系副词when、where、why等引导，定语从句可译为有关词前的前置定语，也可译为并例分句或状语从句。

限制性定语从句

例一　（转译为并例分句）

A multi-purpose machine tool is one which is capable of doing a number of different types of operations. 多用机床是这样一种机床，即能进行很多不同类型操作的机床。

例二　（译为前置定语）

Oxygen is a gas which unites with many substances. 氧是一种能和许多物质化合的气体。

Translate the following sentences into Chinese, and pay attention to the words underlined.

1. He was not at ease with those who made diplomacy their profession, particularly ambassadors.（前置）

2. He lived his life apart from the workers on whose skill he depended.（状语）

3. He′ ll show her the place where they could make her look a proper dame-for next to nothing. (并例)
4. He would be a short-sighted commander who merely manned his fortress and did not look beyond. (条件)
5. There was something original, independent, and heroic about the plan that pleased all of them. (因果)

Reading Material A

Sources of Prestress Force

Prestress force can be applied to a concrete beam in many ways. Perhaps the most obvious method of precompressing is to use jacks reacting against abutments, as shown in Fig. 12-1*a*. Such a scheme has been employed for large projects. Many variations are possible, including replacing the jacks with compression struts after the desired stress in the concrete is obtained or the use of inexpensive jacks which remain in place in the structure, in some cases with a cement grout used as the hydraulic fluid. The principal difficulty associated with such a system is that even a slight movement of the abutments will drastically reduce the prestress force. ①

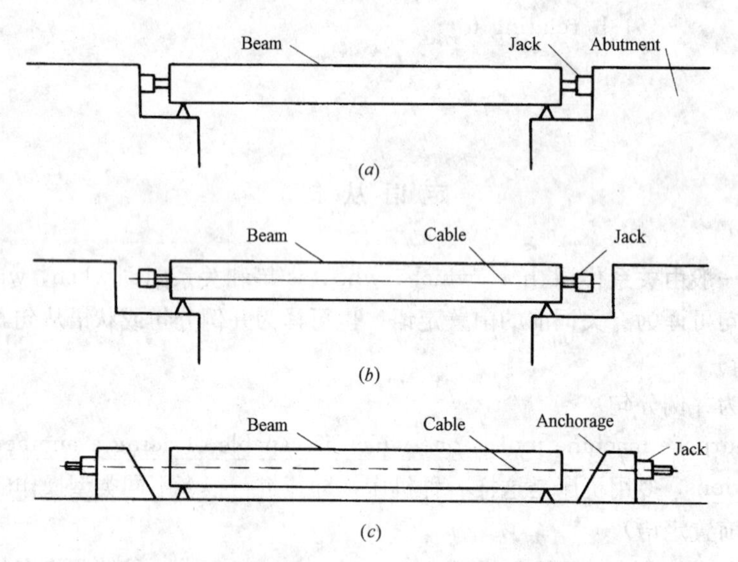

Fig. 12-1 Prestressing methods

In most cases the same result is more conveniently obtained by tying the jack bases together with wires or cables, as shown in Fig. 12-1*b*. These wires or cables may be external, located on each side of the beam; more Usually they are passed through a hollow conduit embedded in the concrete beam. Usually, one end of the prestressing tendon is anchored, and all the force is applied at the other end. After attainment of the desired amount of prestress force, the tendon is wedged against the concrete and the jacking equipment is removed for reuse. ② Note that in this type of prestressing the entire system is self-contained and is independent of relative displacement of the supports.

Another method of prestressing which is widely used is illustrated by Fig. 12-1*c*. The prestressing strands are tensioned between massive abutments in a casting yard prior to placing the concrete in the beam forms. The beam is poured around the tensioned strands, and after the concrete has attained sufficient strength, the jacking pressure is released. This transfers the prestressing force to the concrete by bond and friction along the strands, chiefly at the outer ends.

other means for introducing the desired prestressing force have been attempted on an experimental basis. Thermal prestressing can be achieved by preheating the steel by electrical or other means. Anchored against the ends of the concrete beam while in the extended state, the steel cools and tends to contract. The prestress force is developed through the restrained contraction. The use of expanding cement in concrete members has been tried with varying success. The volumetric expansion, restrained by steel strands or by fixed abutments, produces the prestress force.

Most of the patented systems for applying prestress in current use are variations of those shown in Fig. 12-1*b* and *c*. Such systems can generally be classified as pretensioning or post-tensioning systems. ③ In the case of pretensioning, the tendons are stressed before the concrete is placed, as in Fig. 12-1*c*. This system is well suited for mass production, since casting beds can be made several hundred feet long, the entire length cast at once, and individual beams cut to the desired length from the long casting. ④

In post-tensioned construction, shown in Fig. 12-1*b*, the tendons are tensioned after the concrete is placed and has acquired its strength. Usually, a hollow conduit or sleeve is provided in the beam, through which the tendon is passed. In some cases, hollow box-section beams are used. The jacking force is usually applied against the ends of the hardened concrete, eliminating the need for massive abutments.

A large number of particular systems, steel elements, jacks, and anchorage fittings have been developed in this country and abroad, many of which differ from each other only in minor details. As far as the designer of prestressed concrete structures is concerned, it is unnecessary and perhaps even undesirable to specify in detail the technique that is to be followed and the equipment to be used. It is frequently best to specify only the magnitude and line of action of the prestress force. The contractor is then free, in bidding the work, to receive quotations from several different prestressing subcontractors, with resultant cost savings. It is evident, however, that the designer must have some knowledge of the details of the various systems contemplated for use, so that in selecting cross-sectional dimensions, any one of several systems can be accommodated.

Notes

①这个系统的主要困难是支承面甚至稍微移动就会大大地减小预应力。

②在得到所需量的预应力后，楔入钢丝束，顶在混凝土上，同时拿掉千斤顶设备以便再使用。

③这些方法大体上可分为先张法与后张法两类。

④这种方法适用批量生产，因为台座可制成几百英尺长，整个长度同时浇注，而每根梁从总长度浇注件上切割成所需长度。

Reading Material B

Prestressing Steels

Early attempts at prestressing concrete were unsuccessful because steel of ordinary structural strength was used. The low prestress obtainable in such rods was quickly lost due to shrinkage and creep in the concrete.

Such changes in length of concrete have much less effect on prestress force if that force is obtained using highly stressed steel wires or cables. In Fig. 12-2*a*, a concrete member of length L is prestressed using steel bars of ordinary strength stressed to 20, 000 psi. With $E_s = 29 \times 10^6$psi, the unit strain ε_s required to produce the desired stress in the steel of 20, 000 psi is

$$\varepsilon_s = \frac{\Delta L}{L} = \frac{f_s}{E_s} = \frac{20,000}{29 \times 10^6} = 6.9 \times 10^{-4}$$

However, the long-term strain in the concrete due to shrinkage and creep alonemay be of the order of 8.0×10^{-4}, which would be sufficient to completely relieve the steel of all stress.

Alternatively, suppose that the beam is prestressed using high tensile wire stressed to 150, 000 psi. The elastic modulus of steel does not vary greatly, and the same value of 29×10^6psi will be assumed. Then in this case the unit strain required to produce the desired stress in the steel is

$$\varepsilon_s = \frac{150,000}{29 \times 10^6} = 51.7 \times 10^{-4}$$

If shrinkage and creep strain are the same as before, the net strain in the steel after these losses is

$$\varepsilon_{s,net} = (51.7 - 8.0) \times 10^{-4} = 43.7 \times 10^{-4}$$

and the corresponding stress after losses is

$$f_s = \varepsilon_{s,net} E_s = (43.7 \times 10^{-4})(29 \times 10^6) = 127,000\text{psi}$$

This represents a stress loss of about 15 percent, compared with 100 percent loss in the

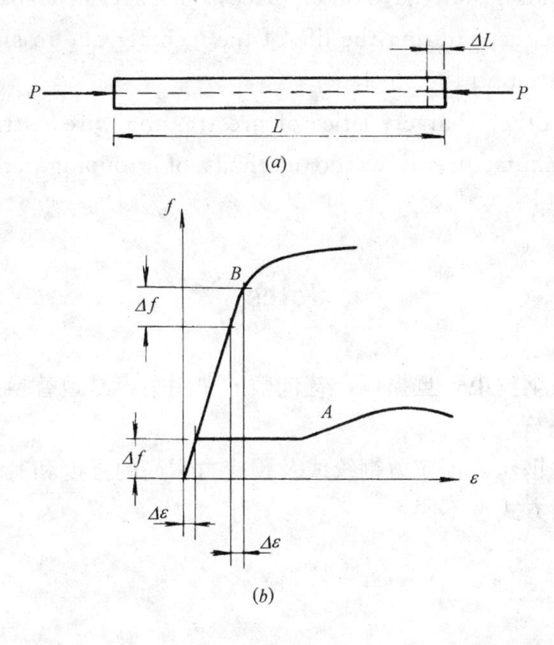

Fig. 12-2 Loss of prestress due to concrete shrinkage and creep

beam using ordinary steel. It is apparent that the amount of stress lost because of shrinkage and creep is independent of the original stress in the steel. Therefore, the higher the original stress the lower the percentage loss. This is illustrated graphically by the stress-strain curves of Fig. 12-2*b*. Curve *A* is representative of ordinary reinforcing rods, with a yield stress between 40, 000 and 60, 000 psi, while curve *B* represents high tensile wire, with an ultimate stress of about 250,000 psi. The stress change Δf resulting from a certain change in strain $\Delta\varepsilon$ is seen to have much less effect when high steel-stress levels are attained. Prestressing of concrete is therefore practical only when steels of very high strength are used.

Prestressing steel is most commonly used in the form of individual wires, stranded cable made up of seven wires, and alloy-steel bars.

The tensile stress permitted by the ACI Code in prestressing wires, strands, or bars is dependent upon the stage of loading. When the jacking force is first applied, a stress of $0.85f_{pu}$ or $0.94f_{py}$ is allowed, whichever is smaller, where f_{pu} is the ultimate strength of the steel and f_{py} is the yield strength. Immediately after transfer of prestress force to the concrete, the permissible stress is $0.74f_{pu}$ or $0.82f_{py}$, whichever is smaller (except at post-tensioning anchorages where the stress is limited to $0.70f_{pu}$). The justification for a higher allowable stress during the stretching operation is that the steel stress is known quite precisely at this stage. Hydraulic jacking pressure and total steel strain are quantities that are easily measured. In addition, if an accidentally deficient tendon should break, it can easily be replaced at small cost; in effect, the tensioning operation is a performance test of the material. ① The lower values of allowable stress apply after elastic shortening of the concrete, frictional loss, and anchorage slip have taken place, when service loads may be applied. The steel stress is further reduced during the life of the member due to shrinkage and creep in the concrete and relaxation in the steel.

The strength and other characteristics of prestressing wire, strands, and bars vary somewhat between manufacturers, as do methods of grouping tendons and anchoring them. ②

Notes

①此外，如果有缺陷的钢丝束一旦损坏，花低廉的费用很容易地替换，实际上，张拉操作是材料的一次性能测验。

②各厂家生产的预应力钢丝，预应力钢绞线及预应力钢筋的强度和其他特性稍有不同，钢丝束的组成及其锚固方式也不同。

UNIT THIRTEEN

Text Fundamentals of Composite Action and Shear Connection

[1] The evolution of satisfactory design methods for composite beams has been a slow process, requiring much theoretical and experimental work in order to provide economic and, at the same time, safe design criteria. The purpose of this Chapter is to describe in some detail the more important fundamentals which have to be taken into account in the design of composite structures.

[2] Historically the first analysis of a composite section was based on the conventional assumptions of the elastic theory which limit the stresses in the component materials to a certain proportion of their failure stresses (yield in the case of steel, crushing in the case of concrete) . ① The assumptions inherent in the elastic method are similar to those for ordinary reinforced concrete. In recent years the concepts of the ultimate load design philosophy have been applied to composite action and a body of experimental evidence has shown it to be a safe, economical basis on which to proportion composite sections. Although at the present time ultimate load design methods are directly applicable only to buildings and not to bridges there seems no reason to doubt that in time the restriction will disappear.

[3] Before dealing in detail with the two design approaches (elastic and ultimate load) certain basic points require consideration.

[4] A clear understanding of the way in which the component materials, steel concrete and shear connection, react to applied load is an essential preliminary to full analysis of the composite section. Of primary importance are the stress-strain relationships, which must of necessity be the product of carefully controlled experiment. These experimental results are not generally suited to direct application and so simplifications and idealisations are adopted in practice. The use of computers has made it possible to reduce the amount of idealisation required with the result that computer 'experiments' can now be performed using material stress-strain relationships of considerable complexity. ②

[5] Composite action between steel and concrete implies some interconnection between the two materials which will transfer shear between them. In reinforced concrete members the natural bond of concrete to steel is often sufficient to do this, although cases do arise in which additional anchorage is required. ③ The fully encased filler joist also has a large embedded area which is adequate for full shear transfer. However, the situation is quite different with the common type of composite beam in which the concrete slab rests on, or at best encloses, the top flange of the steel beam. It is true that there will initially be shear transfer by bond and friction at the beam-slab contact surface. There is, however, a tendency for the slab to separate vertically from the beam and, should this occur, horizontal shear

transfer will cease. ④ A single overload or the fatigue effect of pulsating loading may destroy the natural bond, which once destroyed cannot be reconstituted. The imponderable nature of such shear connection is clearly undesirable; some form of deliberate connection between beam and slab is required with the two objects of transferring horizontal shear and preventing vertical separation. A natural bond will exist in the presence of shear connection but it is neither desirable to count on its existence nor possible in all cases to calculate its value. ⑤ Thus shear connection must be provided to transfer all the horizontal shear force.

[6] It has been pointed out that the paradoxical situation exists that if shear connection is provided it may in fact not come into operation because the natural bond takes all the shear force, and so 'if sufficient shear connectors are provided then they are unnecessary'.

[7] The evolution of shear connection devices has been slow and has necessitated a large volume of experimental work on the static and fatigue properties of a wide range of mainly mechanical connectors.

[8] It soon appeared clear to early research workers that some form of connector fixed to the top flange of the beam and anchored into the slab was necessary. Caughey and Scott in 1929 proposed using, amongst other things, projecting bolt ends. Since then a wide variety of types of mechanical connector has been used in experiment and practice. To some extent the proliferation of types has been the result of steel fabricators using sections which came easily to hand, since initially a purpose-made shear connector was not available.

[9] In any mechanical connection system it is possible to identify parts which transfer horizontal shear and parts which tie the slab down to the beam. Generally, horizontal shear resistance is the ruling criterion of shear connector action and with this in mind mechanical connectors may be classified into three main groups-rigid, flexible and bond.

New Words and Expressions

idealisation [aiˌdiəlaiˈseiʃən]	*n.*	理想化
interconnection [ˌintəkəˈnekʃən]	*n.*	相互作用
encase [inˈkeis]	*v.*	包裹
joist [dʒɔst]	*n.*	小梁
flange * [flændʒ]	*n.*	凸缘，翼缘
pulsate [ˈpʌlseit]	*vi.*	震动
reconstitute [ˈriːˈkɔnstitjuːt]	*vt.*	重新构成；改组
imponderable [imˈpɔndərəbl]	*a.*	不可衡量的；无法估计的
paradoxical [pærəˈdɔksikəl]	*a.*	荒谬的；自相矛盾的
connector [kɔˈnektə]	*n.*	连接键
necessitate * [niˈsesiˌteit]	*v.*	使成为必需，需要
proliferation [prəulifəˈreiʃən]	*n.*	扩散；激增
fabricator * [ˈfæbrikeitə]	*n.*	制造者；制作者；

come to hand　　　　　　　　　　　　　　　　得到；到手

Notes

①句中包含 limit … to 结构。

②required 为过去分词作后置定语；that 引导一个同位语从句修饰 result。

③…bond…to…，……之间粘结；in which 引导一个定语从句修饰 cases；do 强调 arise。

④…should this occur…为倒装句，正常语序为 if this should occur，…。

⑤主要结构为…neither desirable to do nor possible to…。

Exercises

Reading Comprehension

Ⅰ. Choose the best answer.

1. The purpose of this charpter is to describe in some detail ＿＿＿＿＿＿.
   A. the shear transfer between the steel and concrete in the design of composite structures
   B. the mechanical connectors in the design of composite structures
   C. composite section in the design of composite structures
   D. the more important fundamentals in the design of composite structures
2. In the past, the first analysis of a composite section was based on ＿＿＿＿＿＿.
   A. the traditional assumptions of elastic theory.
   B. the fundamentals of composite structures
   C. the reinforced concrete theory
   D. the shear transfer theory
3. For the fully encased filler joist, if the slab is separated vertically from the beam, ＿＿＿＿＿＿.
   A. it will transfer horizontal shear as the common type of composite beam
   B. it won't transfer horizontal shear as the common type of composite beam
   C. it will transfer horizontal shear because it has a large embedded area
   D. it won't transfer horizontal shear because it has a large embedded area
4. The early research workers soon realized clearly that ＿＿＿＿＿＿.
   A. the evolution of shear connection devices had been slow
   B. they should do a large volume of experimental work on the static and fatigue properties of a wide range of mainly mechanical connectors
   C. it was necessary to apply some form of connector fixed to the top flange of the beam and anchored into the slab

D. it was necessary to follow Caughey and Scott and use, among other things, projecting ends

5. Since initially a purpose-made shear connector was not available, the steel fabricators adopted the proliferation' of types because ______.

   A. they wanted to use sections which were easily to get

   B. they wanted to use sections which were easily to deal with

   C. they wanted to use sections which were easily to work on

   D. they wanted to use sections which were easily to connect

Ⅱ. Fill in the blanks with the information given in the text.

1. What are the failure stresses?

   A. ______ in the case of steel.

   B. ______ in the case of concrete.

2. What is it possible to identify in any mechanical connection system?

   A. Parts which transfer ______.

   B. Parts which tie the slab down ______.

Vocabulary

Ⅰ. Choose one word or phrase which is the most similar in meaning to the one underlined in the given sentences.

1. There has been some restriction of entry into medical schools.

A. tests	B. limitation
C. standards	D. prohibition

2. Financial consultants acknowledge that the value of common stock is inherently changeable.

A. relatively	B. unavoidably
C. intrinsically	D. imponderably

3. In designing a machine it is necessary to reduce friction as much as possible.

A. conflict	B. resistance
C. crack	D. rubbing

4. The 20th century has seen a starting evolution in medical research.

A. involvement	B. development
C. revelation	D. exaggeration

5. It was paradoxical that in a country where free speech was enshined in the constitution, people were persecuted for the views.

A. self-contradictory	B. friction
C. conflict	D. imponderable

Ⅱ. Match the words in Column A with their corresponding definitions or explanations in Column B

A	B
1. composite	a. projecting or outside rim to keep sth. in position
2. component	b. cause to vibrate
3. flange	c. outer limit or boundary of a surface
4. pulsate	d. arranged as a system
5. reconstitute	e. helping to form a complete thing
	f. put, bring or come together so that the substance, etc. are no longer distinct
	g. made up of different parts or materials
	h. build up again from parts

Translation

非限定性定语从句

非限定性定语从句一般只能由关系联词 which, when 和 where 加以引导, 用 which 时, 常常用逗号分开, 而用 when 和 where 时, 则不一定用逗号分开。

例一　(译成条件句)

Men become desperate for work, any work, which will help them to keep alive their families.

人们极其迫切地要求工作，不管什么工作，只要它能维持一家人的生活就行。

例二　(译成前置定语)

Last night I saw a very good film, which was about the French revolution.

昨晚我看了一部关于法国革命的非常好的电影。

例三　(译成并例分句)

After melting is completed the steel is transferred to a separate vessel where refining is carried out.

在熔化完毕后将钢水移到另一容器中，在那里进行精炼。

Translate the following sentences into Chinese, and pay attention to the words underlined.

1. He insisted on building another house, which he had no use for.
2. Surely this was his native village, which he had left but the day before.
3. They will fly to Kunming, where they plan to stay two or three days, and then go on to Beijing.
4. We will put off the outing until next week, when we won't be so busy.
5. One herdsman, who looks after 1000 sheep, earns about 10000 yuan each year.

Reading Material A

Other Types of Composite Construction (1)

Although the composite rolled beam or plate girder is probably the most widely used, there are other types of composite system which merit attention. For special purposes many different composite systems have been proposed; some giving even greater economy in steel weight than the conventional beam and slab, others presenting different advantages. At an early stage in the development of conposite construction, novel ideas were put into practice. ① The Kane system, in use in Canada in 1932, had welded lattice beams which were used to support the shuttering for the concrete floor slab and themselves acted compositely with the slab. In addition, the lattice beams were made continuous, either by passing them through the lattice section columns generally used in the system or, for rolled columns, by using steel rods welded to the top chords of the beams and threaded through holes in the columns. The Kane system thus exhibited many of the economic features of composite construction at an early stage in its development.

Prestressing a steel girder by cables has already been referred to in Chapter 3; the idea was to produce in the girder a favourable initial stress distribution opposed to that produced in service. The method described in detail here was used for one particular bridge structure but there appears to be no reason why the system should not be of general application, nor indeed why factory methods of production should not be used to produce composite beams of this type.

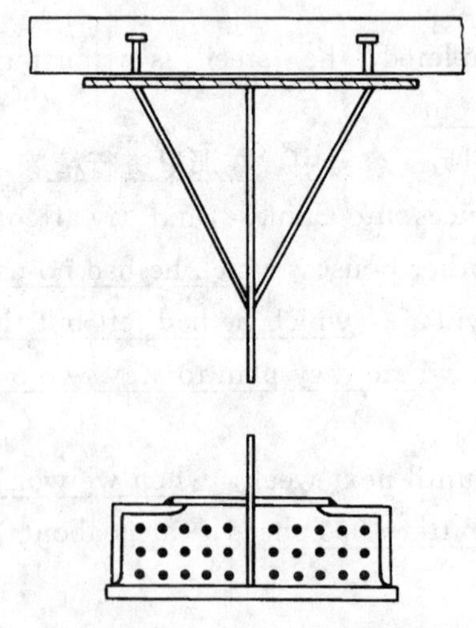

Fig. 13-1 Prestressed tension flange

The girder cross section is shown in Fig. 13-1 The 'delta' top girder has advantages in non-composite construction because of the restraint to lateral buckling provided by the corner plates. While compression flange restraint is generally not a problem in composite structures (the concrete slab fixes the flange firmly) the delta head is still useful in restraining the girder web. However, the important feature is the hollow bottom flange. Initially the bottom flange is left open. Prestressing wire is threaded through and tensioned, then high strength concrete is vibrated into the flange and steam cured. Finally the flange is converted into a closed box by welding cover plates to it. ③

The concrete is thus totally enclosed in a steel jacket, free from atmospheric influence. The prestressing wire, too, is entirely protected from corrosion. Because of its enclosure the concrete will not lose moisture and so creep and shrinkage will be minimised. The steel flange is in compression but is adequately restrained from buckling by its concrete filling, the web plate and the prestressing wire.

The advantage of the prestressed flange lies in the much greater stress range available in the steel. ④ If the flange material has an allowable stress in tension or compression of f then the stress range available is from $-f$ to $+f$, a total of $2.0\,f$ compared with $1.0\,f$ for the non-stressed steel.

The unsymmetrical nature of the composite girder with its neutral axis close to the top flange implies low stresses in the top flange steel. Indeed this flange is little more than a means of transferring horizontal shear between beam and slab and could well be omitted altogether if some other method of shear transfer were available. ⑤

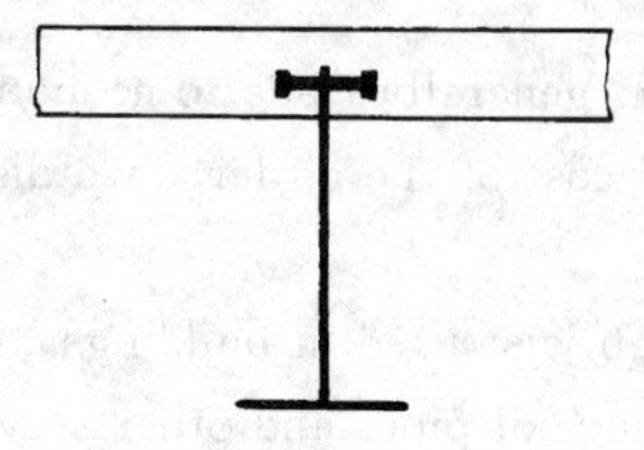

Fig. 13-2 Composite plate girder without top flange

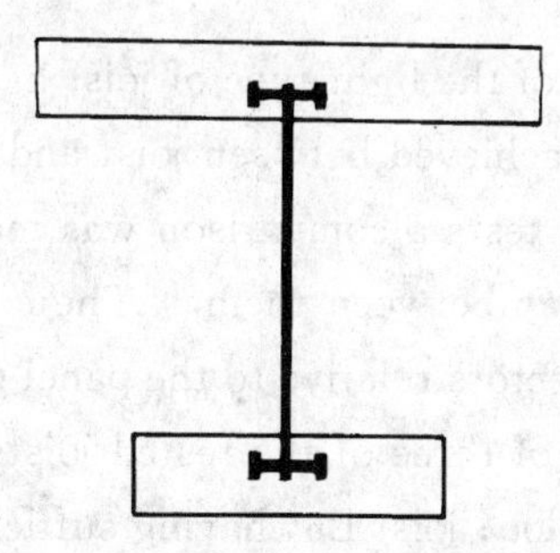

Fig. 13-3 Composite plate girder without top or bottom flanges

A section which has been successfully used in practice is composed of an inverted steel 'T' section (rolled or fabricated) to which the concrete slab is fixed by shear connectors welded to each side of the web (Fig. 13-2). In fact there is no reason why the bottom flange should not also be replaced by concrete as shown in Fig. 13-3.

Tests on a series of hybrid 'T' steel sections of this kind have been reported. Two distinct failure modes were evident, in flexure or in sheaf originating at the shear connectors. Some tentative design rules aimed at suppressing shear failure were put forward. ⑥

Notes

①在组合结构发展的早期，新的思想就得以实施。

②1932 年加拿大使用的克恩系统有焊接格构梁，这些格构梁用来支承混凝土楼板的模板，并与楼板一起起到组合的作用。

③由于焊接上盖板，翼缘成了一个封闭的盒子。

④预应力翼缘的优点在于在更大的应力范围内适用各种钢材。

⑤的确这个翼缘不过是在板与梁之间传递水平剪力，如果有其他剪力传递方法，完全可以省去它。

⑥指出了旨在防止剪力失效的一些临时设计规则。

Reading Material B

Other Types of Composite Construction (2)

The use of open web girders generally leads to economy of steel, though fabrication may significantly affect the final cost of the girder. Two distinct types of open web girder can be distinguished:

(a) The very light open web joist used in buildings, often mass produced and being particularly suitable for the passage of pipes and other service ducts.

(b) The very much heavier lattice girder or truss used in medium and long span bridges.

Research into the behaviour of the light type of joist has shown that , as might be expected, composite action can be achieved between joist and slab if adequate shear connection is provided. In one seri. es of tests a comparison was made between connectors placed either over panel points or midway between them. ① The conclusion from the test results was that the position of the connectors relative to the panel points was of secondary importance. The load deflection curves of three of the tested joists are shown is Fig. 13-4. Joists B1 and B2 failed in shear connection; joist B6, having sufficient shear connection, failed in tensile yield of the bottom chord followed by splitting of the concrete. The considerabl increase in ultimate load capacity of the composite joist when compared with the steel section alone is also shown is Fig. 13-4.

The heavier type of bridge truss may also be designed for composite action. A rigorous analysis requires the effect of concrete creep and shrinkage to be taken into account; the analysis is complicated by the indeterminate nature of the slab acting as a continuous beam elastically supported at each panel point. ② Reference may be made to Sattler (Chapter 2, reference 9) if the effects of creep and shrinkage are considered important enough to be evaluated.

Because of the eccentricity of the slab relative to the centroid of the steel top chord of the truss, bending will be induced in this chord and distributed at each top chord joint to the other truss members.

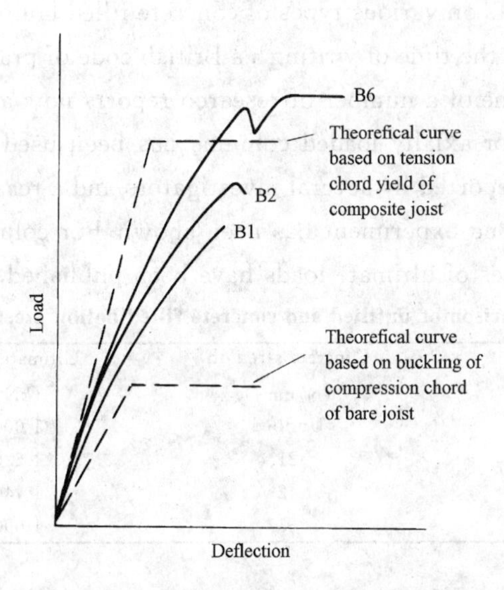

Fig. 13-4 Load-deflection curves of three composite open web joists

Concrete encasement of steel columns has long been a method of protecting the steel from fire. Just as the concrete encasing filler joist floor beams was long ignored in calculating the beam strength, so concrete column casing until recently was left out of assessment of the steel column strength. Even today there are limits on the assistance which the concrete can be assumed to give. BS 449, ('The use of Structural Steel in Building') for example restricts the total axial load on the cased strut to twice that permitted on the uncased steel section. Despite the slowness with which design rules have been officially promulgated, the externally concrete cased steel column is now recognised as a composite section and may be designed as such. ③

Where a hollow steel section is used as a column a more persuasive argument for composite action with an internal filling of concrete can be advanced. The hollow section provides formwork for the concrete and , being itself an efficient compression member, the combination of large diameter high yield steel tube filled with high grade concrete can produce a compact column capable of carrying very large loads. A specific application of such colunms (Fig. 13-5), occurred at the Almondsbury Interchange where high loads had to be carried on columns with the smallest possible lateral dimensions. The maximum load of 32000KN was supported by a composite tube of 1066mm outside diameter and 44. 5mm thick filled with concrete of cube strength 52N/mm^2. On a more modest scale the increase in load carrying capacity of a particular hollow section when filled with concrete is shown in Table 13-1. The axial loads given are ultimate values and must be divided by a siutable load factor to give working loads. ④

The filled hollow section then shows a useful increase in load. It also has an improved fire resistance, although too much should not be made of this aspect as the reduction in the external fire protection required resulting from a concrete infilling is small.

Although many tests on various types of concrete filled hollow sections have been carried out there is not, at the time of writing, a British code of practice for their use. Design must therefore follow one of a number of research reports now available.

A design method for axially loaded columns has been used to compare with a large number of test results reported by several investigators and a reasonable measure of agreement between analysis and experiment has been shown. For columns with combined axial and bending loads, tables of ultimate loads have been published.

Table13-1　　Comparison of unfilled and concrete filled hollow steel seciton

Concrete strength (N/mm^2)	Ultimate load (kN)
Unfilled	1 000
21	1 220
42	1 440
63	1 690

177.8×177.8×6.3mm^3 rectangular hollow section Effective length 3.048m
Steel yield stress 247 N/mm^2

It was at one time believed that containment of the infill concrete by the steel casing would lead to much higher ultimate stresses on the infill because it would be in a state of triaxial stress. At the same time the steel casing would be, by the expansion of the concrete, stressed in hoop tension. These effects do occur, but only with short stocky columns.

Notes

①在一个系列试验中，对连接体放置在节点上或节点中间加以比较。

②精确的分析需要考虑混凝土的徐变和收缩，把板作为支承在每个节点上的弹性连续梁其性质是不确定的，分析起来十分复杂。

③尽管官方迟迟地公布设计规则，外包钢的混凝土柱已被视为组合截面，并可这样来设计。

④给定的轴向荷载为极限值，必须除以适当的荷载系数，以给出其使用荷载值。

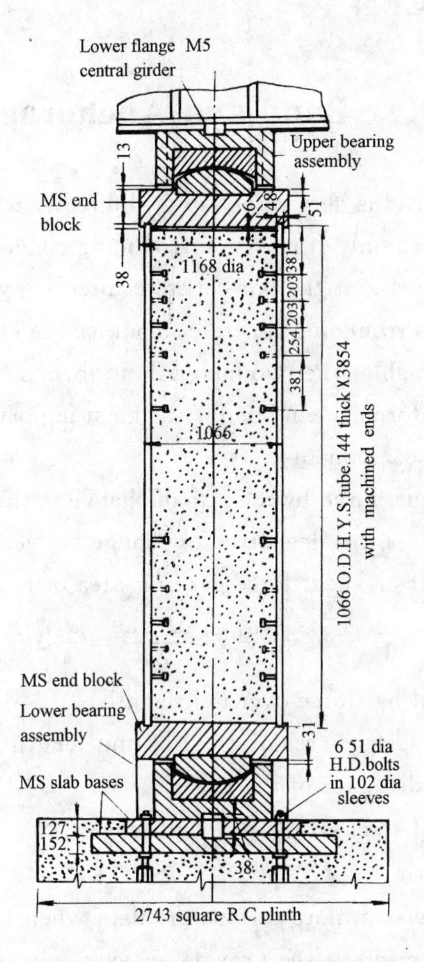

Fig. 13-5 Composite column of Almondsbury Interchange (Dimensions in mm)

UNIT FOURTEEN

Text Bond and Anchorage

[1] Since external load is very rarely applied directly to the reinforcement steel can receive its share of the load only from the surrounding concrete. "Bond stress" is the name assigned to the shear stress at the bar-concrete interface which, by transferring load between the bar and the surrounding concrete, modifies the steel stresses. ① This bond, when efficiently developed, enables the two materials to form a composite structure. The attainment of satisfactory performance in bond is the most important aim of the detailing of reinforcement in structural components.

[2] Bond forces are measured by the rate of change in the force in reinforcing bars. Bond stress will not exist unless the steel stresses change between any two sections. Bond stress u, customarily defined as a shear force per unit area of bar surface, is given by

$$u=\frac{q}{\Sigma o}=\frac{\Delta F_{s}A_{b}}{\Sigma o}=\frac{d_{b}}{4}\Delta F_{s} \tag{1}$$

where q——change of bar force over unit length

Σo——nominal surface area of a bar of unit length

d_b——nominal diameter of the bar

Δf_s——change of steel stress over unit length

A_b——area of bar

[3] Bond strength was a more serious problem when only plain reinforcing bars were used. Bars with a deformed surface provide an extra element of bond strength and safety. On the other hand, the behavior of deformed bars, in particular the introduction of high-strength steels and large diameter bars, presented some new problems. This has necessitated a reexamination of the conventional considerations of bond.

[4] Since existing code requirements are entirely empirical, the full background to numerous design rules is not discussed in this chapter. However, the designer must be aware of the aspects of bond and anchorage that can critically affect structural behavior. Therefore, these are examined in some depth to enable the designer to effectively detail reinforcement.

[5] Several problems in bond that require clarification, have been reported by ACI Committee 408. The report includes a good bibliography.

[6] Bond stresses in reinforced concrete members arise from two distinct situations: from the anchorage of bars, and from the change of bar force along its length, due to change in bending moment along the member.

[7] A bar must extend a distance l_d beyond any section at which it is required to develop a given force, the distance l_d being required to transmit the bar force to the concrete by

bond. If the average bond stress u, assumed to be uniformly distributed over this length, is specified, then considerations of equilibrium (Fig. 14-1*a*) yield the following relationship.

$$T = A_b f_s = u\Sigma o l_d \tag{2a}$$

Hence the development length becomes

$$l_d = \frac{d_b}{4u} f_s \tag{2b}$$

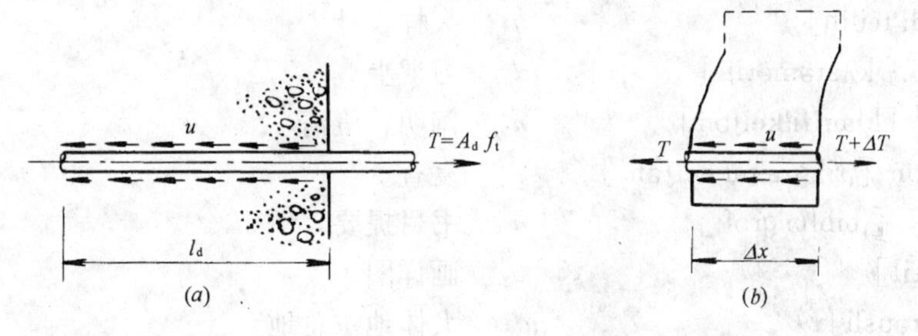

Fig. 14-1 The generation of anchorage and flexural bond

Some codes specify safe values for the anchorage bond stress u, permitting the development length to be calculated from Eq. 2*b*. The ACI code prescribes the minimum development length l_d for various design situations. It was shown that bond forces ΔT are developed along the flexural reinforcement in the shear span of any beam. If it is assumed that the bond stresses u are uniformly distributed between any two sections, close to each other, the equilibrium of a short length of bar (Fig. 14-1*b*) requires that $\Delta T = u\Sigma o\Delta x$. However, if ideal beam action is to take place, the internal tension force T must vary at the same rate as the external bending moment M.

Therefore,

$$\Delta T = \frac{\Delta M}{jd} = \frac{V}{jd}\Delta x$$

hence

$$u = \frac{V}{jd\Sigma o} \tag{3}$$

This equation indicates that when the rate of change of external bending moment (i. e., the shear force) is high, the flexural bond stress can also exhibit high intensity. However, Eq. 3 grossly oversimplifies the situation, and it does not even approximately predict the magnitude of the actual bond stress. This is because the presence of cracks in the concrete at discrete intervals along a member results in additional bond stresses due to the tension carried by the concrete between the cracks. ② Even when the shear force is zero (region of constant bending moment), bond stress will be developed. It has been observed, however, that provided sufficient anchorage length is available for the bars, failure originating from flexural bond stress does not occur. Flexural bond considerations require the anchorage length to be checked in regions of members where the bending moment is zero (at simple supports and at points of contraflexure). In such regions the area of tension steel may be small and the shear force large, resulting in high flexural bond stresses.

New Words and Expresions

bond stress		粘结应力
attainment * [ə'teinmənt]	*n.*	达到
detailing [di'teiliŋ]	*n.*	大样设计
customarily ['kʌstəmərili]	*ad.*	习惯上
clarification [klærifi'keiʃən]	*n.*	阐明、澄清
reeximination [ˌri:igzæmi'neiʃən]		复查
bibliography [ˌbibliə'grəfi]	*n.*	书目提要
detail [di'teil]	*v.*	画详图
grossly ['grəusli]	*ad.*	大体地，总地
oversimplify ['əuvə'simplifai]	*v.*	过渡简化
discrete * [dis'kri:t]	*a.*	不连续的、松散的
contraflexure [kɔtrə'flekʃə]	*n.*	反弯曲

Notes

①句中 which…modifies... 为定语从句修饰主语"Bond stress", by transferring…为从句中的插入语，

②句中 because…为表语从句，从句中 presence of cracks … results in …为主要结构。

Exercises

Reading Comprehension

Ⅰ. Choose the best answer.

1. Bond stress is the name of ________.

A. the transferring load between the bar and the surrounding concrete

B. the external load modifying the steel stress

C. the materials to form a composite structure

D. the shear stress at the bar—concrete interface

2. The most important aim of the detailing of reforcement in structural components is ________.

A. the rate of change in the force in reinforcing bars

B. the attainment of satisfactory performance in bond

C. the clarification of the bond

D. the considerations of equilibrium

3. These are examinated in some depth to enable the designer to effectively detail reinforcement.

   What does the word detail probably mean here?

   A. to make clearer

   B. to tell fully

   C. to draw more clearly

   D. to deal with small things

4. What must the designer be aware of?

   A. The aspects of bond and anchorage.

   B. The structural materials.

   C. The full background to numerous design rules.

   D. The existing code requirements.

5. Which of the statements is not True?

   A. Bond stress will not exist unless the steel stress changes between any two sections.

   B. Bars with a deformed surface provide an extra element of bond strength and safety.

   C. Provided sufficient anchorage length is available for the bars, failure originating from flexural bond stress will occur.

   D. Flexural bond considerations require the anchorage length to be checked in regions of members where the bending moment is zero.

Ⅱ. Fill in the blanks with information given in the text.

1. What is "bond stress"?

   "Bond stress" is ____,

   by ____.

2. Bond stresses in reinforced concrete members arise from two distinct situations:

   from ____,

   and from ____

   ____.

3. This is because the ______________ in the ___________ at ________________ along a ________________ results in ______________ due to ______________ by the ________________.

Vocabulary

Ⅰ. Choose one word or phrase which is the most similar in meaning to the one underlined in the given sentences.

1. The right to speak freely is one of the necessary means to the attainment of the

truth.

A. accomplishment　　B. fulfilment

C. acquirement　　D. attemptment

2. The increase of production necessitates a greater supply of raw materials.

A. compels　　B. requires

C. impels　　D. obliges

3. The president is the nominal head of the club, but the secretary is the one who really runs its affairs.

A. so-called　　B. self-called

C. would-be　　D. in name only

4. All theories originate from practice and in turn service practice.

A. come from　　B. emerge from

C. grow from　　D. benefit from

5. Wages paid to employees, the population of a community, the birth rate, and the like, furnish discrete series of data.

A. separate　　B. disconnected

C. discontinuous　　D. detached

Ⅱ. Match the words in Column A with their corresponding definations or explanations in Column B.

A	B
1. interface	a. a statement of equality between two quantities
2. contraflexure	b. a list of books or articles about a particular subject or person
3. moment	c. a surface lying between two bodies or spaces, and forming their common boundary
4. bibliography	d. the internal forces caused by the external forces which produce the strain
5. detailing	e. a drawing of a part of a building to show more clearly the relationship of parts
	f. a straight line passing from one side to the other through a circle
	g. the action against flexing or bending
	h. (a measure of) the tendency of a force to produce turning motion

Translation

长句译法

长句翻译有它本身的一些规律，最主要的是依据原文的句子结构，分明层次，分析句间的逻辑关系，再按汉语特点译出原文。

常见的长句译法有：顺译法、倒译法、分译法、综合法等。

例一（顺译法）

Many man-made substances are replacing certain natural materials because either the quantity of the natural products cannot meet our ever-increasing requirement, or more often, because the physical properties of the synthetic substance, which is the common name for man-made materials, have been chosen, and even emphasized so that it would be of the greatest use in the field which it is to be applied. 许多人造材料正在取代某些天然材料，这或者因为天然产品的数量不能满足人类不断增长的需要，或者更多地因为合成物（这是各种人造材料的统名称）的物理性能被选中，甚至受到极大的重视，因而使得它会在准备加以采用的领域获得最大量的应用。

例二（倒译法）

Various machine parts can be washed very clean and will be as clean as new ones when they are treated by ultrasonics, no matter how dirty and irregularly shaped they may be. 各种机器零件，无论多么脏，也不管形状多么不规则，当用超声波处理后，都可以清洗得非常干净，甚至象新零件一样。

Translate the following sentences into Chinese, and pay attention to the words underlined.

1.（顺译）

If she had long lost the blue-eyed, flower-like charm, the cool slim purity of face and form,(1) the apple-blossom colouring which had so swiftly and oddly affected Ashurst twenty-six years ago,(2) she was still at forty-three a comely and faithful companion,(3) whose cheeks were faintly mottled,(4) and whose grey-blue eyes had acquired a certain fullness.(5)

2.（倒译）

Time goes fast for one(1) who has a sense of beauty,(2) when there are pretty children in a pool and a young Diana on the edge,(3) to receive with wonder anything you can catch!

Reading Material A

The Nature of Bond Resistance

The bond resistance of plain bars is often thought of as chemical adhesion between mortar paste and bar surface. However, even low stresses will cause sufficient slip to break the adhesion between the concrete and the steel. Once slip occurs, further bond can be developed only by means of friction and by the wedging action of small dislodged sand particles between the bar and the surrounding concrete. ① The frictional resistance depends on the surface conditions of the steel. Fig. 14-2, taken from Rehm's work, displays typical surface profiles for plain round bars under different conditions of rusting. The variation in pitting is significant, and it is not surprising that most designers prefer to use steel in a mildly rusted condition. When plain round bars are subjected to standard load tests, failure occurs when the adhesion and frictional resistance is overcome, and the bars usually pull out from the encasing concrete.

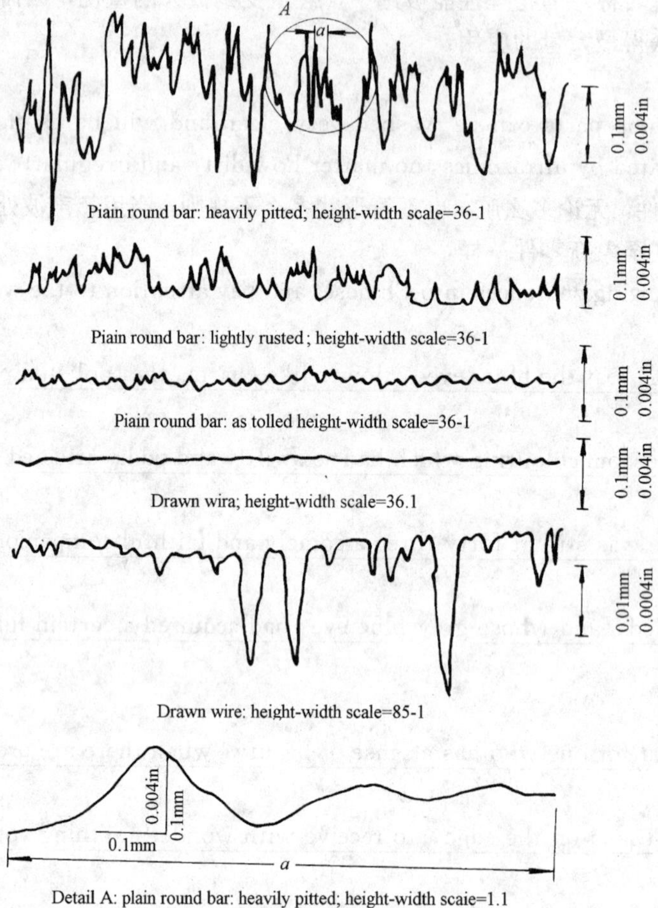

Fig. 14-2 The magnified surface of plain reinforcing bars

Deformed bars have greatly increased bond capacity because of the interlocking of the ribs with the surrounding concrete. The bond strength developed between two ribs of a bar (see Fig. 14-3) is associated with the following stresses:

1. Shear stresses v_a, developed through adhesion along the surface of the bar.

2. Bearing stresses f_b, against the face of the rib.

3. Shear stresses v_c, acting on the cylindrical concrete surface between adjacent

ribs. The relation between these stresses and the force to be transferred to the concrete by bond over a short length of bar between centers of ribs can be obtained from a simple equilibrium requirement as follows:[2]

$$\Delta T = \pi d'_b(b + c)v_a + \pi \frac{d''^2_b - d'^2_b}{4} f_b \approx \pi d''_b c v_c \quad (4)$$

where each term can be identified in Fig. 14-3

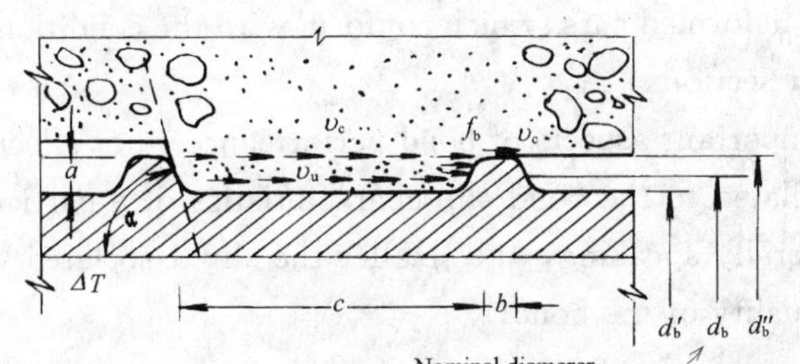

Fig. 14-3 The stresses between two ribs of a deformed bar

As the load is being increased, the adhesion along the bar surface inevitably breaks down. The remaining frictional shear strength is very small in comparison with the bearing strength developed around the ribs; therefore v_a can be ignored for practical purposes. The relationship between the remaining two important components of bond force development, f_b and v_c, can be simplified as follows:

1. Since $b \approx 0.1c$, the rib spacing is approximately c.

2. Since $a \approx 0.05d'_b$ the bearing area of one rib is

$$\pi \frac{d''^2_b - d'^2_b}{4} \approx \pi d_b a$$

where d_b is the nominal diameter of the bar.

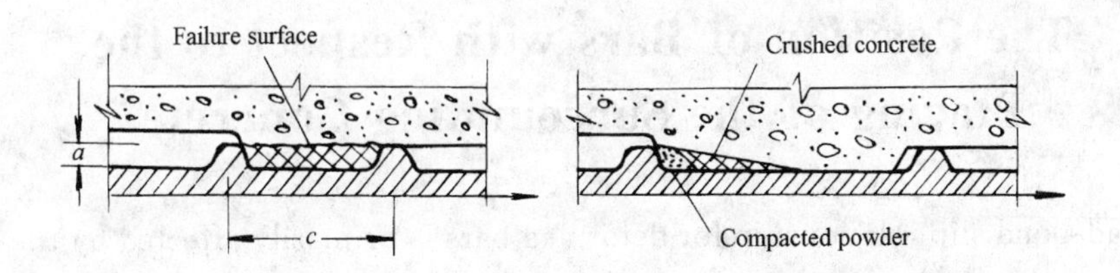

Fig. 14-4 Failure mechanisms at the ribs of deformed bars

(a) $a/c > 0.15$. (b) $a/c < 0.10$

Hence from Eq. 4 we have $\Delta T = \pi d_b a f_b \approx \pi d_b c v_c$; therefore,

$$v_c \approx \frac{a}{c} f_b \quad (5)$$

Rehm succeeded in relating several aspects of the bond problem to the geometric parameter a/c. He found the most satisfactory performance of a bar embedded in concrete over the short length c when a/c was in the vicinity of 0.065. * When the ribs are high and spaced too closely, the shear stress v_c will govern the behavior and the bar will pull out. When the rib spacing is larger than approximately 10 times the rib's height, the partly crushed concrete may form a wedge in front of the rib, and failure is normally brought about by splitting of the surrounding concrete. The concrete in front of the rib can sustain a bearing pressure several times the cylinder crushing strength because of the confined condition of the concrete. ③ The two types of failure mechanism, associated with the rib, are illustrated in Fig. 14-4*a*. Clearly the geometry of deformed bars must be such that a shear pullout failure (Fig. 14-4*a*) cannot occur. The factors that may affect the ultimate capacity and service behavior of deformed bars, which conform with the conditions in Fig. 14-4*b*, are examined in subsequent sections.

One of the most important aspects of bond performance is its effect on crack development. This is closely related to the bond slip characteristics of a particular type of bar in various situations. Generally speaking, the smaller the slip associated with a usable bond force, the better the quality of the bond.

Notes

①一旦出现滑移，只有摩擦力及钢筋与混凝土之间被挤压的小砂粒的楔作用才会产生进一步的粘结力。

②这些应力与肋中间一段短钢筋范围内由粘结传递给混凝土的力之间的关系可以从下面这个简单的平衡条件中得出。

③由于混凝土的这种受约束状态，肋前混凝土可承受几倍于圆柱体抗压强度的承压应力。

Reading Material B

The Position of Bars with Respect to the Placing of the Surrounding Concrete

The load-bond slip relationship for deformed bars is primarily affected by the behavior of the concrete immediately in front of the ribs. The quality of the concrete in this region depends on its relative position when cast. In connection with dowel action, attention was drawn to the effect of water gain and sedimentation under reinforcing bars and under coarse aggregate particles. As a result, a soft and spongy layer of concrete can form under the ribs. When bearing stresses of high intensity are to be developed against such a soft zone, large slips may occur. Fig. 14-5 shows how three bars are affected in different ways by a porous layer of concrete, even though all tend toward the development of the same ultimate load. In these tests the computed bearing stress in front of one rib was in excess of 7 times the compressive cube strength of the concrete. ①

The effect of casting position on bond is even more severe for plain round bars. The ultimate bond strength is drastically reduced in the case of horizontal bars as compared with vertical bars. The upper curves of each pair was obtained for heavily rusted and pitted bars. The lower curve of each pair is for smooth surfaced bars.

It is to be expected that the top bars of a beam will have poorer bond qualities than bottom bars, since the water and air gain will be greater under top bars. In addition, the relative downward movement of the surrounding concrete, caused by settlement of the fresh mixture, can be large. The amount of settlement that occurs will depend on the extent of bleeding of the fresh concrete and the rate at which water is permitted to escape from the formwork. ② Welch and Patten studied this effect and compared the bond performance of bars surrounded by concrete in leaky timber moulds and in well-sealed steel moulds. In the latter they also delayed the placing of the concrete by 40 minutes. Their results demonstrate the profound effect of settlement on bond, particularly for top bars. The ACI Code recognizes this phenomenon by requiring 40% excess development length for top-cast deformed bars.

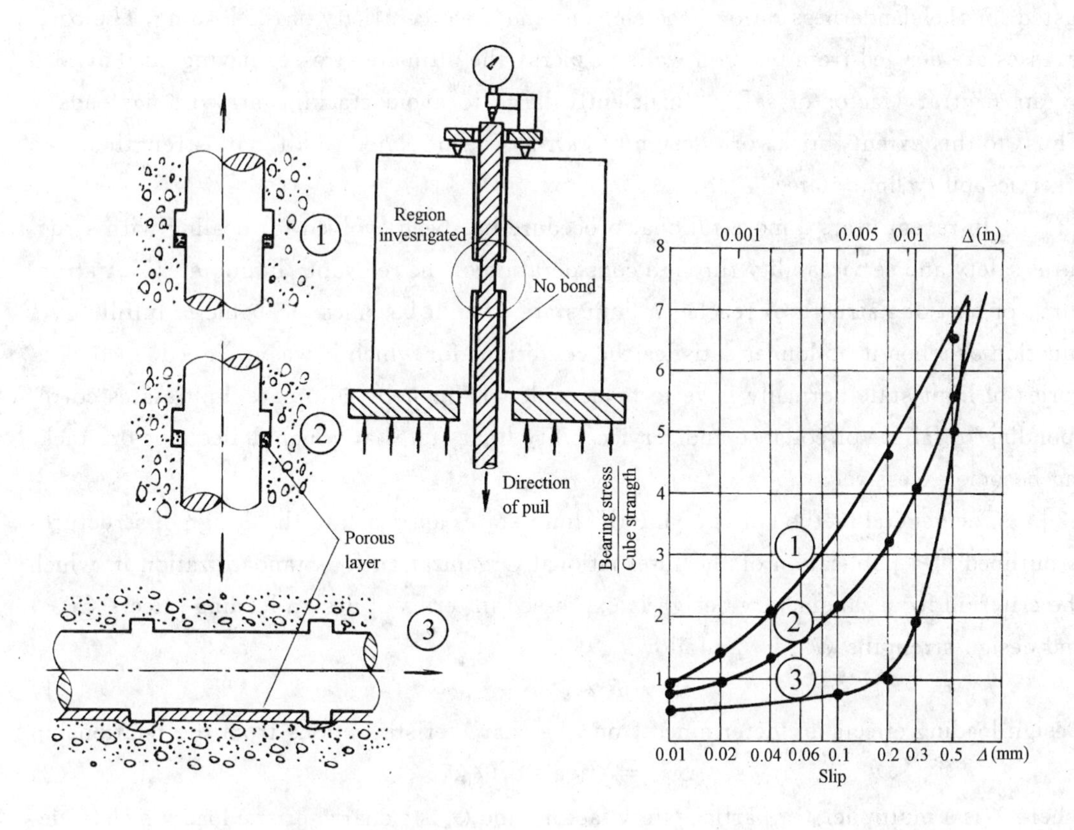

Fig. 14-5 The influence of casting positions on bond performance.

Notes

①在这些试验中，算得的肋前承压应力要超过混凝土立方体抗压强度的七倍。

②下沉出现的多少取决于新浇混凝土的泌水性及水从模板中漏出速度。

UNIT FIFTEEN

Text Limit State Design of Brickwork

[1] The basic aim of structural design is to ensure that a structure should fulfill its intended function throughout its lifetime without excessive deflection, cracking or collapse, and this aim must of course be met with due regard to economy. ① The designer is assisted in his task by the availability of a code of practice which is based on accumulated experience and research. Up to the present time, such codes have sought to ensure the safety and serviceability of masonry structures by specifying permissible stresses for various types and combinations of materials. Thus codes generally give basic compressive stresses for a range of brick-mortar combinations; the basic stress in a particular case has then to be adjusted for the slenderness ratio of the element and the eccentricity of the loading. The basic stresses are derived from tests on walls or piers, the ultimate stresses having been divided by an arbitrary factor of safety sufficiently large to avoid cracking at working loads. ② Thus, to this extent, brickwork design has always been related to ultimate strength and to a serviceability limit state.

[2] In recent years a more rational procedure has been evolved for dealing with structural safety and serviceability through consideration of the relevant 'limit states'. A structure, or part of a structure, reaches a limit state when it becomes incapable of fulfilling its function or when it no longer satisfies the conditions for which it was designed. Two categories of limit state normally have to be considered, namely, ultimate limit states corresponding to failure or collapse and serviceability limit states at which deflections or cracking become excessive.

[3] The general method of applying the limit states approach to the design of structures is outlined in a publication of the International Organization for Standardization in which the criterion for a satisfactory design is expressed in terms of design loading effects ($S*$) and design strengths ($R*$)③ as follows

$$R* \geqslant S* \tag{1}$$

Design loading effects are determined from the characteristic actions from the relationship

$$S* = \text{effects of}(\gamma_f Q_k) \tag{2}$$

where γ_f is a multiplier (or partial safety factor) and Q_k is a characteristic load which, if defined in statistical terms, is given by

$$Q_k = Q_m(1 + k\delta)$$

where Q_m is the value of the most unfavourable load with a 50 per cent probability of its being exceeded once in the expected life of the structure δ is the standard deviation of the distribution of the maximum loading k is a coefficient depending on a selected probability of maximum loadings being greater than Q_k.

[4] It is usual to take the characteristic load as that which will have a 5 per cent probability of being exceeded during the lifetime of the structure. [4] In many situations, however, statistical data are not available and the characteristic loads have to be based on nominal values given in codes of practice or other regulations. The factor γ_f is a function of several partial coefficients.

γ_{f1} which takes account of the possibility of unfavourable deviation of the loads from the characteristic external loads, thus allowing for abnormal or unforeseen actions

γ_{f2} which takes account of the reduced probability that various loads acting together will all be simultaneously at their characteristic values.

γ_{f3} which is intended to allow for possible modification of the loading effects due to incorrect design assumptions (for example, introduction of simplified support conditions, hinges, neglect of thermal and other effects which are difficult to assess) and constructional discrepancies such as dimensions of cross—section, deviation of columns from the vertical and accidental eccentricities

Similarly, design strengths of materials, R^*, are defined by

$$R^* = \frac{R_k}{\gamma_m} \tag{3}$$

where R_k——R_m—ks is the characteristic strength of the material

R_m is the arithmetic mean of test results

s is the standard deviation

k is a coefficient depending on the probability of obtaining results less than R_k

[5] The characteristic strength of a material is usually taken as the 95 per cent confidence limit of the material strength in a relevant test series. The reduction coefficient γ_m is a function of two coefficients.

γ_{m1} which is intended to cover possible reductions in the strength of the materials in the structure as a whole, as compared to the characteristic value deduced from the control test specimen

γ_{m2} which is intended to cover possible weakness of the structure arising from any cause other than the reduction in the strength of the materials allowed for by coefficient γ_{m1}, including manufacturing tolerances

[6] Additionally, ISO 2394 allows for the introduction of a further coefficient γ_c which may be applied either to the design values of loadings or material strengths. This coefficient is in turn a function of two partial coefficients

γ_{c1} which is intended to take account of the nature of the structure and its behaviour, for example, structures or parts of structures in which partial or complete collapse can occur without warning, where redistribution of internal forces is not possible, or where failure of a single element can lead to overall collapse

γ_{c2} which is intended to take account of the seriousness of attaining a limit state from other points of view, for example economic consequences, danger to the community, etc.

[7] Usually γ_c is incorporated into either γ_f or γ_m and therefore does not appear explicitly in design calculations.

[8] The advantage of the limit state approach is that it permits a more rational and flexible assessment of structural safety and serviceability; the various relevant factors are identified and up to a point can be expressed in numerical terms.⑤ Ideally, loadings and strengths should be available in statistical terms but this is seldom possible, so that characteristic values have to be determined on the basis of available evidence. In the case of loads, the evidence generally results from surveys of buildings in service. Characteristic strengths of materials, on the other hand, are derived from laboratory tests, the results of which can sometimes provide a statistical basis for characteristic strength. In the absence of such statistical data, characteristic strengths have to be based on nominal values proved by experience.

New Words and Expressions

availablility * [əˌveilə'biliti] *n.* 可用性，有效性
permissible * [pəː'misəbl] *a.* 可允许的，得到准许的
slenderness [s'lendənis] *n.* 细长度
eccentricity ['eksen'trisiti] *n.* 偏心；偏心率
pier [piə] *n.* 墙垛
category * ['kætigəri] *n.* 种类，类目
standardizatina * [ˌstændədai'zeiʃən] *n.* 标准化
unfavorable ['ʌn'feivərəbl] *a.* 不利的，有害的
abnormal * [æb'nɔːməl] *a.* 反常的；变态的；
unforeseen * ['ʌnfɔː'siːn] *a.* 未预见的，意外的
thermal * ['θəːməl] *a.* 热的；热量的
constructional * [kən'strʌkʃənəl] *a.* 建筑的，建造的
discrepancy * [dis'krepənsi] *n.* 差异的，不符的
tolerance ['tɔlərəns] *n.* 公差；误差
explicitly * [iks'plisitli] *ad.* 明晰地；明确地
additionally [ə'diʃənəli] *ad.* 另外，进一步

Notes

①with due regard to 给……以适当的考虑

②… the ultimate stresses having been divided by … 为独立结构。large to... 作 factor of safty 的定语。

③句中包含 apply... to... 的结构。
④which 引导一个定语从句修饰指示代词 that。
⑤up to a point 在某种程度上。

Exercises

Reading Comprehension

Ⅰ. Choose the best answer.

1. What else should be taken into account in the design of a structure besides its basic aim?
   A. The surroundings that the structure situated.
   B. The working conditions.
   C. The avoidence of wast of money, strength, etc.
   D. The technology.
2. Codes of practice have sought to ensure the safty and serviceability of masonry structure by ________.
   A. giving basic compressive stresses for a range of brick-mortar combinations
   B. by adjusting the basic stress in a particular case for the slenderness ratio of the element and eccentricity of loading
   C. by specifying permissible stress for various types and combinations of materials
   D. by deriving basic stresses from tests on walls or piers
3. During the life time of the structure, the characteristic load ________.
   A. is usually taken as that which will have a 5 percent probability of being exceeded
   B. has to be based on nominal values given in codes of practice or other regulations
   C. is not available because there is no statistical data
   D. is unforeseen because of the possibility of unfavourable deviation
4. The advantage of the limit state approach is that ________.
   A. it provides a more reasonable and adaptable assessment for structural safety and serviceability
   B. it provides a more practical and acceptable assessment for structural safety and serviceability
   C. it provides a more logical and theoretic assessment for structural safety and serviceability
   D. it provides a more changeable and remarkable assessment for structural safety and serviceability
5. Characteristic values have to be determined on the basis of available evidence because ________.
   A. in the case of loads, the evidence generally results from survays of building in ser-

vice

B. it is impossible to get loadings and strengths in statistical terms

C. characteristic strengths of material are derived from laboratory tests

D. the evidence is proved by experience

Ⅱ. Fill in the blanks with the information given in the text.

1. What are the two categories of limit state?

A. ________ corresponding to failure or collaps.

B. ________ at which deflections or cracking become excessive.

2. What is the advantage of the limit state approach?

A. It permits a more rational and flexible ________ of structural safety and serviceability.

B. The various relevant factors are ________ and up to a point can be expressed in numerical terms.

Vocabulary

Ⅰ. Choose one word or phrase which is the most similar in meaning to the one underlined in the given sentences.

1. While they were away on vacation, they allowed their mail to accumulate at the post office.

A. be delivered B. pile up

C. get lost D. be returned

2. The oboe that is most commonly used today is a slender tube about twenty-one inches long.

A. a thin B. a short

C. an elaborate D. an attractive

3. The company is nominally his, but he has nothing to do with it now.

A. in name B. in fact

C. exactly D. normally

4. There was a discrepancy in the two reports of the accident.

A. disagreement B. disorder

C. discriminate D. difference

5. Although many modifications have been made in it, the game known in the United States as football can be traced directly to the English game of rugby.

A. rules B. changes

C. demands D. leagues

Ⅱ. Match the words in Column A with their corresponding definitions or explanations in Column B.

A B

1. thermal a. test the value of
2. explicity b. based on opinion or impulse only, not on reason
3. abnormal c. correct in every detail
4. arbitrary d. different from what is normal
5. assess e. clearly and fully expressed
 f. that can be explained
 g. of heat
 h. more than enough

Translation

长句译法（续）

在英语长句中，有时句子之间关系并不十分密切，翻译时可把句子中的从句或短语化分为句子，分开叙述（分译法）。有些英语长句，单纯用某一种译法都感不便，这时就应综合前面的几种方法来处理句子（综合法）。

例三 （分译法）

As the correct solution of any problem depends primarily on a true understanding of what the problem really is and wherein lies its difficulty, we may profitably pause upon the threshold of our subject to consider first, in a more general way, its real nature; the causes which impede sound practice; the conditions on which success or failure depends; the direction in which error is most to be feared. 任何问题的正确解决方案，主要取决于是否真正了解问题的实质及其困难所在；因此，在开始我们的课题时，先停下来更全面地考虑一下它的实质、阻碍其正常进行的原因、决定其成败的关键条件、最担心发生错误的方面，可能是有利的。（区分为不同的层次，先将原因状语从句译为主句，而后将主句译为结果状语从句。）

例四 （综合法）

By the middle of the year, he warned, the Soviet Union would overtake the United States in the number of landbased strategic missiles, the result of a massive Soviet effort beginning in the mid-1960s, after the Cuban fiasco, to achieve at least parity and possibly superiority in nuclear weapons.

他警告说，到本年年中，苏联将在陆上发射的战略导弹的数量上超过美国，因为苏联在古巴事件中遭到失败后，从60年代中期起就大力发展导弹，目的是为了在核武器方面至少达到同美国均等，并力争超过美国。

（这是一句简单句。有一个插入语 he warned 可以提前。另外有一个表示结果的名词短语，但这个短语中有两个表示时间的短语和一个表示目的短语，需要按逻辑关系来安排。表示结果的名词短语可译为表示原因的句子。）

Translate the following sentences into Chinese.

1. （综合）

This hope of "early discovery" of lung cancer followed by surgical cure, which currently seems to be the most effective form of therapy, is often thwarted by diverse biology behaviours in the rate and direction of growth of the cancer.

2.（分译）

The integrated products quality control system used by thousands of enterprises in the Soviet Union is a combination of controlling bodies and objects under control interacting with the help of material, technical and information facilities when exercising QC at the level of an enterprise.

3.（综合）

But without Adolf Hitler, who was possessed of a demoniac personality, a granite will, uncanny instincts, a cold ruthlessness, a remarkable intellect, a soaring imagination and —until toward the end, when drunk with power and success, he overreached himself—an amazing capacity to size up people and situations, there almost certainly would never have been a Third Reich.

Reading Material A

Methods of Construction

In many of its characteristics, reinforced masonry may be treated, in design, in the same fashion as reinforced concrete. The fundamental behaviour of masonry and concrete under axial load is similar, with both being relatively strong in compression and weak in tension, and of course reinforcement for flexure and shear plays the same role for each material. There are, however, sufficient differences in behaviour to necessitate careful examination of masonry material properties. These differences are partially due to the different component materials, and partially due to the different methods of construction. To fully understand the former, it is necessary to be familiar with the different forms of reinforced masonry common in practice. ①

Here are the two main forms of reinforced masonry construction. Reinforced grouted masonry consists of two skins, or wythes of brick or concrete block, normally solid, separated by a cavity in which the vertical and horizontal reinforcement is placed, and which is grouted as the wythes are built. ② The wythes are normally 2～4 in (50～100mm) thick, and the grout gap $2\frac{1}{2}$～4 in (60～100mm) wide. Reinforced hollow unit masonry is constructed from concrete or brick units with internal vertical voids or cells, some or all of which will contain vertical reinforcement, and will be grouted. The size and design of the units varies considerably, and widths from 4～12 in (100～300mm) are common. Other common structural forms includ masonry infill panels in reinforced concrete or structural steel frame structures, and a modified infill construction method consisting of peripheral reinforced masonry columns and bond beam elements with unreinforced masonry infill.

For seismic resistant structures, the blocks or bricks in both forms of construction illustrated should be laid in running or stretcher bond. ③ Stack bonding, which may be architecturally attractive, creates vertical planes of weakness, particularly in reinforced hollow unit masonry constructed from units with both ends closed. Shear capacity can be reduced virtually to nil, with the stack-bonded wall behaving under earthquakes as a series of independent vertical cantilevers, one unit in section. Several examples of this behaviour were evident in the 1971 San Fernando earthquake. Consequently except at wall ends, or where movement control joints are required, or where seismic shears're low, stackbonding should be avoided. ④

Reinforced grouted masonry has the advantage of providing the designer with greater flexibility in selecting wall widths, and in locating vertical and transverse reinforcement. However, the grout core generally forms a smaller portion of the total wall section area than for reinforced hollow unit masonry, thus reducing its ultimate shear strength, and is a more labour intensive construction form.

In reinforced hollow unit masonry, open-end units (units with one endshell missing, or knocked-out) are to be preferred to standard units because of the poor characteristics, from both strength and waterproofing considerations, of vertical mortared header joints passing through the wall thickness. Horizontal reinforcement is placed in bond-beam units which consist of standard or open-end units with webs knocked-out to approximately half-depth, allowing the horizontal rebar to be located away from the weak horizontal joint plane. Bond beam units may be laid inverted at the bottom course to facilitate clean-out of mortar droppings prior to grouting. In general, walls subjected to in-plane lateral forces under seismic loading should have all cells grout-filled, whether or not they contain vertical reinforcement. This is necessary because of the poor and unpredictable shear strength of ungrouted portions of the wall, and desirable also because of the construction difficulties in placing horizontal reinforcement when some cells are left ungrouted. Exceptions may be made when walls are subjected to faceloading only (veneers) and shear walls subjected to very low shear stresses.

Notes

①要充分地了解不同的组合材料，有必要了解通常使用的配筋砌体的各种不同的形式。
②reinforced grouted masonry　配筋灌浆砌体
③running bond 顺砖砌合，stretcher bond　顺砖砌合
④seismic shear　地震剪力

Reading Material B

The Strength of Materials

The strength of brickwork in compression, tension and shear has been the subject of systematic investigation over a very considerable period. As brickwork structures are primarily stressed in compression, there has naturally been a concentration of interest in the resistance of brick masonry to this type of loading and many investigations have been carried out with a view to establishing the relationship between available brick types and materials, and a variety of mortar mixes. ① These tests have formed the basis for the brickwork strengths used in structural design codes, and in order to reduce the almost unlimited range of brick and mortar combinations to manageable proportions, tables of basic compressive strength have been evolved in which the principal variables are the brick compressive strength and the mortar mix. The strengths of the component materials are defined by standardised tests, which do not necessarily reproduce the state of stress in the component material in brickwork, but which serve as index values in the selection of design stresses.

Although this purely empirical approach has provided an acceptable basis for the structural design of brickwork, it is not altogether satisfactory as it gives little insight into the behaviour of the brick-mortar composite and therefore little guidance either as to the most appropriate kinds of materials test, or as to the ways in which the strength of brickwork could be improved. ② Before examining the results of some of these investigations it may therefore be useful to identify the principal variables which affect the strength of brickwork in compression, and to discuss the mechanism of failure of the material in compression. This discussion will be concerned in the first instance with the crushing strength of short specimens under uniform stress, but consideration will be given to the effects of slenderness and eccentricity of loading on the strength of walls and columns.

Research work has shown that the following factors are of importance in determining the compressive strength of brick masonry

Strength of unit

Geometry of unit

Strength of mortar

Deformation characteristics of unit and mortar

Joint thickness

Suction of units

Water retentivity of mortar

Brickwork bonding.

Some of these factors, such as the unit characteristics, are determined in the manufacturing process, while others such as mortar properties, are susceptible to variations in constituent materials, proportioning, mixing and accuracy of construction. Not all are of equal significance, and in assessing their likely effect on the overall strength of brickwork we may consider the nature of the failure of brickwork in compression.

A number of important points have been derived from compression tests on brickwork and from associated standard materials tests. These include, firstly, the observation that brickwork loaded in uniform compression usually fails by the development of tension cracks parallel to the axis of loading, that is, as a result of tensile stresses at right angles to the primary compression.③ This fact has been well known since the early years of brickwork testing. Secondly, it is evident that the strength of brickwork in compression is much smaller than the nominal compressive strength of the bricks from which it is built, as given by a standard compression test-on the other hand, brickwork strength may greatly exceed the cube crushing strength of the mortar used in it. Finally, it has been shown that the compressive strength of brickwork varies, roughly, as the square root of the nominal brick crushing strength, and as the third or fourth root of the mortar cube strength.

From these observations it has been inferred: (1) that the secondary tensile stresses which cause splitting failure of the brickwork result from the restrained deformation of the mortar in the bed joints of the brickwork; (2) that the apparent compressive strength of bricks in a standard crushing test is not a direct measure of the strength of the unit in brickwork, since the mode of failure is different in the two situations; and (3) that mortar is able to withstand higher compressive stresses in a brickwork bed joint because of the multi-axial nature of the stressing in this situation.

Notes

①由于砌体结构主要是承受压应力,对于砖石砌体的关注自然地集中在其抵抗这种荷载上,并对所应用的砖的类型和材质与各种灰浆之间的关系进行研究。

②虽然这种单凭实验的方法已为砖石砌 体结构的设计提供了可接受的基础,但由于对砖石和灰浆组合性能尚不清楚,所以并不是完全令人满意的,因此对选择材料试验最适合形式或是对提高砖石砌体强度的方法尚缺乏指导性。

③这些包括,第一,观察到在均布压力荷载下砖石砖砌体由于与轴向荷载相平行的受拉裂缝的增大而破坏,即由与主压力呈直角的拉应力所造成。

UNIT SIXTEEN

Text Soil Mechanics

[1] Soil mechanics is a branch of engineering which deals with soils under stress. It did not develop into a science until Terzaghi in the 1920's laid down the principles which still form the basis for most calculations. His principle of of effective stress states that the stress normal to a section of the soil is equal to the sum of the intergranular, or effective, stress transmitted from grain to grain and the neutral, or pore, stress transmitted through the water contained in the soil. ①

[2] Another important idea of Terzaghi concerns the shearing resistance of soils against retaining walls, bulkheads, and braced cuts. ② This lateral pressure increases linearly with depth in retaining walls and parabolically in braced cuts. His results solved many of the disagreements between practice and older theories.

[3] Grain size is the basis of soil mechanics, since it is this which decides whether a soil is frictional or cohesive, a sand or a clay. Starting with the largest sizes, boulders are larger than 10 cm, cobbles are from 5 to 10 cm, gravel or ballast is from about 5 cm to 5 mm, grit is from about 5 mm to 2 mm, sand is from 2 mm to 0.06 mm. All these soils are frictional, being coarse and thus non-cohesive. Their stability depends on their internal friction. For the cohesive or non-frictional soils the two main internationally accepted size limits are: silt from 0.02 mm to 0.002 mm, and clay for all finer material. There are, of course, many silty clays and clayey silts.

[4] Every large civil engineering job starts with a soil mechanics survey in its early stages. The first visit on foot will show whether the site might be suitable, in other words, whether money should be spent on sending soil-sampling equipment out to it. The soil samples and the laboratory results obtained from the triaxial tests, shear tests and so on will show at what depth the soil is likely to be strong enough to take the required load. For a masonry or steel structure, this is where the soil mechanics survey will end, having rarely cost more than 2 per cent of the structure cost.

[5] Generally, the strength of a soil increases with depth. But it can happen that it becomes weaker with depth. Therefore, in choosing the foundation pressure and level for this sort of soil, a knowledge of soil mechanics is essential, since this will give an idea of the likely settlements.

[6] There are, however, several other causes of settlement apart from consolidation due to load. These causes are incalculable and must be carefully guarded against. They include frost action, chemical change in the soil, underground erosion by flowing water, reduction of the ground water level, nearby construction of tunnels or vibrating machinery such as vehicles.

[7] Static load can cause elastic (temporary) or plastic (permanent) settlement, consolidation settlement being permanent. ③ However, when plastic flow is mentioned in English, it generally means the failure of a soil by overload in shear. Consolidation settlement occurs mainly in clays or silts.

[8] From dynamic load alone the commonest settlements are found in sands or gravels, caused by traffic or other vibration, pile driving or other earth shocks. A drop in the ground water level will often cause the soil to shrink and a rise may cause expansion of the soil. Ground water is lowered by the drainage which can be caused by any deep excavation. The shrinkage which can occur with drying is well shown by the clay underlying Mexico City, a volcanic ash. ④ After seven weeks drying this clay shrinks to 6.4 per cent of its initial volume. It is an unusual clay with the very high voids ratio of 93.6/6.4=14.6.

[9] Underground erosion is the removal of solids, usually fines, from the soil by the flow of underground water. The solids can be removed as solids or in solution, though only a few rocks are soluble enough to be removed in this way. Rock salt is the commonest example of a soluble rock. Potassium salts also are soluble.

[10] The permeability of a soil is important for calculations of underground flow, for example, of oil or water to a well, or of water into a trench dug for a foundation, or of water through an earth dam. ⑤ Of the loose soils which can be dug with a spade, clays are the least permeable, silts slightly more, sands yet more, and gravels even more. ⑥ In other words, the permeability is in direct proportion to the grain size of the soil.

[11] When a well is being pumped, the water flows towards it from every direction and the ground water surface (water table) around it sinks. As the distance from the well increases, the water table is lowered rather less, so that around the well it becomes shaped like a funnel, though it is usually called a cone of depression.

New Words and Expressions

frictional * [ˈfrikʃənəl] *a.* 内摩阻力大的
intergranular [ˌintəˈgrænjulə] *a.* 颗粒间的
pore [pɔː] *n.* 孔隙，细孔
bulkhead [ˈbʌlkhed] *n.* 舱壁
parabolically [pærəˈbɔlikəli] *ad.* 抛物线地，抛物面地
disagreement [ˌdisəˈgriːmənt] *n.* 意见不同，不一致
boulder [ˈbəuldə] *n.* 漂石
cobble [kɔbl] *n.* 圆石，卵石
ballast [ˈbæləst] *n.* 石渣，碎石
grit [grit] *n.* 砂粒，粗砂
silt [silt] *n.* 粉粒
silty [silti] *a.* 淤泥的，粉质的

clayey [kleii] *a.* 粘质的
soil-sampling ['sɔilsɑːmpliŋ] *a.* 取土样的
settlement ['setlmənt] *n.* 下沉，沉降
consolidation [kənˌsli'deiʃən] *n.* 固结
incalculable [in'kælkjuləbl] *a.* 难预测的，不可估量的
erosion * [i'rəuʒən] *n.* 侵蚀
drainage ['dreinidʒ] *n.* 排水
excavation [ˌekskə'veiʃən] *n.* 开挖，挖土
underlying * [ʌndə'laiŋ] *a.* 在……的下面
depression * [di'preʃən] *n.* 压低，压下
fine [fain] *n.* 细粒
potassium * [pə'tæsjəm] *n.* 钾
permeability * [pəmjə'biliti] *n.* 渗透，渗透性
trench [trentʃ] *n.* 地沟，深沟
permeable ['pəːmjəbl] *a.* 可渗透的，具有渗透性的
yet [jet] *ad.* 比……还要，更
funnel ['fʌnl] *n.* 漏斗，漏斗形物
cone * [kəun] *n.* 锥形物，锥体

Notes

①在 that 引导的宾语从句中，句子的主要结构为：the stress (normal to...)...is equal to the sum of...the stress transmitted from grain to grain...and the stress transmitted through the water...。

②braced cuts 支撑堑壁。

③Consolidation…being permanent. 为独立结构。

④The shrinkage…shown by the clay…a volcanic ash.
…a volcanic ash. 为"clay"的同位语。

⑤The permeability…for calculation …under-ground flow, for example of oil…or of water into…or of water into…or of water through….
句中四个"of"为并列关系。

⑥Of the loose soils…clays…least permeable 为形容词最高级倒装句。

Exercises

Reading Comprehension

Ⅰ. Choose the best answer

1. According to Paragraph 4, what is mainly talked about?

A. Soil-sampling equipment.

B. Triaxial and shear tests.

C. Soil mechanics survey.

D. Soil samples and laboratory results.

2. A knowledge of soil mechanics is essential to ________ .

A. the strength of a soil

B. this sort of soil

C. the idea of settlement

D. the choose of the foundation pressure

3. Which of the following statements is true?

A. Rise in the ground water level may cause the soil to shrink.

B. Ground water is lowered by the expansion of the soil.

C. The shrinkage can occur with the clay underlying Meico City.

D. Dynamic load such as piledriving is the most common cause for settlement.

4. According to the passage ________ .

A. rocks can be removed in solution

B. most rocks can be removed in solution

C. some rocks can be removed in solution

D. few rocks can be removed in solution

5. Rearrange the permeable soils from the most to the least.

1. sands   2. clays   3. silts   4. gravels

A. 2, 1, 3, 4   B. 2, 3, 1, 4   C. 1, 2, 3, 4   D. 4, 3, 2, 1

Ⅱ. Fill in the table with the information given in the text.

1.

Several other causes of settlement are mentioned in Para. 6. They are…	
1.	2.
3. underground erosion	4.
5.	6. vibrating machinery

2.

Boulders are 10 cm	Cobbles are
Cravel or ballast is…	Crit is…
Sand is…	Silt is…

Vocabulary

Ⅰ. Choose one word or phrase which is the most similar in meaning to the one underlined in the given sentences.

1. Trees help prevent the erosion of soil by running water.

   A. getting away　　B. wearing away

   C. putting away　　D. moving away

2. He looked down into the gapping void at his feet.

   A. emptiness　　B. fullness

   C. darkness　　D. poorness

3. The surfaces of the rocks have some pores.

   A. gaps　　B. circles

   C. spots　　D. lines

4. The loss to the race as a whole is incalculable.

   A. so great that it can not estimated　　B. so many that it can not estimated

   C. so great that it can not counted　　D. so many that it can not counted

5. We should find ways to solve the problem of the settlement of the building.

   A. a gradual sinking　　B. a gradual rising

   C. a gradual twisting　　D. a gradual shaking

Ⅱ. Match the words in Column A with their corresponding definitions or explanations in Column B.

A	B
1. underlying	a. involving three axe
2. triaxial	b. a solid object with a round base and a point at the top
3. potassium	c. a silverwhite soft easily melted metal that is a simple substance
4. linear	d. a flat figure with three straight sides and three angles
5. cone	e. lying beneath or below
	f. a silver-white metal that burns with a bright white light
	g. of lines or of length
	h. hiding away in the ground

Translation

Translate the following sentences into Chinese, and pay attention to the words underlined.

1. The church was built by the Mexican Americans in 1889.
2. Three—phase current should be used for large motors.
3. The number of the buildings in the city has increased by four times since 1978.

4. The output of bulk cement was reduced by 50% this year.

5. Very loud sounds produced by huge planes which fly low over the land can cause damage to houses.

6. In making cement, the mixture of limestone and clay in the proper proportion is pulverized to a fine powder and slowly fed into an inclined revolving cylinder through which hot gases are passing.

7. New York City, which has turned its last 20 years of garbage into the highest peak on the Eastern Seaboard, in a Staten Island landfill that will soon run out of space, is preparing to spend $2.5 billion on the construction of eight trash—to—energy plants, and billions more to operate them. (顺译)

Reading Material A

Footings (1)

Footings generally can be classified as wall and column footings. A wall footing is simply a strip of reinforced concrete, wider than the wall, which distributes its pressure. Single-column footings are usually square, sometimes rectangular, and represent the simplest and most economical type. Their use under exterior columns meets with difficulties if property rights prevent the use of footings projecting beyond the exterior walls. In this case combined footings or strap footings are used which enable one to design a footing which will not project beyond the wall column. Combined footings under two or more columns are also used under closely spaced, heavily loaded interior columns where single footings, if they were provided, would completely or nearly merge. ①

Such individual or combined column footings are the most frequently used types of spread foundations on soils of reasonable bearing capacity. If the soil is weak and/or column loads are great, the required footing areas become so large as to be uneconomical. In this case, unless a deep foundation is called for by soil conditions, a mat or raft foundation is resorted to. This consists of a solid reinforced-concrete slab which extends under the entire building and which consequently distributes the load of the structure over the maximum available area. Such a foundation, in view of its own rigidity, also minimizes differential settlement. It consists, in its simplest form, of a concrete slab reinforced in both directions. A form which provides more rigidity and at the same time is often more economical consists of an inverted beam-and-girder floor. Girders are located in the column lines in one direction, with beams in the other, mostly at closer intervals. If the columns are arranged in a square pattern girders are equally spaced in both directions and the slab is provided with two-way reinforcement, Inverted flat slabs, with capitals at the bottoms of the columns, are also used for mat foundations.

In ordinary constructions the load on a wall or column is transmitted vertically to the footing, which in turn is supported by the upward pressure of the soil on which it rests. If the load is symmetrical with respect to the bearing area, the bearing pressure is assumed to be uniformly distributed (Fig. 16-1*a*). It is known that this is only approximately true. Under footings resting on coarse-grained soils the pressure is larger at the center of the footing and decreases toward the perimeter (Fig. 16-1*b*). This is so because the individual grains in such soils are somewhat mobile, so that the soil located close to the perimeter can shift very slightly outward in the direction of lower soil stresses. In contrast, in clay soils pressures are higher near the edge than at the center of the footing, since in such soils the load produces a shear resistance around the perimeter which adds to the upward pressure (Fig. 16-1*c*). It is customary to disregard these nonuniformities (1) because their numerical amount is uncertain and highly variable, depending on type of soil, and (2) because their influence on the magnitudes of bending moments and shearing forces in the footing is relatively small. ②

On compressible soils footings should be loaded concentrically to avoid tilting, which will result if bearing pressures are significantly larger under one side of the footing than under the opposite side. This means that single footings should be placed concentrically under the columns and wall footings concentrically under the walls and that for combined footings the centroid of the footings area should coincide with the resultant of the column loads. ③ Eccentrically loaded footings can be used on highly compacted soils and on rock. It follows that one should count on rotational restraint of the column by a single footing only when such favorable soil conditions are present and when the footing is designed both for the column load and the restraining moment. Even then, less than full fixity should be assumed, except for footings on rock.

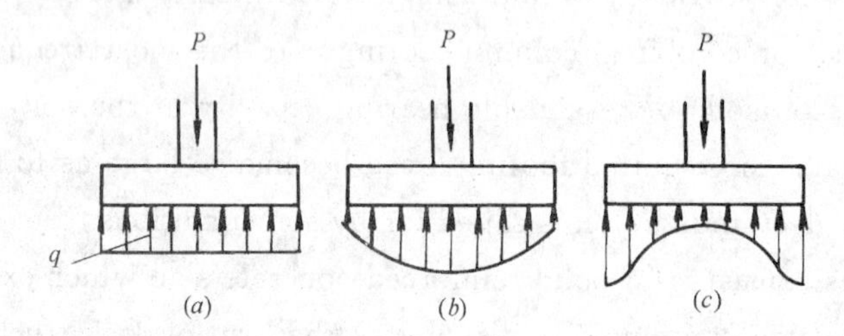

Fig. 16-1 Bearing-pressure distribution:
(*a*) as assumed;
(*b*) actual, for granular soils;
(*c*) actual, for cohesive soils

The accurate determination of stresses, particularly in single-columnfootings is not practical, since they represent relatively massive blocks which cantilever from the column in all four directions. Under uniform upward pressure they deform in a bowl shape, a fact which would greatly complicate an accurate stress analysis. For this reason present procedures for the design of such footings are based almost entirely on the results of two extensive experimental investigations, both carried out at the University of Illinois. These tests have been reevaluated, particularly in the light of newer concepts of strength in shear and diagonal tension.

Notes

①在间距小的重载内柱下也可采用两柱或更多柱的复式基础，如果在这种情况下采用单个基础，它们将完全或几乎完全连成一块。

②人们习惯于不考虑这些不均匀性，因为（1）不均匀性的数值不明，而且由于土质不同变化 很大；（2）不均匀性对基础内弯矩大小和剪力数值的影响较小。

③这意味着单个基础应与柱对中，墙基应与墙对中，而复式基础的基底形心应与柱荷载合力相重合。偏心荷载的基础可用于较密实的土层和岩石之上。

Reading Material B

Footings（2）

Allowable bearing pressures are established from principles of soil mechanics, on the basis of load tests and other experimental determinations. Allowable bearing pressures q-under service loads usually are based on a safety factor of 2.5 to 3.0 against exceeding the ultimate bearing capacity of the particular soil and to keep settlements within tolerable limits. Many local building codescontain allowable bearing pressures for the types of soil conditions found in the particular locality.

For concentrically loaded footings the required area is determined from

$$A_{req} = \frac{D + L}{q_a} \tag{1}$$

In addition, most codes permit a 33 percent increase in allowable pressure when effects of wind W or earthquake E are included, in which case

$$A_{req} = \frac{D + L + W}{1.33q_a} or \frac{D + L + E}{1.33q_a} \tag{2}$$

It should be noted that footing sizes are determined for unfactored service loads and soil pressures, in contrast to the strength design of reinforced-concrete members, which utilizes factored loads and factored nominal strengths. ①This is because for footing design safety is provided by the overall safety factors just mentioned, in contrast to the separate load and strengthreduction factors for member dimensioning.

A_{req}, the required footing area, is the larger of those determined by Eq. (1)or (2). The loads in the numerators of Eqs. (1) and (2) must be calculated at the level of the base of the footing, i. e. , at the contact plane between soil and footing. This means that the weight of the footing and surcharge (i. e. , fill and possible liquid pressure on top of the footing) must be included. Wind loads and other lateral loads cause a tendency to overturning. In checking for overturning of a foundation, only those live loads which contributes to overturning should be included, and dead loads which stabilizeagainst overturning should be multiplied by 0. 9. A safety factor of at least 1. 5 should be maintained against overturning, unless otherwise specified by the local building code.

A footing is eccentrically loaded if the supported column is not concentric with the footing area or if the column transmits at its juncture with the footing not only a vertical load but also a bending moment. ② In either case the load effects at the footing base can be represented by the vertical load P and a bending moment M. The resulting bearing pressures are again assumed to be linearly distributed. As long as the resulting eccentricity $e = M/P$ does notexceed the kern distance k of the footing area, the usual flexure formula

$$q_{\substack{max\\min}} = \frac{P}{A} \pm \frac{Mc}{I} \tag{3}$$

permits the determination of the bearing pressures at the two extreme edges, as shown in Fig. 1a. The footing area is found by trial and errors from the condition $q_{max} \leqslant q_a$. If the eccentricity falls outside the kern, Eq. (3) gives a negative value (tension) for q along one edge of the footing. Because no tension can be transmitted at the contact area between soil and footing, Eq. (3) is no longer valid and bearing pressures are distributed as in Fig. 16-1b. For rectangular footings of size I×b the maximum pressure can be found from

$$q_{max} = \frac{2P}{3bm} \tag{4}$$

which, again, must be no larger than the allowable pressure q_a.

Once the required footing area has been determined, the footing must then be designed to develop the necessary strength to resist all moments, shear, and other internal actions caused by the applied loads. For this purpose, the load factors of the Code apply to footings as all other structural components. Correspondingly, for strength design the footing is dimensioned for the effects of the following external loads

$$U = 1.4D + 1.7L$$

or if wind effects are to be included,

$$U = 0.75(1.4D + 1.7L + 1.7W)$$

In seismic zone earthquake forces E must be considered, in which case $1.1E$ must be substituted for W. The case, that is,

$$U = 0.9D + 1.3W$$

will hardly ever govern the strength design of a footing. However, lateral earth pressure H may on occasion affect footing design, in which case

$$U = 1.4D + 1.7L + 1.7H$$

For horizontal pressures F of liquids, such as groundwater, $1.4F$ must be substituted for

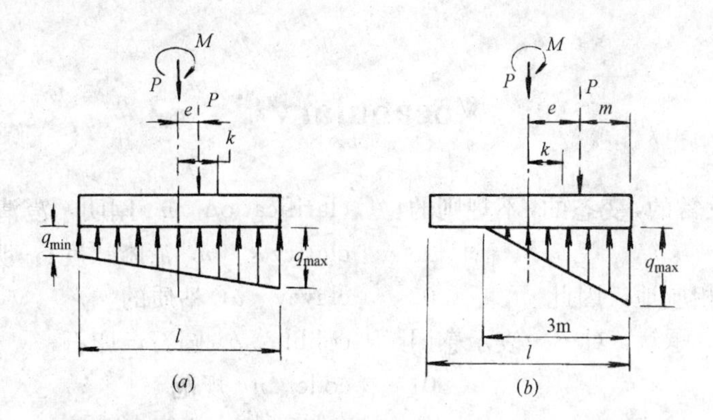

Fig. 16-2 Assumed bearing pressures under eccentric footings

1. 7H in the last equation. Vertical liquid pressures are to be added to dead loads; i. e. , the load factor 1. 4 applies to them.

These factored loads must be counteracted and equilibrated by corresponding bearing pressures of the soil. Consequently, once the footing area is determined, the bearing pressures are rectangulated for the factored loads forpurposes of strength computations. These are fictitious pressures which are needed only to produce the required ultimate strength of the footing. To distinguish them from the actual pressures q under service loads, the design pressures which equilibrate the factored loads U will be designated q_u.

Notes

①应当指出，基础的尺寸取决于使用荷载和土压力。它与钢筋混凝土构件设计不同，后者采用乘以系数的荷载和乘以系数标准强度。

②如果支柱与基础底面不对中或支柱在与基础接合处不但传递竖向荷载，而且传递 弯矩，那么基础就承受偏心荷载。

Appendix Ⅰ Vocabulary

abnormal * *a*. 反常的，变态的，不规则的 15
accordingly *ad*. 相应地，因此 08
acknowledge * *v*. 承认，对……表示感谢 01
actuality *n*. 现实，实际 09
additionally *ad*. 另外，进一步 15
adhesion * *n*. 粘着力，附着力 05
adhesive *a*. 胶粘剂 07
allowance * *n*. 允许，考虑 02
alternatively *ad*. 换句话说，另一方面 03
analytically *ad*. 分析地，解析地 09
anchorage *n*. 锚固 01
appraisal *n*. 鉴定，评价 12
appropriately *ad*. 适合地，正确地， 10
as opposed to 与……相反（相对立） 11
as yet 到目前为止（仍） 11
assessment *n*. 估计，评价 03
assumption * *n*. 假定，设想 04
asymptotically *ad*. 逐渐地 06
attachment * *n*. 附件，辅助机构 06
attainment * *n*. 达到 14
authoritative *a*. 有权威的，可相信的 02
availability * *n*. 可用性，有效性 15
ballast *n*. 石渣，碎石 16
biaxial *a*. 双轴的 10
bibliography *n*. 书目提要 14
bond stress 粘结应力 14
boulder *n*. 漂石 16
bulkhead *n*. 舱壁 16
cantilever *n*. 悬壁（梁） 06
capital *n*. 柱头 08
category * *n*. 种类，类别 15
centerline *n*. 中线 08
certainty * *n*. 肯定，必然 05
clarification *n*. 阐明，澄清 14
clarity * *n*. 清晰（度），明确（性） 01
clayey *a*. 粘质的 16
cobble *b*. 圆石，卵石 16
code *n*. 规范 08
codify *v*. 编撰，整理 01
coefficient * *n*. 系数，常数 06
collaborate *v*. 合作，共同研究 01
come to hand 得到，到手 13
commentary *n*. 评论，评注 02
compatibility * *n*. 相容性 08
complementary * *a*. 补充的，互补的 01
complexity * *n*. 复杂（性） 03
compressive force 压力 05
concurrent *a*. 同时发生的，并存的 01
cone * *n*. 锥形物，锥体 16
connector *n*. 连接键 13
consolidation *n*. 固结 16
constructional * *a*. 建筑的，建造的 15
constructive *a*. 建设（性）的，结构上的 01
construe *vt*. 解释，把……认作 02
contraflexure *n*. 反弯曲 14
corrosion * *n*. 腐蚀，侵蚀 03
counteract * *v*. 消除，抵消 12
countless *a*. 无数的，不可胜数的 02
coverage * *n*. 有效范围 01
criterion * *n*. 准则，标准 10
curvature * *n*. 曲率，弯曲 08
curve-fitting *a*. 曲线配合的 06
cylinder * *n*. 圆柱体，圆筒 10
cylindrical * *a*. 圆柱形的 12
depression * *n*. 压低，压下 16
designate * *vt*. 指明，选定 09
detail *v*. 画样图 14

detailing *n*. 大样设计 14
detrimental * *a*. 有害的，不利的 05
deviation * *n*. 偏差，偏离 05
diagonal * *a*. 对角线的 07
disagreement *n*. 意见不同，不一致 16
disclose * *v*. 表明，泄露 08
discontinuity * *n*. 不连续性，不连续点 08
discrepancy * *n*. 差异，不符合 15
discrete * *n*. 不连续的，松散的 14
dispense *vt*.（使）无必要，不用 05
dissimilar * *a*. 不同的，不相似的 05
dowel *n*. 销栓 09
drainage *n*. 排水 16
dropped panels 加厚的托板 08
ductility * *n*. 延性，延度 11
duplication *n*. 重复，复制品 01
eccentricity * *n*. 偏心，偏心率 15
elastically *ad*. 有弹性地 04
encase *v*. 包裹 13
end anchorage 端部锚固 03
endpoint *n*. 终点，边界线 10
enhancement * *n*. 提高，增强 01
envelope *n*. 包络线 10
equilibrium *n*. 平衡，均衡 08
erosion * *n*. 侵蚀 16
excavation *n*. 开挖，挖土 16
explicit * *a*. 明确的，清晰的 06
explicitly *ad*. 明晰地，明确地 15
exponent *n*. 指数，幂 03
fabricator *n*. 制造者，制作者 13
factored *a*. 乘系数的 11
familiarity * *n*. 精通 01
fine *n*. 细粒 16
flange * *n*. 凸缘，翼缘 13
flexural * *a*. 弯曲的，挠曲的 03
flexure *n*. 弯曲，挠曲 01
fluctuation *n*. 变化 05
footing *n*. 基础，立足点 10
format * *n*. 格式，形式 01
frictional * *a*. 内摩阻力大的 16
functionally *ad*. 功能上，从使用的观点设计地 12
funnel *n*. 漏斗，漏斗形物 16
generality * *n*. 一般（性），普遍（性） 01
geometrically *ad*. 几何学上 11
grid * *n*. 格子，窗格 08
grit *n*. 砂粒，粗砂 16
grossly *ad*. 大体地，总地 14
hairline *n*. 细缝，毛筋 03
hairline crack *n*. 毛细裂缝 05
hatch *v*. 在……上画影线 08
have recourse to 依靠，借助于 09
hinge *n*. 铰（链） 11
homogeneous * *a*. 均质的，同类的 04
hypothetical *a*. 假说的，假设的 03
idealisation *n*. 理想化 13
impair * *vt*. 削弱，损害 07
imponderable *a*. 不可衡量的，无法估计的 13
in conjunction with 共同，一起 12
in lieu of 作为……的替代 06
inadequate * *a*. 不充足的，不适当的 01
incalculable *a*. 难预测的，不可估量的 16
inclination * *n*. 倾斜，趋向 07
indebtedness *n*. 负债，感激 01
ineffective * *a*. 无效的，不合适的 05
innovative * *a*. 创新的 12
instantaneous * *a*. 瞬息的，即刻的 06
intercept * *v*./n. 截断；截线 10
interconnection *n*. 互相连接，相互作用 13
interface * *n*. 相交处 05
intergranular *a*. 颗粒间的 16
interlock * *vt*.（使）连接 05
interrelated *a*. 相关的 12
intersect * *v*. 相交，交叉，横切 09

jointly *ad*. 共同地，联合地 08
joist *n*. 小梁，搁栅 13
keep abreast of 保持与……并列 01
laminate * *v*.（把）分成薄片，用薄片叠成 07
lend onself to 有助于，适于 05
linearly *ad*. 呈直线地，线性地 10
longitudinal * *a*. 经度的，纵向的 04
longtime *a*. 长期的 06
make allowance (s) for 允许，考虑到 11
margin *n*. 储备量，安全系数 03
mechanism * *n*. 机构，机械 11
microcrack *n*. 微裂缝 10
midspan *n*. 中跨 07
modification * *n*. 更改，修正 10
modular * *a*. 模数的 03
modulus *n*. 模数，模量 03
motivation *n*. 动机 01
multistory *a*. 多层的，高层的 12
municipal *a*. 市的，市政的 02
necessitate * *v*. 使成为需要 13
nominal * *a*. 标称的，名义上的，标志的 02
nondimensionalize *vt*. 使无量纲化 10
nonelastic *a*. 无弹性的 05
nonhomogeneous *a*. 非均质的 04
nonparallel *a*. 不平行的 11
nonstructural *a*. 非结构的，不用于结构上的 06
numerical * *a*. 数字的，用数表示的 07
objectionable * *a*. 令人不愉快的，令人厌恶的 12
objectionably *ad*. 该反对地，有异议地 03
octagonral *a*. 八面体的，八面的 10
offensive *a*. 冒犯的，令人不快的 12
orient * *v*. 定向，定位 10
originate * *v*. 开始，创造 01
oversimplify *v*. 过于简化 14
parabola *n*. 抛物线 04
parabolic * *a*. 抛物线的 07
parabolically *ad*. 抛物线地，抛物面地 16
paradoxical *a*. 荒谬的，自相矛盾的 13
parameter * *n*. 参数 06
partition * *n*. 隔墙，隔板 06
permeability * *n*. 渗透，渗透性 16
permeable *a*. 可渗透的，具有渗透性的 16
permissible * *a*. 可允许的，得到准许的 15
perpendicular * *a*.n. 垂直的；垂线 08
pertain * *vi*.（to）关于，属于 02
pier *n*. 墙垛 15
plain *a*. 素的，不配筋的 09
pore * *n*. 孔隙，细孔 16
potassium * *n*. 钾 16
precompression *n*. 预先压缩，预压力 12
premature * *a*. 过早的，不成熟的 12
prematurely *ad*. 不成熟地，过早地 03
prior to 在……之前 03
profound *a*. 深远的，深切的 01
projection * *n*. 凸出物，凸出 08
proliferation *n*. 扩散，激增 13
proportional to 与…成比例 03
proposition *n*. 陈述，定理 05
provision *n*. 规定，条款 01
pulsate *vi*. 震动 13
quadrant *n*. 象限，扇形体 10
qualitatively *ad*. 性质上地，定性地 08
rationale *n*. 基本原理，原理的阐述 11
reconstitute *vt*. 重新构成，改组 13
recourse * *n*. 依赖（靠），救助 09
rectangular * *a*. 矩行的，长方行的 04
redistribution *n*. 重新分布，再分配 09
reexamination *n*. 复查 14
regional *a*. 区域的，地区的 02
remainder * *n*. 剩余物 09
rest with 由……负责 02
revision * *n*. 校订，修改 01

rotational * *a*. 旋转的，转动的 11
segment * *n*. 一部分，段 11
semiempirical *a*. 半经验的 08
settlement *n*. 下沉，沉降 16
shear *a*. 切力，剪力 04
short-time *a*. 短期的 06
shrinkage * *n*. 收缩，减缩 02
silt *n*. 粉粒 16
silty *a*. 淤泥的，粉质的 16
simultaneously *ad*. 同时发生地，同时存在地 06
single-piece *n*. 整块，整段 07
slenderness *n*. 细长度 15
soil-sampling *a*. 取土样的 16
spiral * *a*. 螺旋的 09
standardization * *n*. 标准化 15
standardize *v*. 标准化 12
stirrup *n*. 箍筋，钢箍 09
strand * *n*. 股线，绞合线 12
subdivide *v*. 把……再分，把……细分 01
subscript *n*. 记号，标记 02
supplant *vt*. 代替，取代 05
sustained *a*. 持续不断地 06
tan *n*. 正切，切线 04
tangent * *n*. 正切，切线
a. 切线的，相切的 10
tangential * *a*. 切线的，正切的 04
tentative *a*. 试验性的，初步的 10
thereof * *ad*. 它的，其 05
thermal * *a*. 热的，热量的 15
tolerance *n*. 公差，误差 15
torsional * *a*. 扭转的 09
trajectory *a*. 弧形轨道 07
trench *n*. 地沟，深沟 16
triaxial *a*. 三轴的 10
triaxiality *n*. 三轴性，三维 10
trigger *v*. 引发，导致 12
unacceptable * *a*. 不能接受的，不中意的 12
uncracked *a*. 未开裂的，无裂缝的 03
underlying * *a*. 在……的下面 16
understandable *a*. 能领会的，可被了解的 09
undesirable * *a*. 不合乎需要的，不希望有的 12
unfavorable *a*. 不利的，有害的 15
unforeseen *a*. 未预见的，意外的 15
uniaxial *a*. 单轴的 10
unified *a*. 统一的 08
unreinforced *a*. 无钢筋的，不加固的 09
unreliable *a*. 不可靠的，不可信赖的 09
update * *n*. 最新知识 01
vary over 随……而异 07
verge *n*. 边缘，边际 11
vertically *ad*. 垂直地，直立地 07
yet *ad*. 比……还要，更 16

Appendix Ⅱ Translation for Reference

第1单元

《混凝土结构设计》绪论

本书对以前的版本作了大量的修订、扩充和更新，但它仍保持了相同的基本方法：首先，扎实理解钢筋混凝土结构的性能，进而学习用于现代设计的方法，掌握实用设计的规范和规程。

人们通常认为，要想在专业上取得成功，只进行特殊设计技能和编制工序的训练是不够的。因为这些技能和程序要面对各种不断的变化。为了了解和跟上这些迅猛发展，结构工程师需要有关钢筋混凝土结构材料、部件和构造性能的全面基础训练。另一方面，结构工程师的主要任务是安全、经济和有效地进行结构设计。因此，有了基本的理解作为牢固的基础之后，精通设计程序和应用这些设计程序的技能是十分必要的。这一版和以前的版本一样，都是为这两个目的服务的。

根据作者的教学经验和读者的建设性意见，该版在形式上作了一些变动：以前被分开在前一章中讲解的材料的力学性能和钢筋混凝土性能的部分已并入后面的弯曲和剪切这些有关具体设计等章节中，因而具有更好的连续性，并为掌握每一知识打下坚实基础提供了更便利的参阅资料，避免了重复。在前一版的十二章中，一些过长的章节已重新划分为较短的，更加便于学习和参考的章节。

许多内容的广度和深度都有所提高，而且又增添了有关斜坡板、组合结构、挡土墙和房屋体系这些全新章节。为增加概括性和清晰性，有关柱的那章已做了部分修改。每章中大量扩充的参考目录，为更详细了解背景知识的读者提供了所需文献。对作业题量也做了大幅度地增加，同时，为方便教师和学生，作业题放到了每一章的后面。

所有设计程序、例题和习题都与美国混凝土学会1983年建设规范一致，而桥梁部分则与美国国家公路与运输工作者协会1983年规程一致。这里还包括了许多新的设计方法。因此，这本书对于实习工程师来讲仍不失为一本有价值的案头参考书，因为本书可为他提供现代设计的信息。

教师会发现这本书既适合混凝土结构设计开一个学期的课程，也适合两个学期的课程。如果课程安排只有一个学期（可能在大学四年级时讲授），那么，第一、二章分别关于材料的介绍，第三、四、五章抗弯抗剪和锚固方面的内容，第六章适用性，第八章单向和双向板的介绍，第十二章有关柱的知识，就足已打下一个良好的基础。在课堂上时间可能不允许讲授第十六章框架分析和第十七章房屋体系，但这两部分完全可布置为独立的阅读材料，与前面的章节同时进行。根据作者的经验，这种补充的课外阅读，将会促进学生的学习积极性。

第二个学期的课程（很有可能在研究生的第一年讲授）应该包括第七章扭转这一日趋

重要的问题，第九至第十一章对平板体系的深入研究、第十四、十五章中地基和挡土墙、第十三章中组合结构和第十九章中的桥梁设计。预应力混凝土非常重要，应单设一门课程。但如果课程安排不允许，那么在第十八章中可大体上了解一些最重要的概念。

该书是当初由 Leonard C. Urquhart 和 Charles E. O'Rourke 于 1923 年所编写教材的第十版。那时他们两位都是康奈尔大学的结构工程教授。第二、三、四版牢固地确立了该书作为这一学科领域初级和高级课程主导教材的地位。康奈尔大学的另一位教授 Georage Winter 与 Urquhart 合作修改了第五和第六版，Winter 和本书作者负责第七、八、九版。这一版是继 1982 年 Winter 教授逝世后修改的。

作者非常感谢本书的原作者们。尽管可以肯定地说，就是 Urquhart 和 O'Rourke 也不能辨认本书的许多的细节，但使本书成为独一无二成功之作的学习方法及教育哲学则不会陌生。怀着尤为感激的心情，我要特别提到 Winter 教授对我的影响，与他长期在工作上和私人间的友谊对形成我贯穿于以下各章中的观点有着深刻的影响。

第 2 单元

设计规范与规程以及 ACI 规范安全条款

混凝土结构设计通常要在对材料、结构分析和构件匹配等提供了特殊要求的规范构架内进行。与许多高度发达国家相反，美国没有法定的全国性的制约混凝土结构规范，而是由制定出所需文件的不同专业团体、同业工会以及技术研究院负责和维护设计规程。

美国混凝土协会（ACI）长期以来一直率先进行此方面的努力。作为该活动的一部分，美国混凝土学会发布了得以广泛承认的《钢筋混凝土建筑规范说明》，作为钢筋混凝土建筑设计和施工指南。ACI 规范本身并无法定地位，但却在钢筋混凝土领域中被普遍看作是当前适宜实际应用的权威性声明。因此，该规范已经被依法编入无数确有法定地位的市政及地方建筑法规。所以，其条款事实上已具备法定地位。美国的大多数钢筋混凝土建筑及其相关结构都是按照目前的 ACI 规范进行设计的，而且被许多其他国家用作仿照的样板。ACI 的第二出版物《钢筋混凝土建筑规范说明注释》为规范条款提供了背景材料和理论。美国混凝土学会还出版重要期刊和标准，以及混凝土特种结构的分析与设计建议。

美国的大部分公路大桥都是按照美国各州公路与运输工作者协会的桥梁规程说明设计的。该规程说明不仅包括前面提到的与荷载和荷载分布相关的条款，而且包括混凝土桥梁设计与施工的详细条款。其中很多条款与 ACI 规范大同小异。

铁路桥梁的设计是以美国铁路工程协会（AREA）的铁路工程手册规程为依据的。该手册在大多数方面也模仿了 ACI 规范，但是它却包含了许多为各类铁路建筑所固有的附加材料。

在混凝土结构设计中，没有任何规范和设计规程可以用来取代正确的工程判断。在建筑实践中，常常遇到一些特殊情况，规范条款只能作为指导原则。工程师必须依靠对用于钢筋混凝土或预应力混凝土的结构力学基本原则的深刻理解，以及对材料性质了如指掌。

ACI 规范安全条款是以强度折减系数和荷载系数方程形式给出的。这些系数在一定程度上以统计数据为基础，但在更大程度上是基于经验、工程判断或相互兼顾。也就是说，一个结构或构件的设计强度 ϕS_n 至少必须等于根据设计荷载计算出的要求强度 U。即：

$$\text{设计强度} \geqslant \text{要求强度}$$

或

$$\phi S_n \geqslant U$$

标准强度 S_n（往往有些保守）用可接受的方法进行计算。要求强度 U 的计算是把适当的荷载系数用于各实用荷载：恒载 D、活载 L、风载 W，地震力 E，土压力 H、液压 F、冲击容许量 I 以及可能包括沉降、徐变、收缩和温度变化的环境影响 T。通常，定义荷载包括各种荷载或相关的诸如力矩、剪力或推力的内在效应。因此，用特定术语来表示承受了如力矩、剪力和推力的构件（方程式略）。

其中下标字母 n 分别表示弯曲、剪力和推力的标准强度；下标字母 u 表示乘以系数的荷载产生的力矩、剪力和推力。在计算乘以系数的荷载对右面的影响时，荷载系数可以用于使用荷载本身或根据使用荷载计算出的内部荷载效应。

第 3 单元

适 用 性

目前已经找到确保梁具有适当安全储备的一些方法，以防止弯曲或剪切破坏，或由于钢筋的粘结与锚固不足而引起破坏。为此，假定构件处在虚构的超载状态。

还有一点重要的是，当荷载为实际上所要求的荷载，即荷载系数为 1.0 的正常使用中，构件的性能令人满意。这不能只靠提供足够的强度得以保证。在满载情况下，使用荷载的挠度可能过大，或者由于持续荷载长期挠度可能引起损坏。梁上的受拉裂缝可能过宽，在感观上让人难以接受，甚至使钢筋严重腐蚀。这些以及其他如震动或疲劳等问题都需要予以考虑。

适用性研究是以弹性理论为基础，并假定混凝土及钢筋的应力与应变成正比。可假定中性轴受拉一侧的混凝土未开裂，部分开裂，或全部开裂，这取决于荷载及所用材料的强度。

此前适用性问题的处理是间接的，是将荷载下的混凝土与钢筋的应力限制在得到令人满意的性能的保守值上。目前，由于一般都采用强度设计方法，允许构件更为细长，通过对承载力作出更为准确的估计，用强度较高的材料促使构件的尺寸朝较小的趋势发展，这样的间接的方法将不再适用。较为流行的方法是使构件满足强度要求后，再专门调查使用荷载下的裂缝和挠度。ACI（美国混凝土学会）规范规定反映出想法上的这一改变。

本章将提出一些方法确保钢筋混凝土梁弯曲后引起的裂缝窄些，分布适当。荷载达到满载时，长期和短期的挠度不会太大。

受弯构件的开裂

所有的钢筋混凝土都会有开裂，一般在荷载远远低于适用荷载时就会出现，由于收缩受到约束而引起的开裂甚至出现在荷载之前。由于荷载而产生的受弯开裂，不仅是不可避免的，而且对于有效地使用钢筋也是必要的。在形成受弯裂缝之前，钢筋的受力不能大于相邻的混凝土受力的 n 倍，此处 n 为模量比 E_s/E_c。就目前使用的普通材料而言，n 大约为 8。这样，当混凝土接近其大约 500 磅/英寸^2 的断裂模量时，钢筋的应力仅为 $8\times500=4000$ 磅/英寸^2，此值太低，达不到作为钢筋应有的效力。正常的使用荷载，钢筋应力可为该值的 8 或 9 倍。

设计很好的梁，其受弯裂缝细，称为毛细裂缝，不细心的人几乎看不见，并且，不会使钢筋产生锈蚀。由于荷载逐渐增加大于开裂荷载，裂缝的数量与宽度随之增加，实用荷载的标准是裂缝的最大宽度为大约 0.01 英寸（0.25 毫米）。如果荷载再增加，尽管裂缝的数量大体不变，但裂缝的宽度却随之增大。

混凝土的开裂是一个随机过程，特别易变，而且受很多因素的影响。鉴于问题的复杂性，目前预计裂缝宽度的方法主要以试验观察结果为依据。推导出的大多数方程式都预计可能的最大裂缝宽度，也就是说，通常大约 90% 的构件裂缝宽度低于计算值。然而，有时出现一些超过计算宽度 2 倍的局部裂缝。

影响裂缝宽度的变量

如果设有合适的钢筋弯钩，即使沿全跨粘结受损坏，梁也不会过早断裂。然而，其裂缝宽度大于其他相同的梁，因后者沿其全跨具有良好的抗滑移性能。一般来说，用光滑的圆钢配筋的梁在使用中宽裂缝相当少，而用抗滑移性能好的变形钢筋配筋的梁，会出现许多几乎看不见的微细裂缝。由于这一改进，在目前的实践应用中，常使用表面变形钢筋，其肋的最大间距与最小的高度按 ASTM（美国材料试验学会）标准 A615、A616、A617 的规定来确定。

第二个重要的变量是钢筋的应力。Gergely，Lutz 以及其他科学家们进行的研究证实裂缝宽度与 f_s^n 成正比，此处 f_s 为钢筋应力；n 为幂，在大约 1.0 至 1.4 之间变化。在实际意义的范围内，钢筋受力假定为 20 千磅/英寸^2 至 36 千磅/英寸^2，n 可等于 1.0。根据对弹性开裂部分的分析，便很容易计算出钢筋的应力，反过来，根据 ACI（美国混凝土学会）规范 f_s 可认为相当于 $0.60f_y$。

由 Broms 及其他人所作的实验标明，裂缝的间距和裂缝的宽度都与混凝土保护层的距离（从钢筋中心至混凝土表面）d_c 有关。一般来说，增加保护层就增加了裂缝的间距，也增加了裂缝的宽度。梁中受拉区钢筋的分布是重要的。通常为控制裂缝，最好用大量的小直径钢筋提供所需要的 A_s，而不使用少量的粗钢筋，而且钢筋应均匀地分布在混凝土的受拉区。

第 4 单元

钢筋混凝土的受弯性能

钢筋混凝土梁是非均质梁，它是由两种完全不同的材料构成的。因此，钢筋混凝土梁的分析方法与完全由钢、木或其他结构材料组成的梁的分析方法不同。但所采用的基本原理大致是相同的。概述如下：

任何截面都有内力，可将其分解成法向分量和切向分量。法向分量被称为弯曲应力(在中性轴一侧受拉而另一侧受压)，其作用是抵抗截面上的弯矩。切向分量被称为剪应力，其作用是抵抗横向力或剪力。

关于弯曲和弯剪的基本假设如下：

1. 受荷前为平面的截面，受荷后仍保持平面。即中性轴上方和下方梁中单元的应变与到中性轴的距离成比例。

2. 任一点的弯曲应力 f 取决于该点的应变由材料的应力-应变图给出。如果梁是由均质材料组成的，其拉压应力-应变图如图 4-1a，则下述关系成立。若外纤维处的最大应变小于 ε_p 且在此范围内所给材料的应力与应变成比例，那么中性轴任一侧的压应力和拉应力与到中性轴的距离成比例，如图 4-1b 所示。但如果外纤维处的最大应变大于 ε_p，上述关系不再成立。这种情况如图 4-1c 所示。在梁的外部区域 $\varepsilon>\varepsilon_p$，应力和应变不再成比例。在这些区域，任何截面高度上的应力大小，如图 4-1c 中的 f_2 取决于所给材料应力-应变图在该处的应变 ε_2。也就是说，在梁中，对于一个给定的应变，则该点的应力与材料应力-应变图中相同应变所对应的应力相等。

3. 截面上剪应力的分布依赖于截面的形状和应力—应变图的形状。这些剪应力在中性轴处最大，在外纤维处为零。在任一点，通过水平平面和垂直平面的剪应力相等。

4. 由于剪应力（水平的和垂直的）和弯曲应力的共同作用，梁上任一点都存在斜向拉应力和压应力。最大斜向拉应力和压应力相互垂直。任一点最大的斜应力（或称主应力）的强度为

$$t=\frac{f}{2}\pm\sqrt{\frac{f^2}{4}+v^2} \tag{1}$$

式中 f——法向应力强度；

v——切向剪应力强度。

斜向应力与水平轴的夹角为α，且 $\tan2\alpha=2v/f$

5. 由于水平剪应力和垂直剪应力在中性轴平面上相等，弯曲应力为零。所以在该平面上任一点的斜向拉应力和压应力与水平轴成45°角，其值均与该点的单位剪应力相等。

6. 当外纤维处的应力小于比例极限 f_p 时，梁呈现弹性，如图 4-1b 所示，此时：

①中性轴通过截面的重心

②截面的法向应力强度随离中性轴的距离的增大而增大，在外纤维处达到最大，截面上任何给定点的应力由方程式表示如下：

$$f=\frac{My}{I} \tag{2}$$

式中 f——离中性轴距离为 y 处的弯曲应力；

M——截面的外弯矩；

I——相对于中性轴的截面惯性矩。

最大弯曲应力在最外纤维处，且等于

$$f_{max}=\frac{Mc}{I}=\frac{M}{S} \tag{3}$$

式中　c——中和轴到外纤维的距离；
$S=I/c$——断面的截面模量。

③截面上任一点的剪应力（纵向的等于横向的）v 为

$$v=\frac{VQ}{Ib} \tag{4}$$

式中　V——截面总剪力

Q——通过所求点并与中性轴平行的直线和梁的最近表面（上方或下方）之间的截面部分对中性轴的静矩；

I——对中性轴的截面惯性矩；

b——给定点的梁宽。

④矩形梁截面上的剪力集度沿竖向按抛物线变化，在梁的外纤维处为零，在中性轴处最大，其最大值为$\frac{2}{3}V/b\alpha$，因此，根据公式4，中性轴处$Q=ba^3/8$，$I=ba^3/12$。

第5单元

梁的弯曲分析及设计

结构工程师的主要任务是设计建筑物。所谓设计指确定某一特定建筑物的总体外形及所有的具体尺寸，使之起到应起的作用，并将能在其使用期限中安全地承受所受的影响。这些影响主要是它所承受的荷载和承受的力，以及其他危害因素，如气温变化，基础沉陷，腐蚀影响。结构力学是设计中的主要工具。我们知道，结构力学是使人能准确地预见一给定形状和尺寸的建筑物在承受已知力和其他力的影响时的性能的科学体系。我们真正关心的性能主要有以下几条：（1）建筑物的强度，即引起建筑物失效的给定分布的荷载大小，（2）建筑物在使用荷载作用下的变形，如挠度和裂缝的延伸。钢筋混凝土力学的基本理论如下所述：

1．一个构件的任何截面上的内力，如弯矩、剪力和法向以及剪应力与该截面外荷载效应相平衡。这样说并非假设，而是事实，因为构件中的任何单元体或任何部分只有当作用于其上的所有力是平衡的时候，才能是静止的。

2．一根埋置的钢筋的应变（单位长度的伸长或压缩）与周围的混凝土相同。换句话说，在钢筋和混凝土的界面上存在着完好的粘结力，两种材料之间没有滑移。这样的话，一个变形，另一个也同时变形。除了自然地表面粘结外，现代变形钢筋提供了大得多的咬合力，所以这种假设基本正确。

3．加载以前为平面的构件断面，加载作用之后仍呈平面。精确的测量表明，当一钢筋混凝土构件被加载接近破坏时，这一假设不是绝对正确的。然而这种偏差通常是很小的。基于这一假设所得出的理论结果与大量的实验数据吻合良好。

4．鉴于混凝土的抗拉强度远小于其抗压强度这一事实，构件受拉区的那一部分的混凝土通常会开裂。在设计比较好的构件中，方才提到的这些裂缝都很窄，甚至很难用肉眼看到（他们被称为微裂缝）。这些微裂缝显然使断裂了的混凝土不能承受拉应力。相应地假设混凝土不能抵抗任何拉应力，这种假设显然是实际情况的一种简化，因为事实上开裂前的混凝土和位于裂缝之间的混凝土确实抵抗一小部分拉应力。在稍后的钢筋混凝土梁的抗剪的讨论中，在某些情况下这种假设明显是不能成立的，因为混凝土所具有的适当的抗拉强度是可以利用的。

5. 这一理论实际上基于两种组合材料的应力-应变关系和强度特性，或一些与之相关的合理简化，而不是基于一些理想的材料性能的一些假设。这一点是一个较新的发展。它取代了一种基于假设的分析方法，这种假设即在所有的计算应力范围内，钢筋和混凝土都是弹性的。而非弹性事实上反映了现代理论，假设混凝土不抗拉并考虑两种材料的联合作用，使这种分析方法比由单一的，弹性材料组成的构件的分析方法更复杂，更有吸引力。

只有在一些简单的情况下，上述五种假设才能使人通过计算预测钢筋混凝土构件的性能。实际上钢筋和混凝土这两种材料的联合作用如同它们自身一样是不同的、复杂的，是不能单纯用分析方法处理的。正是因为这个原因，用这些假设所进行的设计和分析方法主要基于大量的和不断的试验研究。这些假设有待于在不断的实验中加以改进和完善。

第 6 单元

长期挠度

长期挠度是由收缩和徐变（主要是后者）引起的。已经指出，混凝土徐变变形与混凝土的压应力成正比。它们随着时间逐渐增加，并且在相同应力下，低强度混凝土比高强度混凝土的徐变变形大。持续荷载引起的长期挠度可以用一个当量的长期模量代替 E_c 来进行计算。在计算 I_{ut} 或 I_{st} 以确定 n 值时，也必须采用这个模量。

在康奈尔大学进行的同样的研究中，大量实验表明，采用下列简化的方法即可估算包括正常的收缩效应在内的长期挠度：(1) 计算由持续荷载引起的瞬时挠度；(2) 将此瞬时挠度乘以系数 λ，得出徐变和正常收缩引起的附加长期挠度，即：

附加长期挠度 $=\lambda\times$ 瞬时挠度

系数 λ 与持续荷载的时间长短有关。也取决于受拉面的受弯构件是否只配有受拉筋 A_s，抑或受压一侧还配有附加的纵向受压筋 A'_s。在后一种情况下，如果配有受压筋，长期挠度就会大大减小，这是因为当没有受压筋时，受压混凝土就不受约束地徐变和收缩。相反，由于钢筋不产生徐变，如果在受压区边缘配有附加受压筋，就会阻碍并从而减少徐变和收缩变形，也就相应地减少了挠度。所以仅考虑这一个原因，就可配置受压钢筋。相应系数值见表 6-1。

《美国混凝土协会规范》根据表 6-1 中所示的实验数据给出了如下的计算长期挠度系数的曲线表达式：

$$\lambda = 2 - 1.2\frac{A'_s}{A_s} \geqslant 0.6 \qquad (a)$$

该式给出的值非常接近于表 6-1 中最后一行的数值。在连续梁的正弯矩区和负弯矩区通常可求得不同的 λ 值，计算时可采用平均值。

较新的研究表明，受压筋含钢率 $\rho'=A'_s/bd$，这一参数较之 A'_s/A_s 能稍为精确地反映出受压筋对徐变和收缩的约束，亦即减小长期挠度的作用。特别是对受拉筋含钢率 A_s/bd 低的构件更是如此。因此建议采用的方程式为：

$$\lambda=\frac{25}{1+50\rho'} \tag{b}$$

但 1977 年的规范继续将（a）式作为估算长期挠度的令人满意的方法使用。

如果梁承受某一持续荷载 P_{sus}（如恒载加桥上的平均交通荷载）和短期高峰荷载 P_{sh}（如一列特殊的重型车辆的重量），在这个短期荷载作用下的最大挠度可按下述步骤计算：

1. 计算由持续荷载 P_{sus} 引起的瞬时挠度 $\delta_{i,sus}$
2. 计算 P_{sus} 引起的附加长期挠度，即 $\delta_{t,sus}=\lambda\delta_{t,sus}$
3. 由荷载持续部分引起的总挠度为 $\delta_{sus}=\delta_{i,sus}+\delta_{t,sus}$
4. 在计算短期荷载 P_{sh} 引起的附加瞬时挠度中，必须注意到开裂后荷载与挠度已不是线性关系了。因此，

$$\delta_{i,sh}=\delta_{i,tot}-\delta_{i,sus}$$

式中　$\delta_{i,tot}$ 为 $P_{sus}+P_{sh}$ 同时作用产生的总的瞬时挠度，计算时采用由 $P_{sus}+P_{sh}$ 引起的弯矩所对应的 I_c。

5. 在短期重荷载和持续荷载作用下的总挠度为

$$\delta_{tot}=\delta_{sus}+\delta_{i,sh}$$

在计算挠度时，必须仔细注意施加荷载的时间顺序和相对大小。为了说明这一点，参照上述的梁，如果短期峰值荷载在随着时间的推移而发生的变形出现之前就作用在梁上，第 3 步的持续荷载作用下的变形 δ_{sus} 就应根据总荷载弯矩图（持续荷载加峰值荷载）采用 I_e 来计算，这是因为在该荷载作用下产生的开裂将会在构件整个使用期间内使构件的刚度减小。如果峰值荷载后来再次应用，第 5 步求出的总挠度 δ_{tot} 就比前者大。

表 6-1　　**附加长期挠度系数 λ**

荷载持续时间	只配 A_s	$A'_s=\frac{A_s}{2}$	$A'_s=A_s$
1 个月	0.6	0.4	0.3
6 个月	1.2	1.0	0.7
1 年	1.4	1.1	0.8
5 年以上	2.0	1.2	0.8

由上述讨论可见，钢筋混凝土结构的挠度大小与许多影响因素有关，不可能进行精确的计算。再说，过高的精度一般也不必要。根据大量的实验数据可以得出的结论是，这里所介绍的方法使计算挠度的精确度大约为±25%，这对大多数设计都可满足要求。更精确但也更复杂的办法可见有关文献。

为了保证挠度符合使用要求，《美国混凝土学会规范》规定了一些按上述方法计算的挠度限值，如表 6-2 所示。在特殊条件下最后两个限值可超过。

表 6-2　　　　　　　　　　最大容许计算挠度

构件类型	挠度类型	挠度极限值
平面屋顶，（未支承或未接触因挠度过大而可能遭到破坏的非结构构件）	由活荷载引起的瞬时挠度 L	1/180
楼板，（未支承或未接触因挠度过大而可能遭到破坏的非结构构件）	由活荷载引起的瞬时挠度 L	1/300
屋顶或楼板结构，（支承或接触因挠度过大而可能遭到破坏的非结构构件）	与非结构构件接触后产生的总挠度中的一部分、所有持续荷载引起的长期挠度之和，以及任何附加活荷载引起的瞬时挠度	1/480
屋顶或楼板结构，（支承或接触不大可能因挠度过大而使其破坏的非结构构件）		1/240

对于不十分重要的构件可以通过限制高跨比来间接控制挠度而不直接进行计算。规范规定，除非进行挠度计算，梁高和单向板厚度不得小于表 6-3 中的规定。采用单位体积重量为 90～120 磅/英尺^3 的轻混凝土构件，表 6-3 中的数值应乘以系数（$1.65～0.005W$）$\geqslant 1.09$，其中 W 为混凝土的单位重量，其单位为磅/英尺^3。对屈服强度不是 60 千磅/英寸^2 的钢筋，表 3 的数值应乘以系数（$0.4+f_y/100,000$），式中 f_y 的单位为磅/英寸^2。

表 6-3　　　　　　　　不计算挠度时梁或单向板的最小厚度

构　　件	最 小 厚 度 h			
	简支	一端连续	两端连续	悬臂
	构件未支承或未接触因挠度过大而可能遭到破坏的隔墙或其他结构			
单向实心板	1/20	1/24	1/28	1/10
梁或单向肋形板	1/16	1/18.5	1/21	1/8

第 7 单元

剪切和斜向拉伸

已经指出，当材料是弹性材料时（应力与应变成正比），除去剪力为零的位置外，在任何截面上既作用着剪应力

$$v=\frac{VQ}{Ib} \tag{1}$$

还有弯曲应力

$$f=\frac{My}{I} \tag{2}$$

根据图 7-1 的分层梁在荷载下的特性，剪应力的作用是显而易见的；这一分层梁由两个沿接触面连在一起的矩形梁组成。如果粘结力相当强，其变形就如同是一根整梁，见图 7-

1a。反之，如粘结力较弱，这两根梁就会分开且相对滑动，如图 7-1*b* 所示。因此，很显然，当粘结效果好时，其中必存在着防止滑动或剪移的力或应力。这些水平剪应力（如图 7-1*c* 所示）分别作用于上部和下部。在整段梁的各个水平面上均发生这样的应力，但这些应力的强度随距中性轴的距离不同而异。

图 7-1*d* 给出矩形整梁的一微分长度单元，其上作用有大小为 V 的剪力。竖直剪应力 v 防止了梁的向上移动，即保持了竖向平衡。剪应力的平均值等于剪力除以横截面面积，即 $v_{av}=V/ab$，但剪应力强度随截面高度而异。用公式 1 很容易计算出，在最外纤维处剪应力为零，在中性轴处为最大值 $1.5v_{av}$，且如图所示，呈抛物线变化。对其他形状横截面可以得到其他值及分布，但剪应力总是在最外纤维处为零，而在中性轴处为最大值。

如果象图 7-2*b* 那样把该梁位于中性轴上的一小块正方单元体分割出来，则根据平衡原理在两个面上的竖直剪应力大小相等，方向相反，作用如图所示。但如果它们是唯一存在的应力，这一单元体不会平衡，它将发生旋转。因此在每两个水平面上存在着大小相同的平衡水平剪应力。即在梁的任一点处，图 7-2*b* 上水平剪应力的大小等于图 7-1*d* 上竖直剪应力的大小。

在以 45°角切下的单元体上，这些剪应力组合起来的效果如图 7-2*c* 所示。这种情况在任何一本材料力学教科书中都可得到证实。即竖直和水平面上两对剪应力的作用与作用在 45°的面上的两对法向应力的作用是相同的。这两对法向应力中的一对为拉应力，另一对为压应力，其数值等于剪应力。假定考虑梁的一个单元体，它既不位于中性轴，也不位于外缘，那么其竖直面不仅要承受剪 应力而且还承受已熟知的弯曲应力，其大小由公式 2 给出（图 7-2*d*）。作用在单元体上的六个应力能再次组合成一对倾斜的压应力和一对倾斜的拉应力，这两对应力的作用方向互成直角。它们被称为主应力（图 7-2*e*）。它们的值由下式给出

$$t=\frac{f}{2}\pm\sqrt{\frac{f^2}{4}+v^2} \tag{3}$$

其倾角 α 由 $\mathrm{tg}2\alpha=2v/f$ 确定。

既然剪应力 v 和弯曲应力 f 的大小不仅沿着梁变化，而且随着它与中性轴的距离也在竖直方向变化，由此产生的主应力 t 的大小及倾角在这一个位置和另一个位置也是不同的。图 7-2*f* 表示承受均布荷载的矩形梁中主应力的走向。即应力轨迹是在任何点上按一定方向画出的一些线，特定的主应力（拉力或压力）沿此方向作用于该点。可以看到在中性轴上梁的主应力总是与中性轴成 45°角，在最外纤维附近，这些主应力在靠近跨中处是水平的。

从上面的讨论得出一个要点。拉应力（由于混凝土抗拉强度较低而需要特别注意）不仅由纯弯引起的水平弯曲应力 f，由于纯剪（中性轴上）或由剪切和弯曲共同作用的结果而产生的不同倾角和大小的拉应力也存在于梁的各个部分，如无足够的措施，此拉应力能削弱梁的整体性。正是由于这种原因，叫做“斜向拉伸”的斜拉应力在钢筋混凝土设计中必须仔细地加以考虑。

第 8 单元

柱支承双向板

当双向板支承在刚度相对较小的扁梁上，或像平板式楼盖及无梁楼盖全部省略柱轴线上的梁时，带来了一些需要考虑解决的新问题。图 8-1（*a*）是楼盖体系的一部分，其中一矩形板支承在四边的扁梁上，梁又在梁轴线的交点处支承在柱上。如果在板上作用面荷载 w，则如前所述，该荷载由假想的短向板条 S 和长向板条 L 分担。注意到由长板条承担的那部分荷载将传递给短梁 B，所以短梁 B 承担的荷载与短向板 S 直接承担的荷载之和等于作用于板上的全部荷载。同理，短向板条 S 将部分荷载传递给长梁 G，该部分荷载与板沿长边方向直接承担的荷载之和亦等于板上的全部荷载。对于柱支承的板，静力学条件显然要求其全部荷载必须在两个方向上由板及其支承梁承担。

图 8-1*b* 所示平板楼盖的情况是类似的，这里省去了梁，但位于柱线上的宽板条起到了与图 8-1*a* 中的梁相同的作用，在这种情况下全部荷载也必须由两个方向分担，在柱子附近图中绘有双向荫影线区采用加厚托板或柱头也不改变这种静力学条件。

图 8-2*a* 表示一块在 A、B、C、D 点由柱子支承的平板楼盖，图 8-2*b* 是沿 l_1 跨度方向的弯矩图，沿该方向，将板看成是宽度为 l_2 的很宽的平板梁，其每英尺长度上相应的荷载为 wl_2。对任意跨度的连续梁，其跨中正弯矩与两端支座处负弯矩的平均值之和，等于相应简支梁的跨中正弯矩。对板而言，这种静力学关系可表示为

$$\frac{1}{2}(M_{ab}+M_{cd})+M_{ef}=\frac{1}{8}wl_2l_1^2 \qquad (a)$$

在相垂直的另一方向上，存在类似关系

$$\frac{1}{2}(M_{ac}+M_{bd})+M_{gh}=\frac{1}{8}wl_1l_2^2 \qquad (b)$$

上述结果并不能表明支座弯矩和跨中弯矩间的大小关系，而经弹性分析可求出静力弯矩分布到各危险截面的值，这需要考虑到相邻板块的相应跨度、荷载分布的形式、柱子的相对刚度及有支承梁时梁和柱的相对刚度。在某些限定条件下也可选择证明是可靠的经验方法求解。

沿危险截面（如 AB 或 EF）的宽度方向，弯矩并非常量，而其分布规律如图 8-2*c*。弯矩的确切分布取决于柱线上是否有梁支承、托板和柱头，以及荷载的集度。为设计方便将每块板划分成图 8-2*c* 所示的柱上板带和中间板带，柱上板带的宽度在柱子轴线两侧各为板宽的四分之一，两柱上板带间的中间板带则为板宽的一半。可以认为在中间板带或柱上板带的宽度范围内，弯矩是常量。当柱线上有梁时则是例外。这时，梁与其相邻的板带必须具有相同的曲率，由于梁的刚度相对较大，与之成正比的梁上弯矩也就较大，弯矩的分布曲线在梁的两侧是不连续的。根据静力学条件，总弯矩与前述相同，所以板的弯矩就相应小些。

ACI 规范第十三章中使用一种统一的方法来处理这样的双向板体系，其条款适用于梁

支承板、无梁楼盖、平板式楼盖，以及双向板肋梁楼盖。尽管在设计中允许使用"满足平衡条件和几何相容条件的任何方法"，但还是特别提到了可供选择的下述两种方法：一种是半经验的直接设计法，另一种是近似的弹性分析方法，即等代框架法。

为了方便设计，这两种方法都将板划分成柱上板带和中间板带。定义柱上板带的宽度沿柱子中线两侧各取为板的尺寸 l_1、l_2 中较小者的四分之一。如果有位于柱线上的梁，该种板带亦将梁包括在内，中间板带则指两条柱上板带之间的部分。在所有情况下，都是将 l_1 定为弯矩分析方向的跨度，l_2 则定为侧向跨度，如不另加注释，跨度都取柱子中线到中线的距离。如果是整体式建筑，梁可能位于板的上方或下方，其尺寸包括梁向两边挑出部分的板长（取大的一边），但不大于四倍板厚。

第 9 单元

钢筋混凝土构件的扭转

为了抵抗扭转，必须采用间距较密的箍筋和纵向钢筋。试验表明，只采用纵向钢筋几乎不能增加抗扭强度，最多也只能增加 15%。这是可以理解的，因为纵向钢筋只能通过销栓作用来提高抗扭强度，如无横向箍筋限制沿钢筋的纵向劈裂，这种销栓作用就非常微弱，也不可靠。

当构件如图 9-1*a* 所示进行了充分配筋时，其混凝土在扭矩等于或稍大于未配筋构件的抗扭强度时开裂。裂缝呈螺旋形。实际上有很多条这样的螺旋形裂缝，相距很近。混凝土一旦开裂，其抗扭力比未开裂构件大约降低一半，剩余部分由钢筋承受。这种内力的重新分布在扭矩-扭转角曲线（图 9-2）中是有反映的：该曲线在开裂时显示出扭矩值保持不变而持续产生扭转，直到钢筋承担了混凝土不再承受的那一部分扭矩为止。进一步增加的任何一点扭矩都必须由钢筋来承担。当构件某处的混凝土沿一条直线（如图 9-1 中的 a-b）被压碎时，构件即告破坏。如果构件设计合理，这种压碎破坏只在箍筋开始屈服以后发生。

通过作用在可能的破坏面上的内力平衡，可分析求出构件的抗扭强度；图 9-1 中的阴影即为可能的破坏面。这一破坏面的边界线，一条是成 45°穿过宽面的拉裂缝，两条是横穿窄面倾角为 ϕ 的裂缝（这一倾角常介于 45°和 90°之间），还有一条是沿 a-d 线的混凝土压碎区。这一破坏与素混凝土类似，基本上是弯曲破坏，混凝土的受压区在 a-d 线附近。

图 9-3 为部分开裂破坏面，包括混凝土受压区（阴影部分）和除了位于受压区内的那些箍筋以外的全部与破坏面相交的箍筋水平肢和竖直肢的拉力 S_h 和 S_v。上面或下面与破坏面相交的箍筋水平肢数量从图上可见 $n_h=(x_1\cot\phi)/S$，而受压区对面的箍筋竖直肢数量为 $n_v=y_1/S$。试验表明，破坏时箍筋竖直肢屈服，而水平肢通常未见屈服。水平箍筋力所产生的扭转力偶相应为

$$T_h = n_h S_h y_1 = \frac{x_1\cot\phi}{S}A_l f_{sh} y_1$$

$$= k_h \frac{x_1 y_1}{S}A_l f_y \qquad (a)$$

式中　A_l——一肢箍筋面积；

f_{sh}——箍筋水平肢的拉应力；

f_y——屈服点；

k_h——$\cot\phi$（f_{sh}/f_y）。

要分析靠近前面的箍筋竖直肢的拉力所产生的扭矩，必须首先注意到在受压区内靠近背面的平衡力尚属未定。至少，这些力包括混凝土的剪力 S_c 和压力 P_c 和该区域内箍筋肢的力。但是根据平衡条件，有一点是清楚的，即所有这些力必须有一个合力 R，与箍筋竖直部分的拉力总和 S_v 大小相等、方向相反。因此，由竖直箍筋力产生的扭矩可表达如下式

$$T_v = n_v S_v x_v = \frac{y_1}{S} A_l f_y K_v x_1 = k_v \frac{x_1 y_1}{S} A_l f_y \tag{b}$$

式中　x_v 为内力 S_v 和 R 的力臂，$k_v = x_v / x_1$。

我们可以看到方程（a）和（b）除了 k_h 和 k_v 之外其余都相同。目前由于所知有限，不能用分析方法来确定其中的任何一个量，只有借助于大量的试验。如令 $\alpha_t = k_h + k_v$，则箍筋提供的总扭矩 $T_s = T_v + T_h$ 为

$$T_s = \alpha_t \frac{x_1 y_1}{S} A_l f_y \tag{1}$$

试验表明，α_t 主要取决于横截面尺寸的比例，可取为

$$\alpha_t = 0.66 + 0.33 \frac{y_1}{x_1} \leqslant 1.50 \tag{2}$$

前面已提到，开裂后混凝土受压区提供的扭矩 T_0 大约等于开裂扭矩 T_{cr} 的一半。保守地取为 40%，可得

$$T_0 = 2.4 \sqrt{f'_c} \frac{x^2 y}{3} = 0.8 \sqrt{f'_c} x^2 y \tag{3}$$

于是总的标称抗扭强度为 $T_n = T_0 + T_s$，或

$$T_n = 0.8 \sqrt{f'_c} x^2 y + \alpha_t A_l \frac{x_1 y_1}{S} f_y \tag{4}$$

根据 T_n 的推导，可以明显看出，只有箍筋排列密度足以使任一破坏截面都有足够数量的箍筋与之相交时，这个标准抗扭强度才能得到实现。为此必须规定箍筋最大间距的限值。

第 10 单元

在复合应力作用下的（混凝土）强度

在许多结构中，混凝土同时受到不同方向各种应力的作用。例如在梁中大部分混凝土同时承受压力和剪应力，在楼板和基础中，混凝土同时承受两个相互垂直方向的压力外加剪力的作用。根据材料力学学习中已知的方法，无论怎样复杂的复合应力状态，都可化为三个相互垂直的主应力，它们作用在材料适当定向的单元立方体上。三个主应力中的任意一个或者全部既可是拉应力，也可是压应力。如果其中一个主应力为零，则为双轴应力状

态。如果有两个主应力为零，则为单轴应力状态，或为简单压缩或为简单拉伸。在多数情况下，根据简单的试验，如圆柱体强度 f'_c 和抗拉强度 f'_t，只能够确定材料在单轴应力作用下的性能。为了预测混凝土在双轴应力或三轴应力作用下的结构强度，在通过试验仅仅知道 f'_c 或 f'_c 与 f'_t 的情况下，需要通过计算确定混凝土在上述复合应力状态下的强度。

尽管人们连续不断地进行了大量的研究，但仍然没有得出有关混凝土在复合应力作用下的强度的通用理论。经过修正的各种强度理论，如最大拉应力理论、莫尔-库仑理论和八面体应力理论（以上理论都在材料力学课本中讨论过）应用于混凝土，取得了不同程度的进展。现在的试验结果表明，极限拉应变（它是平均正应力的函数）可能是一个通用的混凝土破坏标准。目前这些理论中没有一个被普遍接受，其中许多还有明显的自相矛盾的地方。建立一个通用的强度理论的主要困难在于混凝土的高度非均质特性和混凝土在高应力下和断裂时，其性能受微小裂缝和其他不连续现象的影响程度较大。

然而，至少对双轴应力的各种试验确定了混凝土的强度。各种试验结果可用图 10-1 这样的相互作用图的形式表现出来。该图把朝方向 1 的强度表示为作用在方向 2 的应力的函数。所有的应力都根据单轴抗压强度 f'_c 而无量纲化了。在表示双轴压力的象限中可以看出，其强度可达到比单轴抗压强度大 20%左右，强度增加的量取决于 f_2 和 f_1 的比值。在双轴受拉情况下，方向 1 的强度与方向 2 的拉应力无关。当方向 2 的拉应力与方向 1 的压应力同时作用时，抗压强度几乎呈线性下降。例如，大约是单轴抗拉强度的一半的横向拉应力，将使抗压强度减小到单轴抗压强度的一半。这一点在预测深梁或剪力墙内裂缝的出现方面具有非常重要的意义。

混凝土三轴强度的实验研究很少，主要是因为在三个方向同时加荷实际上难以避免由加荷设备产生的很大约束。根据现有资料，关于混凝土三轴强度可得出以下初步结论：(1) 在三轴压应力相等状态下，混凝土的强度可能比单轴抗压强度高一个数量级，(2) 对于双轴压应力相等并在第三个方向上有一较小的压应力的状态，其强度可指望增加 20%以上，(3) 在压应力与至少另外一个方向的拉应力同时作用的应力状态下，中间主应力是无足轻重的，抗压强度可以根据图 10-1 可靠地预计出来。

莫尔-库仑理论可用来近似地描述三轴应力对强度的影响。它代表莫尔理论的特殊形式，规定材料破坏的包络线，使任何一个与包络线相切的莫尔应力圆都代表引起材料破坏的复合应力。对于此处的莫尔应力圆，水平直径的两个端点由三个主应力中的最大和最小主应力所决定，因此应力圆的大小和位置不受中间主应力的影响。图 10-2 中的应力圆 1 表示应力为 f'_t 时简单拉伸引起的破坏，而应力圆 2 表示应力为 f'_c 时的压力破坏。破坏的包络线可以近似地用两条直线表示，如图。试验研究表明，在受压一侧与应力圆 2 相切的直线具有 37°的倾角。在受拉一侧，直线是一截线，与应力圆 1 相切。

第 11 单元

板的屈服线理论

在现行美国混凝土规范中，钢筋混凝土的设计方法是以结构整体的弹性分析结果为基础的，采用的是乘以扩大系数后的荷载，例如取为 $1.4D+1.7L$，其中 D、L 分别指使用恒载和使用活载。实际上，在静不定结构中当某一点或多个点达到抗弯承载力后，弹性曲线在这些对应点处就不再连续，弹性分析的结果就不再成立。如果有足够延性，就会发生弯矩的重分布，直到形成足够多的不连续点，通常称为“塑性铰”，使结构变成机构而破坏。与“弹性分析”对应的术语“极限荷载分析”就是利用即将破坏时的弯矩图作为设计的基础。除了对连续受弯构件在支承处的弯矩重分布作出规定外，现代美国混凝土规范并不允许采用极限荷载分析法。

本章的主要目的是阐述双向板的屈服线理论，虽然美国混凝土规范中尚未采用屈服线理论，但可利用该理论在板的分析中提供所需的资料，这些资料可用于研究各种边界条件下规则或不规则形状板的性能。

对板在极限荷载作用下的弯曲性能的研究可以追溯到本世纪 20 年代，是 K. W. JOHANSEN 将用于板极限荷载设计的屈服线理论的基本概念推进了一大步。在该理论中，假设板的强度仅由弯曲控制，其他诸如剪力和挠度的影响则予以分开考虑，并假定板破坏时沿屈服线上的钢筋完全屈服，且弯矩和扭矩亦沿屈服线均匀分布。

单向板屈服线理论与连续梁的极限分析法并无多大区别，在连续梁中，当梁上某点达到其弯曲强度，例如支座负弯矩区段上的一点，并不一定使梁达到其极限承载力。如果达到弯曲强度的梁截面能够维持抗力不变而继续转动，则其他点也可能达到弯曲强度。从理论上讲，当几个截面屈服（在单向板中亦即沿几条直线屈服）使结构形成非稳定平衡机构后，结构才发生完全破坏。

以图 11-1 所示具有一定宽度的单向板为例，作用于其上的均布荷载沿 AB、EF 产生均布的最大负弯矩，沿 CD 产生均布的正弯矩，CD 与支承边平行。当均布荷载增加到沿 AB、CD 和 EF 的弯矩达到各自的极限值时，各板块将以屈服线为轴线发生转动。一旦达到极限弯矩，抵抗弯矩不再增大而各板块间的夹角仍会发生变化。因此，在这种弯矩不变而板块能够转动的极限状态下，板变成了几何不稳定的体系，该状态称之为“破坏机构”。

对于双向板，因为屈服线一般并不相互平行而是形成屈服线图案，所以屈服线理论需要采取与连续梁的极限分析不同的处理方法。将整个板面划分成几个板块，当处于破坏或不稳定平衡状态时，这些板块能够绕屈服线作刚体转动。

图 11-2*a* 所示是一块支承边非平行的板，破坏时该板将碎成两部分，其中的一块将绕板边Ⅰ转动，而另一块将绕板边Ⅱ转动，正弯矩屈服线则必与直线Ⅰ和直线Ⅱ的交点 O 相交。屈服线Ⅲ的确切位置将依正、负弯矩区域的配筋量和配筋方向而定。

图 11-2*b* 所示是一矩形板，其四支承边简支或连续，破坏机构由四个板块组成。A、B

两点的确切位置则将依支承边的抗弯承载力和两个方向上正弯矩区的配筋而定。

图 11-2c 所示板支承在两边及另外两根独立的柱子上，破坏时板块的转轴一定沿支承边形成（线Ⅰ和线Ⅱ），其余转轴则一定通过独立的柱子。正弯矩屈服线 a、b、c、d 和 e 的危险位置则与配筋量和配筋方向有关，同时，板块作刚体转动时，沿屈服线必须满足变形协调条件。

第 12 单元

预应力混凝土

采用高强材料和逐渐改进设计方法，使现代结构工程向更经济的结构形式发展，构件的截面尺寸减小、重量减轻。在钢筋混凝土结构中，恒荷载在总设计荷载中占据相当大的比例，这种发展趋势就 显得尤为重要。同样，在多层建筑中，构件截面高度减小，并逐层累积，会大大降低结构的总高度，减小作用在基础上的荷载，减少供热、供电和排水管线的长度以及减少墙和间壁的面积。

采用高强混凝土和高强钢筋，并结合能准确预测构件强度的先进设计方法，可取得显著的节省效果。但是，主要由于在使用荷载作用下与开裂和挠度有关的问题，这种发展受到了限制。由于裂缝（裂缝宽度和数量）与钢筋的应变（亦即钢筋的应力）成正比，因而限制了有效地利用高强钢筋。尽管在混凝土结构中通常允许适度开裂，但却不希望发生过宽的裂缝，因为这会暴露钢筋使之锈蚀，并在感观上使人难以接受，还会导致因斜向受拉而过早破坏。挠度问题也会进一步限制高强材料的应用，采用精确的分析方法时更是如此。这样得到的细长构件，可能产生不符合功能要求和视觉要求的挠度。开裂降低了构件的弯曲刚度，这会进一步使挠度增大。

预应力混凝土的发展大大克服了普通钢筋混凝土的这些不足。可将预应力混凝土构件这样定义，在构件中存在着预加的内部应力，其大小和分布能将给定的外部荷载产生的应力抵消到所要求的水平。混凝土基本上是一种抗压材料，其抗拉强度低且不稳定。施加预应力先使构件受压，会降低或消除否则可能存在的不利的拉应力，把使用荷载作用下的裂缝减至最小甚至完全消除，也可以将挠度限制在要求的范围内。事实上，在使用荷载和预应力的联合作用下，可以将构件的挠度设计为零。通过施加预应力实现的对裂缝和挠度的控制，使得工程师能够利用高效、经济的，像钢绞线、钢丝或钢筋之类的高强度钢材，以及较普通混凝土强度高得多的高强混凝土。因而，施加预应力从整体上改善了用于常规跨度和荷载下的结构混凝土的性能，并扩展了混凝土的应用范围，使之远远超过了旧有的限制。这不仅使结构的跨度远远超出了原先的想象，而且允许人们采用新型的结构形式。

施加预应力最初似乎是由美国的P·H·杰克逊，G·R·斯坦纳，奥地利的J·曼德尔和德国的J·凯尼恩于 1886 至 1908 年间提出的。高强钢筋的应用最初是由奥地利的F·恩珀杰于 1923 提出的，大约与此同时，美国的R·H·迪尔提出了施加全预应力以彻底消除裂缝。这些提议当时只停留在纸面上。预应力钢筋混凝土结构的应用主要是由于E. 弗雷辛内特和Y·盖扬（法国），E·霍耶（德国）及G·马格尼尔（比利时）等人得以实际发展。由W·H·休伊特在1923年首创了圆柱形罐，管子的环向预应力，是预应力原理在美国第一次重要的应用。1950年以来T·Y·林在美国多种类型的预应力混凝土结构的设计中做出了重大的贡献。

有趣的是，把欧洲预应力混凝土的发展与美国预应力混凝土的发展作一对照，在欧洲，材料与劳力价值的高比率是普遍的，而在美国却相反。在欧洲，许多先进的设计是使所用材料减至最少，但却要求大量的合格劳力来施工，施加预应力。这样便有了大跨桥梁、平面楼盖体系、壳、甚至空间桁架。在美国是朝着小型预制构件的方向发展，极适合于批量生产。在美国过去的20多年里，几种标准化的预制件占据了预应力混凝土建筑的大部分。这种差异与过去相比不太明显。欧洲工业现在使用美国的完善技术，生产标准化的预制建筑构件、多用电杆、铁路轨枕及其他制品。而这里的工程师在设计主跨特种构件中却使用欧洲经验。

第13单元

组合作用的基础及抗剪连接

寻求组合梁的满意设计方法是一个缓慢的过程。它需要许多理论和试验工作。以此来提供既经济又安全的设计准则。这一章的主要目的是详细介绍一些在组合结构设计中必须考虑的重要基本概念。

过去，组合截面的分析最先用的是基于弹性理论的传统假设。该理论把材料的应力限制在它们的破损应力（钢材即为其屈服点，混凝土即为其压碎应力的某个比例）的一部分。这种在弹性理论中固有的假设和普通钢筋混凝土中的假设十分相似。近年来，极限荷载设计理论已被应用到组合结构中，大量的试验证明，对于匀称的组合截面而言，此方法是安全、经济的。虽然目前极限荷载设计理论仅仅直接用于建筑结构，而还未用于桥梁中，但不容怀疑，这种限制总有一天会消失的。

在详细叙述这两种设计方法（弹性方法和极限荷载方法）之前需先介绍一些基本概念。

清楚地了解组合梁中各部件：钢梁、混凝土板及剪力连接键对外荷载作用的反应是透彻分析组合截面的基础。其中最重要的是应力-应变关系曲线。而该曲线必须是精心试验的结果。这些试验结果并不能直接应用。在实际工作中，必须采用简化和理想化的曲线。因此应用计算机就有可能减少这些所要的假定。由于计算机“实验”可应用复杂得多的材料应力-应变关系。

钢与混凝土间的组合作用是指在两种材料间传递剪力的相互作用。在普通钢筋混凝土构件中虽然有时确有需要附加锚固的情况，但混凝土与钢筋间的天然粘结力足以起到这种作用。完全埋置在混凝土内的现浇肋梁有着较大的锚固面积，这足能传递剪力，然而，这完全不同于普通组合梁。在组合梁中，混凝土板置于钢梁上翼缘之上或将钢梁的上翼缘完全包裹在混凝土板内。最初在钢梁和混凝土板接触面上确有粘结和摩擦力来传递一些剪力。

但上面的混凝土板有和钢梁上下分离的趋势，这样就不能传递水平剪力。超载或振动荷载引起的疲劳作用将破坏混凝土板与钢梁间的天然粘结力。这种粘结力一旦遭到破坏就不可恢复。这种不确定的抗剪连接效果显然不符合要求；所以就需要有意在混凝土板和钢梁间设一些连接键以传递水平剪力和避免二者分离。在抗剪连接中存在着天然粘结力，但不能依靠它，而且在任何情况下都要计算它的数值也是不可能的。这样就必须设置剪力连接键传递所有的水平剪力。

这里应指出一种矛盾现象：若设置了剪力连接键，天然粘结力会承担全部的剪力而使设置的剪力连接键不起作用，所以，如果提供足够的剪力连接键，又是不必要的。

抗剪连接键的研究发展比较缓慢，它需广泛地对大量机械式连接键进行静力和疲劳试验。

早期的研究者很快就清楚地发现：有必要把某种连接键一端固定于钢梁的上翼缘之上，另一端锚入混凝土板中。1929 年 Caughey 和 Scott 在众多的连接键形式中，提出用栓钉连接键。从此，各种机械式的抗剪连接键得到广泛应用。从某种程度上说，连接键形式的多样化是由于钢结构制造商想使用容易找到的部件，因为在研究初期还没有专用抗剪这一目的而特制的剪力连接键。

在任何一种机械式连接体系中，它可以使传递水平剪力和避免使板与梁分开这两个作用统一在一起。一般说来，水平抗剪作用是衡量抗剪连接键的标准。据此，机械式剪力连接键可以分为三大类，即刚性的，柔性的和粘结式的。

第 14 单元

粘结和锚固

钢筋极少直接承受外荷载的作用，而只能分担其周围混凝土的荷载。钢筋与混凝土内表面间的剪应力称为“粘结应力”，它通过在钢筋和其周围混凝土之间传递荷载来改变钢筋应力。有效地发挥这种粘结力可使这两种材料形成一组合结构。达到令人满意的粘结力是结构构件配筋详图设计的最重要的目的。

粘结力是通过钢筋上力的变化率来度量的。除非任意两截面间钢筋应力发生变化，否则粘结应力将不存在。粘结应力 u，习惯上被定义为钢筋表面单位面积上的剪力，由下式给出：

$$u=\frac{q}{\Sigma o}=\frac{\Delta f_{s}A_{b}}{\Sigma o}=\frac{d_{b}}{4}\Delta f_{s}$$

式中 q——单位长度内钢筋力的变化；

Σo——单位长度内钢筋的标准表面积；

d_{b}——钢筋的标准直径；

Δf_{s}——单位长度内钢筋应力的变化；

A_{b}——钢筋面积。

当使用普通钢筋时，粘结力是一个比较重要的问题。表面变形的钢筋具有更好的粘结力和安全性。另一方面，变形钢筋的性能，尤其是高强度钢筋和大直径钢筋的使用提出了一些新问题。这使得有必要重新检查人们通常对粘结力的见解。

因为现有规范中的要求完全是经验性的，本章将不讨论大量设计规则的背景。然而，设计师必须了解对结构性能起决定性作用的粘结和锚固的情况。因此，我们将较深入地探讨这些问题，以便使设计者能有效地绘制配筋详图。

有关粘结的几个需要阐明的问题已在 ACI 408 委员会发表。该报告包括一个很好的参考书目。

钢筋混凝土构件的粘结力来自于两种截然不同的情况：钢筋的锚固和由于沿构件弯矩的变化而产生的沿长度的钢筋力的变化。

钢筋必须从要求钢筋发挥出给定力的截面外延伸出 l_d 的距离，所要求的这一距离 l_d 是为了通过粘结把钢筋的力传给混凝土。如果假定平均粘结应力 u 均匀地分布在这一长度上，那么由平衡条件得下式：

$$T = A_b f_s = u \Sigma o l_d$$

因此延伸长度变成

$$l_d = \frac{d_b}{4u} f_s$$

一些规范规定了锚固粘结应力 u 的安全值，允许按上式来计算延伸长度。ACI 规范规定了各种设计情况的最小延伸长度 l_d。

在前面讲述了任一梁的剪跨区内沿抗弯钢筋产生的粘结力 ΔT。如果假定在彼此靠近的任意两个截面间粘结应力 u 均匀分布，则钢筋在很短长度内平衡要求 $\Delta t = u \Sigma o \Delta x$。然而，如果是理想的梁作用，梁内部拉力 T 必须与外弯矩 M 以同一比例变化。即：

$$\Delta T = \frac{\Delta M}{jd} = \frac{V}{jd} \Delta x$$

因此

$$u = \frac{V}{jd \Sigma o}$$

这一公式表明，当外弯矩的变化率（即剪力）高的时候，弯曲粘结应力也高。然而，此式大大地简化了这种情况，甚至没有粗略地推算实际粘结应力的大小。这是因为在构件方向混凝土中裂缝是间隔一定距离出现的，由于拉力被裂缝间混凝土分担而产生附加粘结应力。甚至当剪力为零时（弯矩为定值区域）也将产生粘结力。然而，可以看出，对钢筋提供足够的锚固长度就可以不发生由于弯曲粘结应力引起的破坏。从弯曲粘结的角度要求检查构件在弯矩为零（在简支点和反弯点）区段的锚固长度。在这些区段，受拉钢筋面积可能小，而剪力大，从而导致高的弯曲粘结应力。

第 15 单元

砌体结构的极限状态设计法

结构设计的基本目的是保证其在使用期间不发生过大的变形、开裂或倒塌，完成预定的功能要求，当然还要适当考虑其经济性。设计者在其工作中可借助于靠积累的经验和科研成果形成的现行规范。到目前为止，这些规范通过规定各种材料及其组合体的允许应力来摸索保证砌体结构的安全性和适用性。因而，规范一般给出砖和砂浆组合范围内的基本抗压应力，在特定情况下基本应力再根据砌体的长细比和荷载的偏心程度予以调整。基本应力根据墙体或墙垛的试验求得，而极限应力则由足以避免在使用荷载作用下发生开裂的适当的安全系数求得。因此，从这种意义上讲，砌体结构设计总是与极限强度和正常使用极限状态联系在一起的。

近年来，通过考虑相应的“极限状态”，即结构或其一部分达到一种不能完成其功能的状态或结构不再满足设计规定条件的状态，形成了一种解决结构安全性和适用性的更合理的设计方法。通常要考虑两类极限状态，即结构将发生破坏或倒塌的承载力极限状态，及结构将产生过大变形或裂缝的正常使用极限状态。

国际标准化组织出版的规范中对结构的极限状态设计方法作了概述，就是用设计荷载效应（S^*）和设计强度（R^*）给出了满足设计准则的表达式，即

$$R^* \geqslant S^* \tag{1}$$

设计荷载效应根据作用的特点由下式给出

$$S^* = \gamma_f Q_k \text{ 的效应} \tag{2}$$

其中 γ_f 为扩大系数（或分项安全系数），按统计学术语 Q_k 为特征荷载，由下式确定

$$Q_k = Q_m(1 + k\delta)$$

式中 Q_m——是在结构使用期内具有 50%失效概率的最不利荷载值；

δ——是最大荷载分布的标准差；

k——为最大荷载大于 Q_k 的概率系数。

在结构的使用期间，特征荷载的取值通常具有 5%的失效概率，但在多种情况下，由于统计资料不足，在实用规范或其他规程中，只给出其名义值。γ_f 是一系列分项系数的函数。

γ_{f1} 考虑了特征荷载可能不利的离散分布，亦即允许存在荷载变异或不可预见的荷载作用；

γ_{f2} 考虑了各种荷载同时达到其特征值在概率上可能性的降低；

γ_{f3} 考虑了由于设计假设不正确（例如采用简化的支承条件、铰、忽略温差等其他难以估计的因素）和截面尺寸、柱子倾斜及偶然偏心等施工误差，用以对荷载效应进行可能的修正。

与此类似，材料的设计强度 R^* 定义为

$$R^* = \frac{R_k}{\gamma_m} \quad (3)$$

式中　R_k——$R_m - ks$　是材料的特征强度；

R_m——为材料强度试验结果的算术平均值；

S——为标准差；

k——为试验结果低于 R_k 的概率系数。

材料的特征强度通常根据相应的试验结果取为具有95％保证率的值。材料强度的降低系数 γ_m 是以下两个系数的函数。

γ_{m1}　用以考虑结构中的材料与试件相比可能的强度降低；

γ_{m2}　用以考虑除由系数 γ_{m1} 决定的材料强度的降低外，包括制造误差在内的其他因素可能对结构的削弱。

另外，ISO2394还允许采用另一个系数 γ_c，它可用以调整荷载或材料强度的设计值。该系数也是以下两分项系数的函数。

γ_{c1}　用以考虑结构的特征和性能，例如结构或结构的一部分在没有预兆时可能全部或部分倒塌，这种情况下不可能发生内力重分布，或者说单个构件破坏将导致整个结构倒塌；

γ_{c2}　用以从其他方面考虑结构达到极限状态后的严重程度，例如经济后果，对社会的危险性等。

通常将 γ_c 计入 γ_f 或 γ_m 中，因此它并不在设计计算中直接出现。

极限状态设计法的优点是允许对结构的安全性和适用性作出更合理和灵活的估计，对各种有关的系数作了统一化处理，在一定程度上可用数值表示。理想情况是荷载和强度应该由数理统计方法给出，但实际上这几乎是不可能的，因此其特征值只得根据一些手头资料确定。对荷载而言，这些资料通常来源于对使用中的建筑物进行观测；但对材料的特征强度而言，是根据试验结果得出的，试验结果有时会成为特征强度数理统计的依据。在缺乏这样的统计资料时，特征强度只得依赖于经实践验证的名义值。

第16单元

土力学

土力学是论述应力下土的一门工程力学。直到在本世纪20年代，Terzaghi为其制定了原理之后才使它成为了一门学科。今天许多的运算还基于这些原理。他的有效应力原理表明，垂直于土某截面的应力等于土颗粒间传递应力（即有效应力）与通过土所含水分传递的消压应力（即孔隙应力）之和。

Terzaghi的另一重要概念是有关作用在挡土墙、舱壁和支撑壁上的土的抗剪力。这个侧面上的压力随挡土墙的高度按线性增大，随支撑壁的高度按抛物线增大。他的这些结论解决了许多实践与旧理论间的不符之处。

粒径大小是土力学的基础，因为正是这一点决定了土是内摩阻力大的还是有粘聚性的，是砂土还是粘土。从最大的粒径开始，漂石大于10cm，卵石5～10cm，砾石或石碴5mm～5cm，石屑大约2～5mm，砂0.06～2mm。这些土内摩阻力都大；因为粒粗，所以没有粘聚性。它们的稳定性取决于其内摩阻力。对于粘聚性的或内摩阻力小的土，国际上采用的两个主要粒径极限是：粉土0.002～0.02mm，比这更细的便是粘土。当然也有多种砂质粘土和粘质砂土。

每一项大型的土木工程施工在初期阶段都从地基勘察开始。通过第一次踏勘，将会查明场地是否适宜建筑，换句话说，是否值得投资把取土样的设备送到那里去。取出的土样和三轴试验、剪力试验等实验结果将表明，土在什么深度有可能具备足够的强度以承受必要的荷载。对于砖石结构和钢结构，地基勘察就此可以结束，所需费用通常不超过结构费用的2％。

一般说来，土的强度都随其深度而增加。但是强度随深度而减小的情况也可能发生。因此在选择基础压力和这类土的层位时，土力学的知识就很重要，因为这将使人们对可能发生的沉降有所了解。

但是，除了荷载所造成的固结之外，还有一些其他沉降的原因。这些原因是难以预测的，所以必须仔细防范。这包括冻结作用、土的化学变化、流水的地下侵蚀作用、地下水位的降低、附近的隧道施工或车辆等会产生的振动的机械。

静荷载可能引起弹性（暂时的）或塑性（永久的）沉降，固结沉降是永久性的。但是，当英文里提到塑流时，它一般指的是剪切超载引起的土体破坏。固结沉降主要发生在粘土或粉土中。

单纯由动荷载引起的最常见的沉降发生在砂或砾石中，由来往车辆或其他振动、打桩或地层震动所引起。地下水位下降常会引起土的收缩，而水位上升则引起土的膨胀。地下水由于排水而下降，排水可能是深挖土造成的。墨西哥城下面的粘土（一种火山灰）清楚地表明了由于干燥产生的土体收缩。经过七周的干燥之后，这种粘土收缩到原体积的6.4％。这是一种不寻常的粘土，具有特别高的孔隙比：93.6/6.4＝14.6。

地下侵蚀是指由于地下水的流动使固体物质（通常是细粒）从土中流失。固体物质可能作为固体或溶液流失，不过只有少数几种岩石的溶解度大到足以成为溶液而流失。岩盐是可溶岩的最常见的例子。钾盐也是可溶岩。

土的渗透性对于计算地下潜流很重要，例如计算石油或水流入井中，或者计算水流入打基础所挖的基坑，或计算水流过土坝等。在用锹能挖掘的疏松土中，粘土渗透性最小，粉土稍大，砂再大一些，砾石则更大。换言之，渗透性和土的粒径大小成正比。

当用泵抽井水时，水从四面八方向井流来，井周围的地下水位（潜水位）就下降。离井的距离越远，潜水位的下降越少，以致潜水面在井周围形成漏斗状，不过它通常被称为下降锥。

Appendix Ⅲ   Key to the Exercises

UNIT ONE

Reading Comprehension

Ⅰ 1.C 2.A 3.A 4.D 5.A

Ⅱ 略

Vocabulary

Ⅰ 1.D 2.A 3.A 4.D 5.C

Ⅱ 1.c 2.e 3.a 4.f 5.d

Translation

1. 如不添煤，炉子就会熄灭。
2. 他在这场战斗中消灭了五个敌人。
3. 这地区的路面还有一半没有修好。
4. 她尽力为她丈夫被控抢劫申冤。
5. 扮演“奥赛罗”这个角色，劳伦斯·奥利维花了一个多小时化妆。

UNIT TWO

Reading Comprehension

Ⅰ.1.D 2.B 3.C 4.A 5.C

Ⅱ.略

Vocabulary

Ⅰ.1.B 2.C 3.A 4.D 5.C

Ⅱ.1.g 2.h 3.a 4.f 5.c

Translation

1. 写这样一封生气的信简直是毫无道理。
2. 去 Fatty 餐厅就餐，七年中已成为了他生活中惯常的事情。
3. 那个箱子又大又笨重，装的都是书，不过他随身带的箱子却是另一回事。
4. 此方法的发明者所表现的远大眼光和广阔知识，给人以十分良好的印象。
5. 机器的发明使世界进入了一个新纪元，即工业时代，金钱成了主宰一切的权威。

UNIT THREE

Reading Comprehension

Ⅰ. 1. B　2. D　3. C　4. A　5. C

Ⅱ. 略

Vocabulary

Ⅰ. 1. B　2. C　3. A　4. C　5. D

Ⅱ. 1. e　2. f　3. h　4. a　5. b

Translation

1. 所有磁铁，不论大小，其性质都一样。（增补连词“不论”，表示让步状语）
2. 人们认为镭的射线可以用来治疗各种疾病。（原文中 it 为形式主语，译文增补人称主语“人们”）
3. 第一批电子计算机于 1946 年开始使用。（添加“批”字表示多台计算机）
4. 气压低，沸点就低。（联系动词 get 和 become 省略）
5. 重力是向下的力，〔所以〕任何物体都会向下运动。（and therefore 省略）

UNIT FOUR

Reading Comprehension

Ⅰ. 1. D　2. D　3. A　4. D　5. C

Ⅱ. 略

Vocabulary

Ⅰ. 1. D　2. A　3. B　4. A　5. C

Ⅱ. 1. f　2. e　3. a　4. b　5. h

Translation

1. 不是许多东西在刚发现时就是有用的。
2. 这两台仪器不都是精密的。（一台精密，一台不精密）
3. 十年前关于电子计算机还知道得不多。（释译这类否定句时须要特别注意的是，一定要搞清否定的对象。一般说来，使用上列否定词时，那是对全句的否定，而不是仅只否定动词或其他句子成分。）
4. 所有的答案都不对。
5. （=Not all these metals are good conductors。）这些金属并不都是良导体。

UNIT FIVE

Reading Comprehension

Ⅰ. 1. C　2. A　3. B　4. C　5. A

Ⅱ. 略

Vocabulary

Ⅰ.1.B 2.C 3.D 4.A 5.D

Ⅱ.1.g 2.h 3.f 4.d 5.a

Translation

1. 电子和原子的行为，多少有点象一组波。（动→名）
2. 他们十分熟悉这类晶体管放大器的性能。（形→动）
3. 激光是近年来最轰动的科学成就之一，因为它可以应用于许多科学领域，也适合各种实际用途。（名→动）
4. 中国丰富石油资源的发现也是和石油工人的努力"争气"分不开的。（名→副）
5. 这里的发电厂供给全市的电力。（副→形）

UNIT SIX

Reading Comprehension

Ⅰ.1.B 2.C 3.A 4.D 5.D

Ⅱ. 略

Vocabulary

Ⅰ.1.B 2.A 3.C 4.D 5.C

Ⅱ.1.g 2.e 3.c 4.f 5.a

Translation

1. 关于这个问题的争论已在工程界持续了许多年。（定→状）
2. 这些反应器的内径为140mm。（定→主）
3. 转子的结构设计得很好。（表→主）
4. 在我们所能看到的任何物体中，分子的数目都是大得难以想像的。（状→补语）

UNIT SEVEN

Reading Comprehension

Ⅰ.1.C 2.A 3.D 4.B 5.A

Ⅱ. 略

Vocabulary

Ⅰ1.D 2.C 3.B 4.A 5.C

Ⅱ1.c 2.d 3.e 4.f 5.g

Translation

1. 他们把沙发收拾一下，让这位不速之客睡觉。

2. 我们不得不加快车速，以弥补在波士顿所耽误的时间。
3. 把原料加工成成品的最简便方法是精密铸造。
4. 太阳给我们带来了温暖和光明。（增补“带来了”三个字，补足谓语动词“gives”的语意）
5. 原子是元素的最小的粒子。（the 和 an 省略）
6. 这种材料什么地方都没有。（全部否定）
7. 在力的作用下，没有一种材料不或多或少地变形。（即任何材料都或多或少地变形）（双重否定）
8. 把这两种物质混合起来时没有发生其他变化。（名→动）
9. 这些原料的性质有很大的差异。（状→主）
10. 它们的具有重大意义的化学成分根本不同（它们的根本不同的化学成分具有重大的意义）。（表→定）

UNIT EIGHT

Reading Comprehension

Ⅰ. 1. C　2. A　3. D　4. B　5. D

Ⅱ. 略

Vocabulary

Ⅰ. 1. C　2. A　3. D　5. D　5. C

Ⅱ. 1. e　2. c　3. h　4. d　5. f

Translation

1. 几天以内全国武装起来了。
2. 这一发现在科学界得到很高的评价。（被评价→得到评价）
3. 如果（人们）不强烈地感到损失，那倒是奇怪了。
4. 人们说，数控就是机床用数字加以操纵。（添加泛指人称代词“人们”作主语）
5. 问题的解决办法终于找到了。

UNIT NINE

Reading Comprehension

Ⅰ. 1. A　2. C　3. D　4. B　5. D

Ⅱ. 略

Vocabulary

Ⅰ. 1. C　2. B　3. A　4. D　5. B

Ⅱ. 1. g　2. e　3. d　4. a　5. b

Translation

1. 因此它的用途被限于制造首先要求重量小的物件。
2. 去年这个地区遭受到60 年来最严重的旱灾。
3. 其他方法将简单地加以讨论。
4. 一部分的光或全部的光可能被其去路的东西和物体所反射、吸收或透射。
5. 很久以来，流水就被用来转动工业上用的轮子。

UNIT TEN

Reading Comprehension

Ⅰ. 1. B　2. D　3. C　4. A　5. D

Vocabulary

Ⅰ. 1. D　2. B　3. B　4. D　5. A

Ⅱ. 1. g　2. f　3. e　4. a　5. c

Translation

1. 产量增长了 56000 万吨。
2. 铬掩模的使用寿命为乳胶掩模的 10～100 倍。
3. 中国 1984 年的煤产量为1959 年的十倍。（或：“1984 年中国煤产量比 1959 年增加了九倍。”）
4. 试验大楼为宿舍的三倍高。
5. 1965 年以来机床产量增加了 5 倍。

UNIT ELEVEN

Reading Comprehension

Ⅰ. 1. D　2. A　3. C　4. B　5. C

Ⅱ. 略

Vocabulary

Ⅰ. 1. C　2. B　3. A　4. D　5. B

Ⅱ. 1. d　2. f　3. a　4. e　5. h

Translation

1. 此法少用了 22%的燃料。
2. A 是 B 的三分之一（A 比 B 小 2/3）。
3. 金属损耗降低到 15%。
4. 新型晶体管的开关时间缩短了一半。
5. 待冷却气体的总热函也会减小到原来的 1/5～1/4。

UNIT TWELVE

Reading Comlprehension

Ⅰ. 1. C　2. A　3. B　4. D　5. C

Ⅱ. 略

Vocabulary

Ⅰ. 1. A　2. B　3. C　4. D　5. B

Ⅱ. 1c　2a　3e　4b　5g

Translation

1. 他同那班以外交为职业的人特别是大使们搞不来。
2. 他不跟工人们在一起生活，虽然他依靠他们的熟练技巧。
3. 他可以把她带到那个地方去，在那里他们会把她打扮成一个漂亮的少女，而且花不了几个钱。
4. 谁如果只守城堡而不往远处看，那他就是一个目光短浅的指挥员。
5. 这个方案富于创造性，独出心裁，很有魄力，所以使他们都很喜欢。

UNIT THIRTEEN

Reading Comprehension

Ⅰ. 1. D　2. A　3. B　4. C　5. A

Ⅱ. 略

vocabulary

Ⅰ. 1. B　2. C　3. D　4. B　5. A

Ⅱ. 1. g　2. e　3. a　4. b　5. h

Translation

1. 他坚持要再造一幢房子，尽管他并无此需要。
2. 这明明是他的家乡，他不过在前一天离开的。
3. 他们将乘飞机去昆明，在那儿计划呆两三天，然后再去北京。
4. 我们打算把郊游推到下周，那时我们不会这么忙。
5. 一个牧民，看一千只羊，每年约挣一万元。

UNIT FOURTEEN

Reading Comprehension

Ⅰ. 1. D　2. B　3. C　4. A　5. C

Ⅱ. 略

Vocabulary

Ⅰ.1.C 2.B 3.D 4.A 5.C

Ⅱ.1.c 2.g 3.h 4.b 5.e

Translation

1. 分析：这个句子是由一个主句、一个状语从句和三个定语从句组成的。"她依旧是个好看而忠实的伴侣"是主句，也是全句的中心内容。主句前面是一个假设状语从句，其中又包含一个定语从句，这个定语从句较长，所以，在译文中加破折号放在被修饰语之后。全句共有五层意思：(一) 她早已失掉了那蔚蓝色眼睛的、花儿般的魅力，也失掉了她脸儿和身段的那种玉洁冰清、苗条多姿的气质和那苹果花似的颜色；(二) 26 年前这些东西曾迅速而奇妙地影响过艾舍斯特；(三) 在 43 岁的今天，她依旧是个好看而忠实的伴侣；(四) 不过两颊淡淡地有点儿斑驳；(五) 灰蓝的眼睛也已经有点儿饱满了。原文各句的逻辑关系、表达顺序与汉语完全一致，因此可按原句顺序译出。

译文：如果说她早已失掉了那蔚蓝色眼睛的、花儿般的魅力，也失掉了她脸儿和身段的那种玉洁冰清、苗条多姿的气质和那苹果花似的颜色(1)——26 年前这种花容月貌曾那样迅速而奇妙地影响过艾舍斯特(2)——那么在 43 岁的今天，她依旧是个好看而忠实的伴侣(3)，不过两颊淡淡地有点儿斑驳(4)，而灰蓝的眼睛也已经有点儿饱满了(5)。

2. 分析：这个句子是由一个主句、两个定语从句和一个状语从句组成。"时间是过得很快的"是主句，也是全句的中心内容。全句共有四层意思：(一) 时间是过得很快的；(二) 如果你懂得什么是美的话；(三) 当你跟可爱的孩子们站在池子里，又有个年轻的狄安娜在池边好奇地接受东西；(四) 你所捉上来的东西。按照汉语先发生的事先叙述，以及条件在先结果在后的习惯，这句句子可逆着原文顺序译出。

译文：当你跟可爱的孩子们站在池子里，又有个年轻的狄安娜在池边好奇地接受你捉上来的任何东西的时候(3)，如果你懂得什么叫美的话(2)，时间是过得很快的！(1)

UNIT FIFTEEN

Reading Comprehension

Ⅰ.1.C 2.C 3.A 4.A 5.B

Ⅱ. 略

Vocabulary

Ⅰ.1.B 2.A 3.A 4.D 5.B

Ⅱ.1.g 2.e 3.d 4.b 5.a

Translation

1. 人们希望“早期发现”肺癌，随即进行外科治疗，因为外科治疗目前似乎是最有效的疗法。然而，由于肺癌生长速度和生长方向等生物学特征有很大差异，“早期发现”的希望往往落空。(分译为两句：第一句顺译，第二句倒译)
2. 苏联成千上万家企业采用的产品质量综合管理体系，是通过在整个企业范围内实行质量管理、把企业内各个管理机构和各种管理对象联结起来的综合体，这种联结是借助于材料部门、技术部门和信息部门实现的。(按原文含义分为两个层次，先译主要部分，后译次要部分。)
3. 分析：这个句子由一个主句、一个非限制性定语从句和一个状语从句组成。插入主句中间的是一个由 who 引起的非限制性定语从句。这个从句较长，中间又插入了一个用破折号分开的、由 until 引起的时间状语从句。这个状语从句对非限制性定语从句的后面部分作了些补充说明，因而虽然具有相对的独立意义，仍可根据逻辑关系将该句译文置于句尾。全句有两层主要意思：(一) 如果没有希特勒，那就几乎可以肯定不会有第三帝国；(二) 希特勒在性格、智力、能力等等方面具有某些特点。原文各句的逻辑关系和表达顺序与汉语大致一致，但因从句是插入成分，和汉语表达习惯不同，所以翻译时顺中有逆，可以综合处理。

译文：然而，如果没有阿道夫·希特勒，那就几乎可以肯定不会有第三帝国。因为阿道夫·希特勒有着恶魔般的性格、花岗石般的意志、不可思议的本能、无情的冷酷、杰出的智力、深远的想象力以及对人和局势惊人的判断力。这种判断力最后由于权力和胜利冲昏了头脑而自不量力，终于弄巧成拙。

UNIT SIXTEEN

Reading Comprehension

Ⅰ. 1. C　2. D　3. D　4. C　5. B

Ⅱ. 略

Vocabulary

Ⅰ. 1. B　2. A　3. A　4. A　5. A

Ⅱ. 1. e　2. a　3. c　4. g　5. b

Translation

1. 这所教堂由美籍墨西哥人建于一八八九年。(汉语被动句)
2. 大型电动机应当使用三相电流。(汉语主动句)
3. 自一九七八年以来这座城市建筑物的数量增加四倍。
4. 今年散装水泥的产量减少 50%。
5. 巨型飞机低空飞行时产生的巨大轰鸣，足以摧毁房屋。(译为时间状语从句)
6. 在制造水泥时，把适当配比的石灰石与粘土的混合物粉碎成细粉，并缓慢地喂入到一个有炽热气体从其中通过的斜置旋转圆筒中。
7. 纽约市过去二十年中已经用它的垃圾把斯塔登岛填土场堆积成东海岸最高的山峰，而且该填土场很快没有空地了。因此，该市正准备耗资 25 亿美元修建八座垃圾发电装置，并且打算再花费几十亿美元来运转这些装置。(分译成两句，并将 which 引导的非限制性定语从句与主语合译为一句。)

图书在版编目（CIP）数据

建筑类专业英语．建筑工程．第2册/乔梦铎，王久愉主编．—北京：中国建筑工业出版社，1997（2005重印）

高等学校试用教材

ISBN 978-7-112-03030-9

Ⅰ．建…　Ⅱ．①乔…②王…　Ⅲ．①建筑学-英语-高等学校-教材②建筑工程-英语-高等学校-教材　Ⅳ．H31

中国版本图书馆CIP数据核字（2005）第118878号

本书即《建筑类专业英语　工业与民用建筑》第二册，系根据国家教委印发的《大学英语专业阅读阶段教学基本要求》编写的专业阅读课教材，按照建筑类院校共同设置的五个较大专业对口编写。本册包括设计规范与规程、钢筋混凝土的弯曲性能、梁的弯曲分析及设计、长期挠度、板的屈服理论、粘接和锚固等方面内容。全书安排16个单元，每单元除正课外，还有两篇阅读材料，均配有必要的注释。正课文还配有词汇表和练习，书后附有总词汇表、参考译文和练习答案。语言难度大于第一册，本册还对科技英语翻译技巧作了简要说明，并增加例句和翻译练习题。供本专业学生三年级上半学期使用。

高等学校试用教材

建筑类专业英语

建　筑　工　程

第二册

乔梦铎　王久愉　　　主编

王凤友　李英贤　李　斐
周桂兰　祝恩淳　高　伟　　　编

计学闰　　　主审

*

中国建筑工业出版社出版、发行（北京西郊百万庄）

各地新华书店、建筑书店经销

北京建筑工业印刷厂印刷

*

开本：787×1092毫米　1/16　印张：$12\frac{1}{2}$　字数：304千字

1997年6月第一版　2014年2月第十五次印刷

定价：**18.00**元

ISBN 978-7-112-03030-9

(14854)